BROADWAY'S BEST
1960

Broadway's Best

★ ★ 1960 ★ ★

THE COMPLETE RECORD OF

THE THEATRICAL YEAR

BY

JOHN CHAPMAN

★

1960

Doubleday & Company, Inc.

Garden City, New York

FOR GEORGIA
with infinite love and great gratitude

Library of Congress Catalog Card Number 57–12462
Copyright © 1960 by John Chapman
All Rights Reserved
Printed in the United States of America
First Edition

CONTENTS

FOREWORD

THIS is a critical and statistical survey of the New York theatrical season which began June 1, 1959, and ended May 31, 1960. The Golden Dozen plays and musicals which I have selected for extended critical and descriptive examination are my own choice, as being most representative of one theatergoer's year. As always is the case, there are hits among them, and failures, too. In the distressing hit-or-flop economy to which the Broadway stage has fallen victim several honestly and decently wrought dramas have not had the chance their quality warranted. They will be remembered only by their authors, producers, and actors and by the comparative handful of theatrical followers who bought tickets to something even though it was not described in the reviews as "a smash!" "a must!" or "a wow!" Inclusion in this volume may extend the memory of them somewhat, but this will be no solid, measurable advantage to the authors, producers, and actors who risked their enthusiasms and lost. But if there *were* no risk in the theatre, artistically and commercially, the stage would finally be dead after all these centuries of striving. The sure thing, the walkover, the cinch, is the least interesting possibility in life, simply because it contains no possibility. Venture provides the spice of life, and there *was* venture now and then in the stage season which is being chronicled and commented upon herewith.

JOHN CHAPMAN

New York, June 1960

A VIEW OF THE SEASON

EVERYBODY kept saying this was a bad season, and so it was; but the adjective needs clarification. The year was very much worse financially than it was artistically. Among the many failures there were very few which seemed to have a total lack of merit, including a musical, *Happy Town*, which was incredibly amateurish, and a drama, *The Long Dream*, which was downright offensive. But any season which can offer us such plays as *The Miracle Worker, The Tenth Man*, and *The Best Man*, and such original musicals as *Fiorello!* and *Bye Bye Birdie* can not be described as bad in an artistic sense. Our classical repertoire was, as it has been for some time now, dismayingly thin, but it did include exciting productions of *Much Ado About Nothing* and *Heartbreak House*.

On Broadway commerce should beget art and art should beget commerce—but something went wrong with commerce. As the season approached its Memorial Day close there were threats of a strike by Actors Equity. The actors wanted a rise in minimum wages and a pension scheme financed by the producers. The producers, operating as the League of New York Theatres, maintained that they could not meet the new demands. They argued that they would have to pass any increase in production cost along to the ticket buyer, and that any further increase in the price of tickets would drive more theatergoers away from the box offices.

In defense of their position, the managers put out a set of statistics which was appalling. Thirty-nine plays, musicals and revivals closed with a total loss of $5,200,500, while only six successes had worked up a profit of $244,000. In addition, nine attractions did not even try to open on Broadway, but closed after discouraging out-of-town tryouts with a loss to investors of $1,085,500.

I think there was more than one reason for this frightening financial record, but the main one was, once again, the hit-or-flop economy of the commercial stage. Ticket prices have become so high that the average theatergoer will not risk his money on anything but a guaranteed success—something which has won a majority of favorable reviews. When critical opinion is divided—a healthy division! —the play suffers.

In an easier economy, the attraction which is favored by a few would have a chance; it might start slowly and hope to build public favor. But the financial risk is now too great for a manager to indulge in such hopefulness; his weekly operating costs prohibit chance-taking among all but the most daring.

Besides ticket costs, the theatergoer often faces a further discouragement—the benefit party. Before it opened, the Rodgers-Hammerstein-Mary Martin *The Sound of Music* had sold 300 performances to theater parties. This was financially comforting to those who had risked the production but it was dispiriting to the showgoer. It meant that he had to do one of two things if he really felt he had to see this attraction: Join a benefit group and pay an even higher price or wait several months. If he wanted to go to a Saturday matinee he would have to wait a year. The playgoer has developed extraordinary patience in the last decade, but I believe that, like Cousin Egbert, he can be pushed just so far. I think he is reaching the point where he says, "The hell with it. I don't *have* to go to the theater. I can do plenty of other things. Anyhow, I might be in bed with a cold or be called out of town when my turn comes."

Another important reason for the crisis in the theater, and perhaps the gravest of all, is the *kind* of drama we have been offered; if it is not downright seamy and smudgy it is discouraging to the point of nihilism. I advanced this opinion in a newspaper article which was syndicated through the country, and the response it gained was remarkable—and instructive. What I had written was this:

"Today being Sunday, it is a good time for a sermon on how the Broadway theatre has been sinking to hell, with a suggestion or two about possible salvation.

"One always hopes for the better, for an upturn; but as of the moment I am writing this has been the most disastrous drama season in the memory of professionals who go back to the turn of the century.

"The diasters have been colossal, financially speaking—but a backer and his money are soon parted and this is nothing to be concerned over. Investors are a nickel a dozen and when one has emptied his wallet another stands eager to take his place. The fact that the theatre has lost several million dollars this year is of small importance.

"The important fact—the basic reason for these failures, these bad and unpopular plays—is something which must be searched out. Nobody has found it for sure as yet, but I may be on the right track in thinking that our theatre is appallingly lacking in spirituality and forgetful of the nobility of man.

"We have been told so often that we are living in a disillusioned age, in which none of us is sure that he won't wake up dead tomorrow morning that we may have been persuaded that this is so. And the theatre, which is supposed to mirror or interpret our life, has assumed this attitude of dis-illusion.

"I think that this is wrong and this is why the stage has been failing—not only failing as a commerce in tickets but failing in its interpretation of the life we are living. The hard facts, the dirty facts, the evidences of human depravity and spiritual loneliness, have been the main subjects of our drama. Baseness, cruelty and frustration have been the bases of many of our plays— and it is encouraging to me, rather than discouraging, that so many of these have failed. It is an indication that people are not finding in the theatre what they hope to find, and are staying away in such numbers that a Broad-way run of five performances is a long one. We are beginning to discover that life in these puzzling times cannot be interpreted by a patient on a psychoanalyst's couch.

"Amidst the welter of failures there have been some great successes which must be puzzling to the merchants of Broadway because, according to all the rules of commerce, they should have been flops. One of these, put on a couple of seasons ago, was *J. B.* According to the rules, this one should have lasted a couple of weeks. It was in verse by a man of whom Broadway had hardly heard, Archibald MacLeish. It was a retelling of a chapter in the Bible, the Book of Job. It had no more chance than a snowball in a pizza oven.

"Yet *J. B.* found a great audience. It had no jokes, it had no sex and it told of incredible suffering. But it did sing of the unconquerable nobility and hope and courage in the spirit of mankind. And because of this it found a great audience.

"Two of the most successful plays of this season should have been failures in the world of disillusion which is Broadway. One is set in a synagogue and concerns itself with the exorcism of an evil spirit in an elaborate religious rite. The other tells of how a sightless deaf-mute is taught to talk. Nothing could have smaller commercial prospects than these two—yet they are at the top of the best-seller list among plays.

"I do not believe the success of these two ventures is an accident, a freak or a paradox. They are selling out because they are hymns to the spirit of man. They tell us that something still is right in the world—and not in a Pollyanna fashion. We must look for the right and find it.

"The first of these plays, Paddy Chayefsky's *The Tenth Man*, is a modern twist on an old Hebrew fable which first was dramatized in Russian by S. Ansky. It concerns a dybbuk, or devil, which has possessed a human soul and must be driven out according to prescribed rite. Chayefsky has put a de-lightful twist in the legend by suggesting that the dybbuk may be residing somewhere else, rather than where a wonderful congregation of old Jews thinks it is.

"The dybbuk is exorcised, fair enough—but not by rite or incantation. It is driven out by love, which is the one great and indestructible heritage of man. We want it, and when we can find it in the theatre it makes us happy.

"The second play is William Gibson's *The Miracle Worker*, which tells how a teacher of unconquerable will and dauntless love fought her way into the seemingly impenetrable prison which held a little girl named Helen Keller. She fought her way in and led the little girl out. She released a spirit which was to have enormous effect in and upon the world. She proved that the mind of man must have no bonds.

"Neither of these plays is a preachment; both are sheer entertainment, and they are most admirably acted. But when we see them they give us pride and hope and dignity—a feeling that we are not altogether damned and lost in this world. Last week a well-meaning and intelligently made—but structurally defective—drama about Harlem juvenile gangs, marijuana peddlers, poverty and dope addiction, *The Cool World*, lasted two performances. I think it should have run longer, for it was not done cheaply . . . but it had no spirit. When man loses all pride in himself he will go—and his theatre is already going fast."

When the mail reaction to this article became appreciable, with such letters as "I have given up theatergoing because I find no pleasure in it any more—or in movies, either," I followed with another column of comment which ended with a warning: "Turn around, boys. There is handwriting on the back wall of the box office."

Nor was I alone in my estimate of dramatic quality. Tom F. Driver of *The Christian Century* wrote an objection to the assumption on the part of so many dramatists and novelists "that compassion isn't really compassion until it has been consummated in sexual unions."

In *Theatre Arts* P. G. Wodehouse wrote, "I wish the boys who are writing today would stop being so frightfully powerful and significant and give us a little comedy occasionally. I am all for incest and wrecked lives and tortured souls in moderation, but a good laugh from time to time never hurt anybody. And except for revues like *La Plume de Ma Tante* and *A Thurber Carnival*, has anyone laughed in a Broadway theater in years? All you hear now is the soft, sibilant sound of creeping flesh, punctuated now and then by a sharp intake of the breath as somebody behind the footlights utters one of those four-letter words hitherto confined to the cozy surroundings of the lower-type barroom."

There also are many supporters of the psychoanalytical-nihilistic drama who maintain, with right on their side, that the theater at its best is a place for looking for truth and telling it. Its subject matter must not be circumscribed. It can be a moral force, as Shaw and many others have demonstrated. But if it *is* a moral force it should point the way toward something, hope to gain something. Much of our theater—even more off Broadway than on—is morally, intellectually beatnik.

This defeatist theater has not been without its attractions and it has given us some moving moments of compassion and a little beauty now and then. But I think, after all the years since *The Glass Menagerie*, we have had it. We seem to have explored it thoroughly, for nothing new has come out of it lately, and now we—the people who go to plays—want something different. The theater is quick to sense a change in public desires. After last season at the box office it is bound to alter its sights. One can always hope it will raise them. One can always hope, too, that somewhere will be found a dramatist who has, in addition to the necessary technical skill, the gift of *writing*—of making our incomparable language an instrument of beauty and grace.

MONTH BY MONTH

SUMMER was as usual. A sufficient variety of hits for tourists and conventioneers coasted along. In Central Park there were some praiseworthy productions of Shakespeare, with no admission charged. A season of musicals and ballet put on in a theatre-in-the-round built over the Park's outdoor skating rink was not a success, although I thought one of them, *Can Can*, was good. One or two critics who have been long-time champions of theatre-in-the-round complained that the setting was wrong—that the towered skyline of Manhattan to the south was more dramatic than the shows which competed against it.

There was only one new offering in September, a very stylish revival of *Much Ado About Nothing*, with Margaret Leighton and Sir John Gielgud. This was an exceptionally adept feat of direction by Gielgud, and Miss Leighton was a perfect and wondrously handsome high-style comedienne.

October opened with *The Gang's All Here*, a drama about a Presidential administration not unlike that of Warren G. Harding. The writers, Jerome Lawrence and Robert E. Lee, told of a Chief Executive who was betrayed by his pals, the cabinet ministers. As the luckless President, Melvyn Douglas had the first of two political roles of the season. Later he appeared as a candidate for nomination in a better drama, *The Best Man*. *The Gang's All Here* did not stir me up too much, for I thought that Maureen Watkins had done a better play—also a failure—on the Harding story in the 1920s, when she adapted Samuel Hopkins Adams' novel, *Revelry*. Next in October came the Phoenix production of O'Neill's *The Great God Brown*. This was a confused and confusing drama to begin with, and the new production clarified no points. *Happy Town*, a musical about a Texas town which didn't have a millionaire to its name, was an incredible mistake. And then came Michael Flanders and Donald Swann in *At the Drop of a Hat*, the two-man entertainment they had kept running for years in London. This little mixture of wit, satire, song, and personality was one of the most lighthearted events of the season. It was appreciated to the utmost by "the carriage trade" but it broke no box office records.

Anita Loos once adapted a story by the French Colette, *Gigi*, which had a long Broadway run, made a star of Audrey Hepburn and then was converted into one of the best musicals ever filmed. This time, in October, she tried two Colette stories, called them *Chéri* and lived to regret it. There was an amiable Navy farce, *The Golden Fleecing*, but it struggled to its end. A splendid all-star revival of Shaw's *Heartbreak House* was a distinguished failure. Then *The Miracle Worker* opened and the American theater came alive. Only one other October entry showed quality and staying power—a musical version of O'Neill's *Ah, Wilderness!* titled *Take Me Along*. With Jackie Gleason, Walter Pidgeon, Robert Morse and Eileen Herlie in the cast, it was a fine sentimental journey back to the early 1900s in New England.

November began with a revue, *The Girls Against the Boys*, starring Nancy Walker and Bert Lahr. Good title for a show with these two low-down comedians—but the writers weren't up to the talents of the performers. Dore Schary got worried about the fallout of strontium 90 in *The Highest Tree*, but the worst he suffered was the fallout of his drama. The night after Schary's scary work we found one of the great delights of the year, Paddy Chayefsky's *The Tenth Man*. This was original and charming and splendidly acted by nobody worth mentioning on a billboard, and it gave a great lift to a playgoer's spirits.

Following *The Tenth Man* was *The Sound of Music*, rated in advance as the greatest thing since the invention of the paper dollar. One had to join a benevolent organization to get in. Late November entries included *A Loss of Roses*, one of the better tears-and-sympathy dramas of the season, and the robust and cheerful musical about Mayor La Guardia, *Fiorello!*

At the beginning of December we were in for more tears and sympathy, with the English import, *Five Finger Exercise*, to be remembered among them. Not much could be said or done for *Silent Night, Lonely Night*, in which a woman and a man committed adultery out of commiseration, or *Jolly's Progress*, a comedy-drama about a Negro Liza Doolittle. The musical version of Edna Ferber's novel, *Saratoga Trunk*, was a $400,000 failure because it seemed more preoccupied with the novel than it was with the stage. One of the very few novels to become a stage success without heartless cutting and revision was John Steinbeck's *Of Mice and Men*—and Steinbeck wrote his novel as a play in the first place.

Rex Harrison tried manfully as a retired general who could not cope with the present in Jean Giraudoux's *The Fighting Cock*, but the play seemed a warmover of another and better one by the same author, *The Waltz of the Toreadors*. The final entry of 1959 on Broadway was a good one, *The Andersonville Trial*, a slice of Civil War history performed by an all-male cast.

The new year clunked in with a comedy, *A Mighty Man Is He*. It was written by two good and admired humorists, Arthur Kober and George Oppenheimer, but they left something out. It is my opinion that they left out the principal character, the mighty man of the title. He was only an offstage figure, and since he was more interesting than anybody onstage the play suffered. Next came another quick failure, *A Distant Bell*, which struck me as having some of the best and most original writing of the year. In our hit-or-flop economy, this sensitive and imaginative drama did not have a fair chance at a fair hearing.

Among nine plays which ventured forth in February, only two seem important to the historian. These were *The Deadly Game* and *Toys in the Attic*. The first-mentioned was by Friedrich Duerrenmatt, the German-writing Swiss who provided the Lunts with *The Visit*. This was a skillful piece of melodramatic fiction—and our theater, Mr. Wodehouse, needs melodrama as much as it needs comedy. *Toys in the Attic* was a workmanlike job by Lillian Hellman, and it won the Critics Circle award as the best American play of the year.

Late February also brought the American answer to Britain's *At the Drop of a Hat*, *A Thurber Carnival*. It had been Burgess Meredith's idea to take a selection of James Thurber's memoirs, fiction, philosophies, and drawings—all of them conceived for the printed page—and present them on the stage with live actors. This transition from page to stage was a thorough and civilized delight. Not so in-

spired, though, was the Leap Year offering of February 29, *There
Was a Little Girl*. This was a shoddy little drama about what happened to a nice girl after she had been abducted and submitted to
a fate worse than death.

One of the most ballyhooed of the season's plays inaugurated
the month of March—*The Good Soup*. Adapted by Garson Kanin
from a long-run French sex comedy, and starring Ruth Gordon and
Diane Cilento, it was expected to be the utmost in worldly humor.
It was an elaborate bore, strengthening my belief that French dramatists—and perhaps all the French—have a naïve, childlike attitude
toward sex.

Another elaborate musical failure was another adaptation of a best-
selling novel, B. J. Chute's fantasy, *Greenwillow*. It had good Frank
Loesser songs and presented Anthony Perkins as a singer, but the
story line was muddled. A muddled story line in a musical is fatal.

Katharine Cornell and Brian Aherne brought in *Dear Liar*, which
they had trouped successfully across the country in a specially built
bus. It was a "reading" of some of the letters between two egoma-
niacs, Mrs. Pat Campbell and G. B. Shaw. It was caviar, unsalted.
March went out like a lion with the production of Gore Vidal's political comedy-drama, *The Best Man*, in which Melvyn Douglas, having
committed suicide while in the White House in *The Gang's All Here*,
now was trying to get *into* the White House.

There were two good ideas among the April entries which turned
out to be quite dreadful in execution. One was to make a satirical
farce out of the advertising business, appropriately titled *Viva Madison Avenue!* I have a long-nurtured belief that such things as radio,
television, and advertising cannot be satirized because they are satires
in themselves, and one should not paint the lily. The only good
satire about the movies was *Once in a Lifetime*, and this was a
straight comedy and not a criticism. *Viva Madison Avenue!* was not
very funny; you cannot make jokes about people who lead desperate
lives. The other good idea in April was to put on a revue called *From
A to Z* and to have a song or sketch or blackout for every letter of
the alphabet. Unfortunately, the people who wrote the material
were not equal to the idea, and the star of the enterprise, Hermione
Gingold, went through her little collection of grotesqueries quite
some time before the evening was over.

But April did shower a blessing here and there. One was *Bye Bye
Birdie*, a musical comedy with the year's most unlikely title, which

had to do with Elvis Presley and his teen-age idolaters. Somebody else might have said, "Let's do a satire on Presley and rock-and-roll" and flop would go another show. One cannot satirize satire. The authors and composers of *Birdie* decided to look upon Presley and his young admirers with an understanding, sympathetic eye. They proved, in a very happy show, that we may not have to worry too much about our young. Not as much, indeed, as our young should worry about us, if one is to believe contemporary playwrights.

The important part of the year ended with *Duel of Angels*, a consciously mannered French discussion of sex in which Vivien Leigh, the Bad Girl, was opposed to Mary Ure, the Good Girl. This adaptation by Christopher Fry from a sardonic comedy by Jean Giraudoux was gracefully written and admirably performed.

The season closed with admirable City Center revivals of *Finian's Rainbow* and *The King and I*. *Finian's Rainbow*, a fantasy involving a magic pot of gold and a leprechaun, seemed as fresh musically and in story as it was when it was produced in 1947; heartened by the critical and public reception, a new management took the musical over from the City Center and established it at the Forty-sixth Street Theatre for a Broadway run.

And then, on June 1, came a one-performance actors' strike of one play, *The Tenth Man*. The actors, battling with managers over pay rises and pension provisions, planned a tactic of "harassment" in which it would call out the cast of one attraction each night until Equity and management should come to terms. The managers, however, refused to sit still for this type of warfare; on June 2 they closed all plays and musicals on Broadway—twenty-two of them. This was the first theater blackout since August 1919, when the actors struck for a month and gained recognition of their union by the producers.

OFF BROADWAY

BY CHARLES McHARRY

BETWEEN September 9, 1959, and May 26 of this year, seventy events were presented in the little houses which constitute off-Broadway. As was true of last season, most of the offerings were new plays by American authors. Five new musicals appeared and five original revues were presented.

Europe's playwrights were represented by Ionesco, Duerrenmatt, Anouilh, Genet, Betti, Fabbri, Beckett and Ronald Duncan, and there were revivals of classics by Chekhov, Tolstoy, de Musset, Pirandello, Shakespeare, and Ibsen.

Tobacco Road and *Camino Real* turned up among the dramas originally staged on Broadway, and Cole Porter's *Gay Divorce* and the Gershwins' *Oh, Kay!* were dusted off and brought forth for inspection.

Dorothy Raedler and her American Savoyards prospered at the Jan Hus with a fine repertory of Gilbert and Sullivan, and there were other features such as *The Mime Theatre of Etienne Decroux* which fit into a category best described as odd-ball.

As usual, the fatality rate was high, with at least fifty of the entries folding quickly. Others lingered for respectable runs without achieving financial success. Only two and possibly three of the offerings have paid off.

The highly acclaimed double-bill at the Provincetown Playhouse consisting of Samuel Beckett's *Krapp's Last Tape* and Edward Albee's *The Zoo Story* was quick pay, and so was Rick Besoyan's *Little Mary Sunshine*. Both have played to capacity since opening.

David Ross' production of Chekhov's *The Three Sisters* was said to have regained its production cost, and it is highly probable that Circle in the Square's *The Balcony*, a drama of assorted sexual depravities by French author Jean Genet, will make money.

Other likely winners are Chekhov's *A Country Scandal*, a late spring arrival receiving its first professional production in this country, and *The Fantasticks*, an off-beat musical by Tom Jones and Harry Schmidt.

U.S.A., the John Dos Passos-Paul Shyre collaboration, gave 246 performances at the Martinique Theatre and wound up in the red, and the revival of Tennessee Williams' *Orpheus Descending* was seen 230 times at the Gramercy Arts Theatre and also was a loser.

Most notable of the short-lived events, in this reviewer's opinion, were Sam Spewack's *Under the Sycamore Tree*, William Gibson's *Dinny and the Witches*, Ronald Duncan's *The Death of Satan*, and the revival of Australian playwright Ray Lawler's *Summer of the Seventeenth Doll*.

Robert Penn Warren's adaptation of his novel, *All the King's Men*, was well received, as was the revival of Paul Vincent Carroll's *Shadow and Substance*, featuring the Irish Players. Also listed among the good trys were Francis Gallagher's *Vincent* and Viña Delmar's *The Confederates.*

The only play to live down original devastating notices was *The Connection,* a Living Theatre presentation dealing with jazz and narcotics. Easily the most avant-garde piece in town, *The Connection* was vigorously condemned by all but one of the newspaper arbiters who attended its opening performance. It found friends among the weekly reviewers, however, and its audiences, small at first, began to build, and it has continued to run in repertory with other Living Theatre projects.

Sophie Treadwell's expressionist *Machinal* was exhumed and acclaimed (except in this corner), and off-Broadway even revived an off-Broadway original, this being Arthur Schnitzler's *La Ronde,* first staged by José Quintero at Circle-in-the-Square in 1953.

The phenominal *The Threepenny Opera* breezed through its fourth year at the Theater de Lys and is now in its fifth, and it still sells out. Another holdover was *Leave It Jane,* in its second year at the Sheridan Square Playhouse.

One of the most controversial plays of the season was Warner Le Roy's adaptation of Diego Fabbri's *Between Two Thieves,* a drama which asks if Jesus Christ was guilty of a crime according to the laws of His time and who actually was responsible for His crucifixion.

Off-Broadway itself continued to be a subject of controversy, its critics maintaining in the public prints that it has no direction or purpose and that it is overpriced and amateurish. Its defenders answered back that it remains young, daring, professional, imaginative, and more purposeful than Broadway.

The movement once again demonstrated its showcase value, introducing such players as Elisa Loti (*Come Share My House*), Rochelle Oliver (*Vincent*), Eileen Brennan (*Little Mary Sunshine*), Donald Davis (*Krapp's Last Tape*), George Maharis and William Daniels (*The Zoo Story*), Gerry Orbach (*The Fantasticks*), and Mark Lenard (*A Country Scandal*).

Rick Besoyan was hailed for his music, authorship, and direction of *Little Mary Sunshine,* and Edward Albee established himself as a playwright with *The Zoo Story.* Young author Jack Richardson was acclaimed for *The Prodigal,* a drama which I failed to appreciate and therewith was branded an idiot minority of one.

José Quintero distinguished himself further with his staging of

The Balcony and the beauteous Salome Jens was summoned to Hollywood as the result of her role in this show.

An estimated 800,000 patrons attended the little houses last season and about $800,000 went down the drain with losing productions.

In addition to the seventy shows which opened, a handsome new off-Broadway theatre made its debut. This was the Maidman Playhouse, on West 42d Street near Ninth Ave. The Maidman opened February 6 with *Russell Patterson's Sketchbook*, a revue which lasted three performances.

Since *Sketchbook*, the Maidman has been host to Anouilh's *Jeanette* (four performances), a one-woman show by Claire Luce (six performances) and Belgian playwright Hugo Claus' *A Bride in the Morning* (two performances).

A rough initiation? Yes, but typical.

The Phoenix Theatre, although located on lower Second Avenue, is a big house and its operation is no way typical of off-Broadway. Its permanent acting company is paid considerably more than the $45-a-week minimum established for off-Broadway by Actors Equity, and it is partially subsidized by regular subscribers. It also received a $120,000 grant last season from the Ford Foundation.

Phoenix productions last season consisted of O'Neill's *The Great God Brown*, Aristophanes' *Lysistrata*, Ibsen's *Peer Gynt*, and Shakespeare's *King Henry IV, Parts 1* and *2*. With the exception of *Lysistrata*, all were critically blessed.

FUTURE PRODUCTIONS

WHEN it first became apparent that Equity might force a shutdown of theaters, the League of New York Managers called a halt in new production. Casting was stopped—even though casting is normally at its height in the early summer months. But many plans and some casts were already set. Here are some of the attractions likely to arrive in 1960–61:

Advise and Consent, dramatization of Allen Drury's Pulitzer Prize novel.

Anatol, musical version of Schnitzler's *The Affairs of Anatol*, with songs by Arthur Schwartz and Howard Dietz.

Camelot, musical by Alan Jay Lerner and Frederick Loewe, of

My Fair Lady fame. It concerns King Arthur and his knights, and was announced to open November 17 at the Winter Garden.

The Emperor Jones and *Hughie*, short plays by O'Neill, starring Myron McCormick.

I Give It Six Months, a comedy by George S. Kaufman and Leueen MacGrath.

Rhinoceros, by Eugene Ionesco, with Eli Wallach and Anne Jackson.

Tenderloin, by the authors of *Fiorello!* Adapted from the late Samuel Hopkins Adams' last novel, it is a period piece about crooked cops, a newspaper man, and a crusading minister patterned after the famed Dr. Parkhurst.

The Unsinkable Molly Brown, with music and lyrics by Meredith (*The Music Man*) Willson. Tammy Grimes plays the real Mrs. Brown, a chambermaid whose husband struck it rich in Colorado, and who became a heroine of the *Titanic*.

BEST OF BROADWAY

THE MIRACLE WORKER

By William Gibson

MY COLLEAGUES, the members of the New York Drama Critics Circle, made their annual mistake by disagreeing with me and giving their best play citation to the wrong drama. A year ago they bestowed their blessing on *A Raisin in the Sun* when MacLeish's *J. B.* should have had it. (This error in thinking was compensated for when *J. B.* won the Pulitzer Prize.) During the season now under contemplation the critics gave their doubtful blessing to Lillian Hellman's *Toys in the Attic*, an excellent piece of workmanship. They might better have voted for one of two other plays which were equally well made and which had greater spiritual force. One of them was Paddy Chayefsky's *The Tenth Man* and the other was William Gibson's *The Miracle Worker*. My own ballot in the critics' lottery was cast for *The Miracle Worker*.

William Gibson was born in the Bronx and educated at the College of the City of New York. A poet and novelist, he also wanted to write for the theater, but it took fifteen years of trying before he won his first Broadway production—the enormously successful *Two for the Seesaw*, in which a new actress, Anne Bancroft, became a star for her extraordinary playing of a Jewish girl possessing a forthright philosophy. Gibson's first success was a novel, *The Cobweb*, a best seller which was made into a movie. He made added profit from *Seesaw* by writing a book about the creation and production of the play, *The Seesaw Log*.

Gibson, his wife and two children live in Stockbridge, Massachusetts, and it was in the public library there that he found a book of letters from Annie Sullivan, Helen Keller's teacher, and the story of Miss Sullivan's fight to bring forth the consciousness of a blind deaf mute struck him as being prime dramatic material. As he had done with *Seesaw*, he first wrote *The Miracle Worker* as a television drama, and it won acclaim. So producer Fred Coe and director Arthur Penn set about bringing the play to the stage.

Their choice for the role of Annie Sullivan was Miss Bancroft,

a young woman of Italian descent who found no difficulty in making
the transition from the Jewish girl in *Seesaw* to the Irish girl in *The
Miracle Worker*. Another acting find was Patty Duke for the role of
Helen Keller. Miss Duke was born on New York's East Side and she
got into television acting because her older brother Raymond had
got into television acting. She had a marked East Side accent but
she licked it and became a successful TV actress. She also appeared
in three motion pictures, *The Fourth Dimensional Man, The Goddess*,
and *Happy Anniversary*. When *The Miracle Worker* opened in
October 1959, her biography in the program stated that she was
ten years old; some months later, when called upon to testify at a
Congressional investigation of "payola," she said she was a couple
of years older than that—but this advanced age did not make her
any the less remarkable as an actress.

Like all plays based upon fact, *The Miracle Worker* contains elements of fiction—but it is the kind of fiction which makes the drama
seem more believable than it would be if it clung strictly to fact.
Helen Keller was born in Tuscumbia, Alabama, June 27, 1880. She
was a normal child, but when she was still a baby a disease diagnosed
as "brain fever" bereft her of sight and hearing—and so it was
she could never learn to talk. "Brain fever" was held to make idiots
of its victims, but Helen's parents did not take the easy way and put
her in an institution. As she grew into childhood she was wild and
almost unmanageable.

Then, when Helen was nearly seven, her parents brought her a
teacher, a girl of twenty named Anne Sullivan. Miss Sullivan had
been blind and had been educated in a school for the blind, the Perkins Institution in Boston. She had regained her sight through surgery,
and now she was engaged to try to teach Helen Keller something.

She communicated with the child by using the manual alphabet,
pressing the fingers into the hand. Helen could spell what she was
taught, like "doll," but she did not know that she was spelling
a word which stood for something—or even that words existed.

One day teacher and pupil were standing by the pump outside
the Keller house, where someone else was drawing water. Annie put
Helen's hand into the flow of cool, wet stuff and then spelled out
"water" repeatedly. Suddenly the girl knew that the spelled-out word
stood for something. She touched the earth and asked its letter-name.
Before this miraculous day ended she had learned thirty words.

You will see, as the play reaches its climax, what use Gibson has made of the incident at the pump.

Helen Keller was brilliant. She learned reading and writing and Braille. In 1890 she surprised Annie Sullivan by asking to be taught to speak. Somehow she had learned that a deaf and blind Norwegian girl had learned how to talk. Sarah Fuller, of the Horace Mann School in New York, was Helen's first speech teacher—but it was Annie Sullivan who was always with her, even through Radcliffe. In 1904 Miss Sullivan married John A. Macy, the literary critic, and Miss Keller went to live with the Macys.

With the exception of one, the newspaper reviews of *The Miracle Worker* were ecstatic. The dissenter was the *Times'* Brooks Atkinson, who, after giving great praise for the performances of the Misses Bancroft and Duke, said, "If the journeymen who made an acceptable play out of *Two for the Seesaw* had gone to work on *The Miracle Worker* they could probably have made something more acceptable than the disarray that is now on the stage. It has the loose narrative technique of a TV script."

Walter Kerr, of the *Herald Tribune*, reported, "All reviewers are adjective-happy, and most of us overpraise. . . . How, then, are you going to believe me when I tell you that *The Miracle Worker* is really and truly powerful, hair-raising, spine-tingling, touching and just plain wonderful?"

My first-night notice began, "My first impulse in beginning to write this report was to say that it is a beautiful play. Then I reminded myself that Helen Keller, who learned words in a way that passes belief—and who therefore must use her words more carefully than a spendthrift with four fingers on a typewriter—might choose another adjective. She might call it a loving play."

THE PLAY: ACT 1

The time is the 1880s, the locale in and around the Keller homestead in Tuscumbia, Alabama; also, briefly, the Perkins Institution for the Blind in Boston. The playing space (designed by George Jenkins) is divided into two areas by a diagonal line. The area behind the diagonal is on platforms and represents the Keller house, including a family room and a bedroom. Outside a porch is a water pump. The other area, in front of the diagonal, is neutral ground;

it accommodates various places as designated at various times. Gibson's instructions were, "The convention of the staging is one of cutting through time and place, and its essential qualities are fluidity and spatial counterpoint. . . . Locales should be only skeletal suggestions, and the movement from one to another should be accomplished by little more than lights."

As the curtain rises it is night, and three people are grouped about a crib, in lamplight—Kate Keller, her husband, Captain Arthur Keller —a newspaper editor—and a doctor. To the immense relief of the parents, he announces that the child in the crib will live, and should be all right by morning. She has had acute congestion of the brain and stomach. When the doctor leaves Captain Keller accompanies him to his buggy, and the mother bends over the crib and talks lovingly to the child. Then something puzzles her: when she moves her hand before the baby's face the child does not seem to see it. She tries again with no reaction. She screams for her husband, and the infant doesn't blink at the scream. And this is how the Kellers learn that their Helen has gone blind and deaf. The light dims.

The light comes up on a day five years later. Helen is six and a half, and now in a terse scene we realize the calamity which has fallen upon her—and upon her home. She is out by the pump with two Negro children, Martha and Percy. While Martha cuts out a paper doll and "operates" on it with her scissors, Percy offers advice and asks questions. Helen wants to get in on it. She senses that they are talking and wants to learn the trick. She puts her fingers inside Martha's mouth, and Martha pushes the hand away. She tries it with Percy and he bites her fingers. So she fingers her own lips as she soundlessly moves them, and, in sudden rage at her failure she bites at her own fingers. This alarms Martha, who pushes Helen's hand down; whereupon Helen pounces on her, pins her to the ground and grabs the scissors—and Percy leaps to the porch to sound the alarm by pulling the bell string there.

In this one moment one feels the impact of Miss Duke's performance; she *is* blind and deaf and dumb.

Inside the house are Kate Keller, her husband, her indolent young stepson, James, and a benign visiting relative, Aunt Ev. As Patricia Neal plays Kate, sitting by the crib of a new baby and darning socks, one can see what five years have wrought in her. She is, as Gibson intends, "a woman steeled in grief." With the sound of the bell she is out of the house in a flash, to lift Helen off Martha and take the scissors from her and lead her into the house.

Aunt Ev has finished a rag doll she has been working on and gives it to the little girl, who sits on the floor and explores it with her fingers. She is puzzled because it has no face.

The problem of Helen is uppermost in the minds of all. Aunt Ev (Kathleen Comegys) thinks a famous Baltimore specialist may be able to cure the girl's blindness; Captain Keller (Torin Thatcher) has abandoned such hope after having engaged specialists all over Alabama and Tennessee. James (James Congdon), being only a half-brother, is plain tough about the afflicted one; he thinks she should be put in an asylum.

Helen finds her way to Aunt Ev, fingers her dress and tears two buttons from it and tries to push them into the doll's face. Her mother, sensing immediately that the girl wants her doll to have eyes, takes two of her own buttons from the sewing basket and sews them in place. Helen, overjoyed that her doll has eyes, now croons over it happily—but not for long. She comes upon the baby's crib and tips it over, spilling the baby out; she wants to put her doll in the crib. Thwarted by her mother, she utters a weird noise, collides with a chair, falls and lies weeping on the floor.

The lights dim, and come up on a skeletal setting of the Perkins Institution for the Blind. The Baltimore specialist has suggested to the Kellers that they might find here a governess who might somehow teach Helen something. On a chair, suitcase beside her, is Annie Sullivan, being told by an Institution doctor of the job in store for her. She is twenty—a rather obstinate, combative, impudent but humorous girl who has recently recovered her sight. But her eyes still hurt, and often she keeps them closed to shut out the pain of light. She wonders if this child she is going to is bright or dull. When the doctor reminds Annie that the girl is like a locked safe that no one can open, he adds that perhaps Annie can unlock the safe and find a treasure inside. The Irish girl speculates that it might be empty, too.

Annie has been the favorite of the little blind children at the Institution, and they have taken up a collection for two going-away presents. Before she leaves they give them to her and listen as she opens them. One is an elegant doll with movable eyelids for Helen; the other is a pair of smoked glasses for herself.

Kate and James go to the station to meet Annie, and Kate seems taken aback by the girl's youth—and, being a Southern gentlewoman, by her look of being working-class Irish. But in a few moments of talk she decides she is going to like this girl. What, she asks, will Annie try to teach Helen first? "First, last and in between, language," says the new governess. Language seems far away to Kate, for nobody yet has got through to Helen to teach her to sit still.

Annie's first glimpse of her new charge reveals a messy, tumble-haired girl who has come onto the Keller porch in groping pursuit of a dog. Annie lugs her suitcase, with the doll in it, across the yard and drops it heavily on the porch. Helen feels the jar and comes to grope at the piece of luggage. Annie touches Helen's hand, and the girl grasps Annie's and explores it with her fingers. Then she explores the arm, the dress, the face . . . and the eyes beneath the dark glasses.

With Helen insistently helping, Annie gets her suitcase upstairs to the bedroom which has been prepared for her, and here she gives Helen a key to the case. The child unlocks and opens it and explores its contents, coming at last upon the elegant doll. By holding Helen's hand to her face and nodding, she tells Helen the doll is hers. And now begins the first lesson: spelling words with fingertips in the palm of a hand.

D-O-L-L. Helen catches on immediately and soon is spelling out the word with her fingers in the air. She is *bright*, Annie decides. So the two begin to find out about each other—and each has a strong will. When Annie takes the doll from Helen, hoping that the child will ask for it by spelling out the word, Helen becomes raging angry. At Annie's insistence, the girl finally spells the word, and when she gets the doll she promptly bangs Annie in the face with it, knocking out a tooth. This is going to be a war. Helen wins the first battle by scuttling out of the bedroom and locking Annie inside. The indignant Captain Keller finally has to bring her down for dinner by carrying her down a ladder from her window.

After dinner, in the dusk, Annie finds Helen alone by the pump, playing with the doll with innocent contentment. Presently the child stands up, groping to see if anyone is near, and Annie avoids her touch. Satisfied that she is alone, Helen takes the bedroom key from her mouth, lifts a loose board over the well, drops the key in and hugs herself gleefully.

"You *devil*," says Annie.

The Curtain Falls

ACT II

The warfare continues. It is not a war of hatred, but a clash between two strong wills, with each combatant wanting her own way. Annie's problem is to find a way, somehow, of disciplining her charge without breaking her spirit. There are scenes of tempest, such as Helen spilling Annie's writing ink or stabbing her with a needle. Annie tries to get through with the difference between a "good girl" and "bad girl" by letting Helen feel her face. If it is a smiling face, it means good girl; if the mouth is turned down it means bad. And always Annie is spelling into Helen's palm.

Kate Keller watches one of these spelling bees and announces she would like to learn the finger alphabet. But what good will it do? Are any of the words getting through? Annie explains that this spelling is like talking baby-talk to a baby: The baby doesn't understand for a long time, but after a million words or so it begins to catch the meaning. If Kate will learn finger-spelling it will cut Annie's million words in half. Helen can now spell brilliantly, but she won't know what spelling is until she knows what a *word* is. In writing a letter—probably a report to the Institution in Boston—Annie declares, "The more I think the more certain I am that obedience is the gateway through which knowledge enters the mind of the child."

One morning Viney, the colored cook, has the table set for breakfast and has filled the water pitcher from the pump. The family and Annie begin to eat, but Helen wanders around the table, exploring the contents of the various plates. Her parents and half-brother pretend not to notice her messy investigation; but when Helen gropes for Annie's plate, Annie lifts the plate out of reach and thrusts the girl's hand from the table. Soon Helen begins to make angry noises and flail at the governess. It has been the family's habit, just to keep peace at mealtime, to let Helen pick up what she wants where she wants it; but Annie is bound to keep *her* plate for herself.

Miss Sullivan shows her first burst of temper toward her employers when Captain Keller admonishes that she should have some pity. "For this *tyrant?*" the governess shouts. She makes a point when she says it is less trouble to feel sorry for Helen than to try to teach her anything better. Still holding the struggling girl, she surprisingly demands that everybody else leave the table and the room. While Helen kicks in a tantrum on the floor, she locks both doors of the room and removes all plates from the table. The showdown has come.

It is a violent physical showdown with no holds barred, and it is exciting to watch it played by Miss Duke and Miss Bancroft. It seems to be a more real, more bruising fight than any of the faked-up barroom matches that one sees on TV Westerns. When Helen lands a roundhouse on Annie's ear, the governess retaliates by giving the girl a good hard slap in the face. Another slap and Helen begins to think things over: somebody besides her can fight. She tries to escape from the room and finds it locked.

Repeatedly Annie thrusts Helen into her proper chair and puts her hands beside the breakfast plate she has set in place, and repeatedly the child escapes around or under the table. Soon the room is in great disorder. Not in years has there been such a rough-and-tumble on a New York stage—and between a little girl and a young woman! All Annie wants Helen to do is to sit in her own chair and use her own spoon on her own plate. She doesn't win the bout—even after she flings the pitcher of water into the astonished child's face.

But the morning is yet young. All morning the family room doors remain locked. Come dinnertime at noon, Viney has the meal ready and the family all are waiting. Finally the door to the porch opens and Helen comes blundering out "like a ruined bat out of hell." She is followed by Annie, smoked glasses in hand, and, though considerably undone, she looks as though she had taken Vicksburg. She announces to Mrs. Keller: "She ate from her own plate. She ate with a spoon. Herself. And she folded her napkin." Annie goes to her room to start packing—either to quit or be fired.

The afternoon wears on. Annie has had her showdown with Helen and now she faces one with the girl's father. Captain Keller and Kate are in a summerhouse on the homestead, discussing the noontime events. Keller is red-faced, angry and determined to get rid of the governess forthwith. Perhaps the only place for his daughter is an asylum—but Kate objects that the girl is not mentally defective; she *did* fold her napkin. And before she was stricken, and at a surprisingly early age, she did learn one word, water, which she called wah-wah.

Being summoned, Annie appears at the summerhouse, determined now to fight her job through. After considerable bluster, Keller offers her another chance—if she undergoes a radical change of manner. Annie lays down her own condition: If she stays, she must be in complete charge of the girl; Helen must be dependent on her and her alone.

In a speech passionately spoken by Miss Bancroft, Annie tells the parents what life in an asylum would be like—and she knows, for she and her now-dead little brother lived in one, the state almshouse. They played with the rats there because they had no toys.

Dubiously, Keller agrees to Annie's bargain. They will make the summerhouse suitable for permanent living. Helen will be taken there after a long journey, so she won't know where she is, and she and Annie will be *alone*. The parents may see their child, of course, but Helen must never know they are there. Keller agrees to the deal— for two weeks only. "Two weeks," says Annie. "For only one miracle?"

Furniture is moved from the main house to the summerhouse, including a box of toys with the doll at the top of the pile. Annie and Helen and the small Negro boy, Percy, will be here alone. Helen is brought here by her parents after a two-hour drive in the country, and, being in a strange place, she begins exploring with great curiosity. She is overjoyed at finding her doll, but appalled when she feels Annie—for Annie is the person she hates and fears. Locked alone in the house with her governess, Helen has another wild tantrum, going on a rampage of destruction until at last she sinks exhausted on the floor, doll in arms.

At two in the morning, in her nightgown, Annie tries an approach to Helen, still sleeping on the floor. At her touch the girl awakens and quickly scrambles away under her bed. But Annie *must* touch Helen, communicate with her, somehow. She calls to Percy in the next room and the sleepy-eyed lad finally responds. She suggests that, as part of a new game, he crawl under the bed and touch Helen.

When the boy does this the girl utters an animal-like sound and crawls farther under the bed—but she starts sniffing. When Percy touches her again she sniffs his hand, recognizes him and comes out from under to hug him with delight.

Now Annie takes Percy's hand—the one Helen isn't holding— and begins teaching the puzzled boy the manual alphabet. Helen knows something is up and her curiosity is consuming. She spells "cake" into Percy's other palm. Before long, so jealous is she of the attention Percy is getting, she is holding up her hand for Annie to spell something into. Annie spells "milk." Helen spells it back to her, and Annie promptly fetches her a mug of milk.

After drinking, the child climbs into her bed. Relations have been resumed . . . and dependence established. Up in the main house, shafts of moonlight pick out Kate, James, and Captain Keller in various places. They all are still awake, wondering what is happening.

The Curtain Falls

ACT III

The two weeks are up and it is breakfast time. In the main house the Kellers are edgy, wondering, half-expectant. In the summerhouse Annie is talking aloud to Helen, and spelling to her, too. W-A-T-E-R. "This is water. It has a name. The name stands for the thing. There's only one way out for you, and it's language."

Kate goes for a look through the window at the last day in the summerhouse. She finds Helen on her bed, crocheting intently, and Annie readying the girl's breakfast. When Annie brings a chair and a tray, Helen drops her work, sits in the chair, tucks a napkin in her neck and feels for a spoon. Annie has withheld it. So Helen folds her hands in her lap and quietly waits. Not until she has been given her spoon does she begin to eat, neatly. No more eating with her fingers.

It has been a busy fortnight, with Helen keeping herself clean, stringing beads, climbing trees . . . and spelling, always spelling. But she doesn't know the *meaning* of a word.

Keller comes to the little house, too, but Annie bars him from entering; this last day isn't officially up until six o'clock. Good-humoredly calling the governess a tyrant, Keller expresses his gratitude for what Annie has done. What can they do to repay her? Give her another week, she suggests, but the parents are too hungry for their child to agree.

With so few hours left, Annie Sullivan is desperate. She has wanted to teach Helen everything the earth is full of—and she *could*, too, with only one word.

At six o'clock Helen is taken home, and the girl and her mother embrace each other tightly, gratefully. Annie, alone in the summerhouse, tired and defeated, bathes her burning, aching eyes. Her dejected solitude is broken by the appearance of Captain Keller, bringing her an envelope for her first month's salary—the first month of her new engagement. They want her to stay on.

Dinner that night in the main house is a gala one, with Viney having cooked some of Helen's favorite dishes. They all are seated, with Annie next to Helen, and Annie puts a napkin around the girl's neck. With a devilish gleam, she throws it on the floor, and when Annie picks it up and puts it back on the child again discards it.

Annie's Irish begins to rise. After the third such maneuver, she removes the child's plate of food over the protests of her parents. After all, this is a special occasion; can't she be indulged just once? Vehemently, Annie points out that Helen is just testing them—trying to see if she can get away with her old tricks.

Captain Keller recovers the napkin and puts it on his daughter, who accepts it quietly. In triumph he gives her a fork. With wicked glee she flings down the fork and, plunging a hand into her plate, crams a fistful of food down her mouth. Next she reaches out the other hand and raids Annie's plate. This is too much for the governess, and she seizes Helen's wrist. With the other hand the girl grabs the water pitcher and aims a blow at Annie, who manages to fend it off with an elbow. But water gets splashed all over her dress.

Thoroughly angry, Annie picks Helen out of her chair with one arm, grabs the pitcher and heads for outdoors. Savagely polite, she advises the Kellers not to undo anything more that she has done. She is going to take Helen out to the pump and make her fill the pitcher again. Keller is all for interfering, but, surprisingly, his son James bars his way.

Grimly hauling, Annie puts Helen's hand on the pump handle and forces her to work it. When the water starts coming she puts the pitcher in the girl's other hand and holds it under the flow. Next she takes the pump handle from Helen and spells W-A-T-E-R into the thus-freed hand.

The light changes to dusk . . . and a new light comes over Helen's face. Something inside her is struggling, and her lips tremble. Finally she says "Wah . . . wah. Wah . . . wah." The miracle has come.

Eager with new discovery, Helen drops to the ground, pats it and then holds up her palm, imperiously demanding what *that* is. "Ground," Annie spells. Trembling with excitement, the girl heads for the house and stumbles at the porch. What did she stumble over? A step, Annie tells her.

Annie cries exultantly toward the house and the family come hurrying out. Now eager for all knowledge, Helen Keller demands to know what everything is and who everybody is, and Annie spells out the answers. M-O-T-H-E-R. P-A-P-A. And who is she? T-E-A-C-H-E-R. The drama ends with pupil and teacher in an embrace, with Annie spelling into the little fist "I love Helen."

The Curtain Falls

FIORELLO!

Book by Jerome Weidman and George Abbott; *music by* Jerry Bock; *lyrics by* Sheldon Harnick.

WISEACRES like myself figured that the most important award in the theater, the Pulitzer Prize, would go to one of three plays, *The Miracle Worker, The Tenth Man,* or *The Best Man.* The judges foxed almost all of Broadway by anointing *Fiorello!* There were no cries of outrage at this decision, for this is an excellent and original musical; the award came as a surprise because only two other musicals, *Of Thee I Sing* and *South Pacific,* had been honored by the Pulitzer judges.

Fiorello! is original in two ways: It is not in the standard music-show pattern and it was created by two writers who did not adapt it from some already-published work. These two, novelist Jerome Weidman and George Abbott, seventy-three-year-old author, co-author, adapter or director of many a hit, simply started with the idea that Fiorello H. La Guardia, rumpus-raising mayor of New York, had been such a colorful character that he would make a good subject for a show. Moreover, the times during which he quarreled, campaigned, and reigned were extraordinarily lively in New York. The administration which "The Little Flower" unhorsed may have been crooked, but it had zip.

It goes without saying these days that anything Abbott takes a hand in will be produced by the most successful music-show producing team in the theater, Robert E. Griffith and Harold S. Prince—for these two have learned about the theater from Abbott himself, having been stage managers for many of his productions.

For the songs, the talents of Jerry Bock, composer, and Sheldon Harnick, lyricist, were enlisted. They collaborated for the first time two years ago on a musical which failed during its tryout, *The Body Beautiful.* Bock's first full music-show score was for *Mr. Wonderful,* starring Sammy Davis, Jr. Harnick's first Broadway lyric was "The Boston Beguine" in *New Faces of 1952.* He has contributed to a few revues, on Broadway and in night clubs, and has written lyrics for Ray Bolger, Hermione Gingold, and Eddie Fisher. The songs of *Fiorello!* are not juke-box hits, but they do have one admirable quality: they fit. And there is good sound satire in two of their numbers, "Politics and Poker" and "Little Tin Box."

This was a first venture into the theatre for Weidman, author of sixteen novels, including the famed *I Can Get It for You Wholesale, The Enemy Camp,* and the recent *They Told Me You Were Dead.* And a stroke of casting genius by director Abbott, who would rather find and develop a new actor than hire an established one, was the discovery of an off-Broadway and stock player, Tom Bosley, for the title role. On the opening night Bosley looked like La Guardia, sounded like him, and acted like him—due to research among newsreels and news pictures made when Bosley was very young. Subsequently he received several awards for his performance. When he was given an Antoinette Perry "Tony" by the American Theatre Wing, his speech of thanks was, "If it weren't for Mr. Abbott I'd be just another chubby actor."

Even when *Fiorello!* was well received out of town and on its opening night, one doubt gnawed at authors and producers: Would it hold up? After all, such Manhattan personalities as La Guardia, Judge Samuel Seabury, and Jimmy Walker are no longer present, and the time of the story spans ten years beginning shortly before World War I—the First German War. The plot might arouse warm memories among those who were around at the time, but what about a generation which might not even have *heard* of La Guardia, Seabury, and Walker? Would they enjoy the show?

The box office kept selling out, except during the actors' strike. Public response heartened the same group of authors and producers in their next project, a musical version of the late Samuel Hopkins Adams' last novel, *Tenderloin.* This also was a story of malfeasance in Manhattan, set in an even earlier time—the time of the crusading minister, Dr. Parkhurst.

THE LIBRETTO: ACT I

The curtain rises on a dark stage. A voice, Bosley's, gives an uncanny imitation of La Guardia's during the memorable moments when, during a newspaper strike, the Mayor read the comic strips to the children over the city's radio station. The lights come up for an instant on this radio station scene; then they dim and throw the time back to just before World War I. The setting is the two-room law office of Fiorello H. La Guardia in Greenwich Village.

It is late afternoon. One sees Neil, a bright young law clerk (Bob Holiday) at the telephone switchboard; Morris, the doleful office manager (Nathaniel Frey), is talking on the phone. A squat, fiftyish matron is seated on the clients' bench. Two shabby men join her there, all wanting Mr. La Guardia to solve their troubles. Morris observes that Mr. La Guardia never has time for people who pay their bills, and in song Neil assures the petitioners in a number called "On the Side of the Angels" that their rights will be protected. This clients' bench, sings Neil, is a regular wailing wall.

Next to arrive is Marie (Patricia Wilson), the attractive, efficient secretary. She brings with her the boss's cornet, which has been repaired. At last La Guardia himself bursts in. As a director, Abbott has two hallmarks—pace and playing it straight, even in the broadest, most farcical roles. La Guardia always had pace and he took things with violent seriousness.

In one whirlwind instant Fiorello promises help for his petitioners and even takes on the case of a friend of Marie's, Thea, whom a crooked cop has arrested for soliciting while she was peacefully picketing a shirtwaist factory. Then he announces briskly that he must see Ben Marino, Republican leader in the Fourteenth Congressional District, because he wants the nomination for Congress. Incredulous, the secretary points out that Tammany has the Fourteenth sewed up and no Republican *ever* went to Congress from there. In another flash Fiorello is out of his office and on his way to see Marino.

He goes to the musty political meeting house of the Ben Marino Association on West Third Street. Here he finds five of Ben's political hacks playing five-card stud at a big round poker table. Ben (Howard Da Silva) declines to take a hand. He must settle on a candidate and nobody wants to be one. The hacks play, Ben urges the seriousness of his problem—and they all do it in one of the best songs in the show, "Politics and Poker," in which they observe that politics is more predictable than poker because in politics one can stack the deck.

Marie, who knows Ben, has come with Fiorello and introduces him. One of the card players looks contemptuously at him and says something about a little wop with a big hat. Fiorello counters that there are only *big* wops—and he has come here to get the nomination.

Ben, cynical and seasoned, shrugs "Why not?" As Fiorello and Marie hurry out, Ben takes a sixth hand and the sextet resumes harmonizing "Politics and Poker."

Now Fiorello puts his mind on the strike at the Nifty Shirtwaist Factory, next door to which the girls have set up headquarters. Several of them are parading in the street carrying "Unfair" signs. Women going on strike is something new, and there are many hecklers among the men passing by. Even Floyd, the cop, (Mark Dawson) is unfriendly, and he prods a girl for loitering when she stops to adjust the cardboard in the hole of one shoe. Another striker, Dora (Pat Stanley), angrily tells the cop they "got a right" to march.

When Floyd threatens to arrest Dora for wiggling she dares him to do it—and performs a vigorous wiggle. Fiorello breaks in on this row and announces he will take charge. He orders the girls into their headquarters for a meeting, then turns on Floyd and threatens him with a writ of interdictum—which makes this dumb cop uneasy.

Marie, figuring that a lot of girls may be arrested, heads for the office to line up some bail bondsmen, and just as she is going Fiorello asks if she will have dinner with him tonight; he has always wanted to know her better. She accepts promptly.

Soon Thea, the girl who was arrested (Ellen Hanley) appears in the tow of Morris, who has arranged her bail. Inside strike headquarters, Fiorello brightens when he learns that Thea is from Trieste —now, she says darkly, being ground under the heel of Austria. Fiorello tells her he was U. S. Consul in Fiume and knows Trieste well.

He also brightens at the prospects ahead—a fight for the strikers, in whom he believes, which should incidentally help his campaign for Congress. He wants to know more about the problems at the factory, and Thea asks him to take her to dinner tonight so she can explain things. After a small hesitation he makes the date.

Fiorello now addresses the girls in an inflammatory song about misbegotten misers and sweatshops. They must howl at the top of their voices, he urges—and they do.

In the La Guardia office Marie and Morris have finished lining up bail in case some of the strikers are arrested, when Fiorello telephones his secretary. We don't hear what he says, but it is obvious from watching the girl's face that he has reneged on the dinner date. She sweetly tells Mr. La Guardia it is perfectly all right—but after she has hung up she begins to get angry. "There ought to be a law," she exclaims—and this notion develops into a duet by her and Morris. She has a number of laws she'd like to write—such as throwing into jail any man who breaks a date.

A little time passes and La Guardia's campaign begins. On a street corner Neil, of La Guardia's office, tells a small gathering what a great man the great man is. Ben Marino is on hand to observe and help with applause. Next speaker will be Thea, and while she is mounting the stepladder platform Floyd, the cop, and his erstwhile enemy, Dora, have a talk. He has heard that the strike has been won, and, shaking hands with Dora, hopes there are no hard feelings.

Thea is more enthusiastic than Neil about Fiorello. She tells the assemblage that he is the man who came to the rescue of girls who were working twelve hours a day for four dollars a week. And at last the candidate scurries aloft and begins an attack on Tammany in the form of a quick and tricky patter song. Soon he has the crowd with him.

The lights go down quickly and come up again on another part of the stage and in another part of Greenwich Village. The audience is Italian this time, and Thea harangues it about La Guardia, the friend of Trieste. Up on the platform next bounces Fiorello and he repeats his campaign song—but in Italian! On another street the crowd is Jewish and the little man makes his pitch in Yiddish. Obviously, he is a formidable campaigner. (The real La Guardia was half Italian, half Jewish.)

Another street scene: This time Ben Marino and his henchmen appear, wearing dazed looks and carrying newspapers, and they give us the news in a song called "The Bum Won." Instead of being elated, Ben is worried. What good will Fiorello's election to the House of Representatives be if the little fireball isn't grateful to Ben and his organization? It would be a calamity if the victor proved to be independent.

For a musical, Fiorello! hasn't been very romantic up to now—which may be the key to its Pulitzer Prize. Fiorello breaking a dinner date with Marie and that is all. Now we encounter a bit of he-she stuff on the dreary roof of a Village tenement, where a table has been set and Dora is serving a second cup of tea to, of all people, Floyd, the dumb cop. He wants a kiss, but she protests it is daylight. They talk of Marie, who is coming by to borrow a hat so she can go to Washington and see Representative La Guardia.

Floyd, a Tammany man, has nothing nice to say about Fiorello.

He's trying to get us into the war. They hate him in his own district, which he stole right from under Tammany's nose because the Wigwam was overconfident. Floyd can't tarry, for his partner is waiting downstairs, but he leaves Dora in a happy mood. When Marie arrives to pick up the hat in Dora's apartment, Dora says she is happy but miserable, too. This is a song, "I Love a Cop," which pert Pat Stanley delivers pertly.

Marie picks one of Dora's two best hats, then confides that she is going to Washington to see Ben Marino, not Fiorello. Ben thinks Marie may have influence enough to tell La Guardia what to say in Congress.

We switch you now, as they say on radio and TV, to Washington, where Fiorello is in his office, busy as usual, and busiest most about being himself. He brushes off a dignified Senator who tells him freshman Congressmen should be seen but not heard. And he *has* been heard, arguing that France and England are almost worn out and we must get into the war to save our nation. And the fair and honest way of sending American men into a war would be a Draft Act.

Marie and Ben turn up, also, to talk about the Draft Act. Marie says the constituents in New York are upset over Fiorello's attitude, and Ben adds further arguments. To which Fiorello replies, with unusual quietness, that he is no longer the choice of a few people in one district; he is now a Congressman, and he must think about the whole country.

Angrily and cuttingly, Ben asks what his thinking would be if the Draft Act applied to Congressmen. Fiorello stops him cold by announcing, "I enlisted this morning."

The Draft Act has been passed, boys are in uniform and F. H. La Guardia is going to war—so the Ben Marino Association is giving him a farewell party at the clubhouse. One can hear the cheers of people in the yard outside. Fiorello is in the uniform of a flier. He has definite plans ahead. First, there is the war to be won and Trieste to be regained as a personal gift to Thea, the striker. He has kind words for Marie, too, but not loving ones. His big plan, he tells Thea, is to come back from the war and marry Thea.

In *Fiorello!* World War I is the fastest conflict on record. The act ends with a montage of real and staged pictures on a movie screen— La Guardia closing his desk in Washington, La Guardia with his squadron grouped by a biplane somewhere in France, an aerial dog-fight in which Fiorella bags a Hun, King Victor Emmanuel reclaiming Trieste, the Armistice Day celebration in Times Square. The screen is pulled up and here, walking down a real gangplank, comes the uniformed Fiorello. He takes Thea into his arms.

ACT II

Ten years have gone. It is the first day of a new political campaign in New York, and the setting is the La Guardia home. Thea, now Mrs. La Guardia, is setting breakfast. Fiorello, wearing shirt, tie, and everything else but his pants, comes out of the bedroom to ask his wife where his black suit is. She sent it out to be pressed. How, he asks, does she expect him to beat that tinhorn tailor's dummy, Jimmy Walker, if he wears pressed pants?

Dora drops in to report joyfully the latest rise in the career of the dumb Tammany cop, Floyd. Because he knew how to keep his mouth shut, he rose in the police ranks, then shifted to sewers. And now, says Dora, he has been promoted to garbage, having been given the city's disposal contract for lower Manhattan. It is obvious that the two are now married—and Floyd and Dora have a penthouse apartment.

Ben thinks he is running Fiorello's campaign again, but Fiorello pays him no mind; he will run it his own way and is looking high and low for crooks.

In this scene it is established that Thea is not well, but she minimizes her trouble to Dora, saying she is tired and the doctor says all she needs is a rest. At the close she is alone, singing a nice but not sensational ballad, "When Did I Fall in Love?"

Floyd and Dora McDuff really have it good. Here they are on their terrace preparing a party with the help of a very proper butler. Floyd is pleased that Tammany big shots are coming—but Dora drops a nasty remark that she doesn't think a gangster like Frankie Scarpini is a big shot. (Michael Scrittorale plays Frankie very cool and menacing a little later.)

The guests, in dinner jackets, begin to arrive—a judge, a commissioner, a politician among them. They talk bitterly about La Guardia, and wonder if they can shut him up by "getting something" on him or letting him get hit by a truck.

Floyd has provided fine entertainment for his party. There is the musical comedy star, Mitzi Travers (Eileen Rodgers) and she has brought along a chorus of dancing cuties. The number she does is right out of the Jimmy Walker era, jazzy and zippy, and it is called "Gentleman Jimmy."

After the song, Frankie Scarpini arrives with a couple of body-guards, and he talks guardedly with one of the guests, the commissioner. (Commissioner of what is not established.) Dora eyes him and frankly tells her husband she thinks he is a terrible-looking man, and Floyd warns her to pipe down. Does she want to get him bumped off?

Frankie and the commissioner talk over their plan. When La Guardia speaks next week at 105th Street . . . a roof right over the speaker's platform . . . somebody up there to drop something . . .

We return to the La Guardia law office. It is just about the same as it was ten years ago, except that the staff are now older and there is a new girl on the switchboard. Neil and Morris and Marie, the loyal secretary, are there, and so is Ben Marino, Fiorello's political lieutenant. Ben now calls Fiorello Major and he still thinks his man is all wrong as a campaigner. Why should he call Alderman Marconi a crook when Alderman Marconi is so popular with Italian voters?

Fiorello denies that he called Marconi a crook; he said he was a thief. Ben is certain that Fiorello will lose this election for the simple reason that he just will not play ball. The little man is so confident, however, that he tells a reporter who has come to interview him that he will win the mayoralty of New York City by at least 350,000 votes.

Tonight is the night that Fiorello will make his speech at 105th Street and Madison Avenue. His wife, Thea, would like to come, but she still is ill and he tells her on the telephone to stay home in bed.

Dora comes into the office. She is distraught because she is torn between loyalty to her husband, Floyd, the ex-cop, and the champion of the shirtwaist strikers, Fiorello. Fiorello has won in this case, and she tells Marie something she has heard some men talking to her husband about. Tonight, at the speech on 105th Street, somebody will turn in a fire alarm. During the confusion when the fire apparatus arrives, some thugs on a roof are going to tip over a baby carriage filled with paving blocks right on La Guardia's head.

When Marie relays the news to her boss he is undaunted. He orders Neil to stand by the fire alarm box on the corner and stop anybody who tries to pull it, even if there is a real fire; and he orders

Morris to get somebody at Police Headquarters to put guards on the roof.

When speech-time comes Neil mounts guard over the fire alarm and prevents two or three shady characters from pulling it. But he leaves his post when Morris appears to tell him the awful and unexpected news that Thea has died. Fiorello can be heard offstage making his speech, and his two loyal men leave the corner to break the news to him. As soon as they have gone somebody pulls the alarm, and the scene ends with the sound of sirens in the audience's ears.

After the speech Fiorello goes back to the office. The murder plan nearly went through: Somebody *did* push a carriage full of paving blocks off the roof, but the little man had a lucky escape. He got his face and his clothes smudged with dirt, but was unhurt; and now he is fighting mad. Why did Neil let somebody pull the fire alarm? They break the news to him that his wife has passed away.

In the usual play or musical comedy, this would be the time for the hero to win—for La Guardia to become mayor of New York. But it didn't work out this way in history and it doesn't in the show. In this campaign James J. Walker was returned to office in a landslide, and Fiorello is left a widower, defeated at the polls—but not crushed. After the returns are in he tells his staff, "If we can't fight them in City Hall we'll fight them in the courts."

And this is what happens. We find out about it in another poker-playing scene in the Ben Marino Association's clubhouse. Ben and his followers are here again, playing stud and talking politics. This time they are talking about Judge Seabury's investigation of Tammany and are reading about it in today's newspapers. This was a relentless probe in which Seabury asked Tammany officeholders how it happened that, with their salaries, they happened to have so much money.

The Ben Marino boys, being Republicans, relish Seabury's twisting of the Tiger's tail. They put on a burlesque of the investigation, with Ben impersonating various witnesses who have been asked for an accounting by Seabury. This is the musical and satirical highlight of *Fiorello!*—the number called "Little Tin Box." With mock glibness, Ben tries to explain his wealth—his ability to buy yachts, Rolls-Royces and women—by saying that he went without lunch, stopped smoking or cashed in on his empty milk bottles and put the savings in a little tin box.

The next few minutes are devoted to wrapping up the show and wrapping up history, with no disservice to either. The history is that, some three years after the Seabury investigation began, La Guardia was asked to run for the mayoralty once more, on a Fusion ticket. The history also is that the bouncy little scrapper was married a second time—to Marie, the secretary who had been in his employ for so long . . . for so many years after he had broken a dinner date with her to talk to the militant striker from Trieste.

The Curtain Falls

(Mrs. F. H. La Guardia was way down front and center on the opening night of *Fiorello!* She enjoyed it very much, and must have been touched by it much more than any of the rest of us, for she was the ex-secretary who was at her husband's side through a fabulous reign at City Hall and up to the time of his ultimate defeat in 1947—by cancer.)

THE TENTH MAN

By Paddy Chayefsky

WHILE he was living in Paris before World War I, a Russian playwright, S. Ansky (real name, Solomon Z. Rappaport), delved into the Dreyfus case and this led him down a bypath of exploring Jewish folklore. He was struck with the legend of the dybbuk, an ancient one which has its counterpart among other peoples, and in 1914 he wrote a drama called *Between Two Worlds*. Back in Moscow three years later, he reworked it into a play called *The Dybbuk* for the Moscow Art Theatre at Stanislavsky's request. The censor banned it, so it was translated into Yiddish for the Vilna Troupe, and again it was suppressed. Bialik, noted Hebrew poet, tried a Hebrew adaptation and this, too, was banned.

Ansky liked the Hebrew version best of all, so he translated it into Yiddish. It became the main drama of the great Habima Players after they first performed it in Warsaw in 1920. In 1921 it was performed by New York's noted Yiddish Art Theatre. In 1925 the Neighborhood Playhouse presented an English version with Mary Ellis as the girl who is possessed.

The story of *The Dybbuk* is a poetic tragedy telling of two lovers, Chanan and Leah. Thwarted in his love for Leah, Chanan dies, and his spirit, or dybbuk, takes up residence in Leah's body. When her family arranges a rich marriage for her, the dybbuk in her cries out against the match. A rabbi is called in to exorcise this objecting spirit and he does so; but after the exorcism Leah dies. Thus it is that love at last has its way, for Leah's spirit joins Chanan's.

Also interested in ancient dybbuk lore, Paddy Chayefsky set out to present the tale as a modern one, and to rationalize it with psychiatry; and he wanted a human story, not a lofty tragedy. The success of his enterprise was complete. He had written a warm and lovely play, and its performance, under the direction of Tyrone Guthrie, was almost miraculously unified and orchestrated. The newspaper criticisms could be summed up by quoting from Walter Kerr's review in the *Herald Tribune*: "If we are serious about wanting a theatre

that ignores business as usual in favor of freshness, literary adventur-
ousness and independence of vision, we must both respect and support Mr. Chayefsky's uncompromising haymaker."

This is Chayefsky's second Broadway play. His first, *Middle of the
Night*, also was a success despite my disapproval of it. Chayefsky, a
New Yorker born in 1923, served in the Army during World War II.
Wounded by a booby trap in Germany, he spent his convalescence
writing the book and lyrics of an Army musical, *No T. O. for Love*.
Garson Kanin then got him to help on an award-winning documentary, *True Glory*. After the war he got into writing for the movies,
radio, and television. His TV script, *Marty*, later became an Oscar-
winning film.

THE PLAY: ACT I

The setting, beautifully evoked by David Hays, is a synagogue in a
Long Island town—but no lofty, imposing, stained-glass structure.
It is a make-do place of worship belonging to a small, poor congregation. Before it became a church it was a one-story store. A railed-off
raised platform contains the lectern and the Holy Ark. Surrounding
it are plain, wooden folding chairs. On the far side of this altar is an
old desk at which the Rabbi presides when teaching Hebrew school.
A partitioned cubicle is the Rabbi's study, with a battered desk and
chair, piles of prayer books and a worn leather armchair and sofa.
There are two metal heating units, one in front and one in back.

The curtain rises at 6:30 A.M. on a cold Winter day. The Cabalist
(Arnold Marlé), a bearded old gentleman with the serene face of a
scholar, clad in a white linen prayer shawl with black stripes, is praying
silently from a heavy prayer book he rests on the railing of the altar.
He does not seem to be well, for at one moment he clutches the
railing to keep from falling.

Three men hurry in from the bitter cold outside. They are Schlissel
(Lou Jacobi), Zitorsky (Jack Gilford) and the Sexton (David Vardi).
The first two are in their seventies; the Sexton is forty-eight—small,
nervous, bespectacled, and carrying a huge ring of keys which is the
token of his office. While he goes about turning on lights and tending
the heater, Schlissel and Zitorsky have a little small talk about the
upcoming prayer meeting. Davis won't be here this morning. His
daughter-in-law says he has a cold. Zitorsky utters a pious wish that

his daughter-in-law may grow rich and buy a hotel with a thousand rooms and be found dead in every one of them. Schlissel doesn't care for his son's wife, either.

And Forman won't be here this morning, either. This is the day— the day he is taking his granddaughter back to the institution. This girl, a schizophrenic, has been in and out of mental abodes since she was eleven, and now she is becoming violent again. Another member of the congregation, Alper, a patrician little old man with a Vandyke beard (George Voskovec), arrives. In the Rabbi's office, the Sexton makes a phone call to a man named Harris. He should come on down today, for Forman and Davis won't be here and they need ten men for the morning prayers. Another phone call to somebody named Kessler: he and his brother should come, for a quorum of ten is needed for prayers.

After he hangs up, the Sexton counts on his fingers and then announces to nobody in particular that he is going out to get a tenth Jew off the street somewheres.

Into the synagogue comes a sixth old Jew—Forman, a frightened wisp of a man (Jacob Ben-Ami) who is obviously in a state. After terrified looks all about, he darts outside and brings back with him a girl of eighteen who also appears distracted. The others all are busy with individual prayers or other affairs, so he manages to get the girl across the room and into the Rabbi's office unseen. He leaves her in the room, almost rigid with terror, and closes the office door behind him.

Furtively, Forman confides to Alper that he has brought the girl here—taken her out of his son's house and put her in the office. Alper's view is that he has made a mistake. He knows how dear the girl is to him, but, after all, she is insane. He should telephone his son and tell him where she is. But Forman protests that his granddaughter is possessed; she has a dybbuk in her. He knows, for this morning the dybbuk spoke to him. He had gone to see his grandchild in her room, and while he was there she fell into a faint and then began talking in a voice not her own. She was, said this voice, the soul of Hannah Luchinsky, whom Forman once dishonored and to whom the gates of heaven have been closed.

Alper remembers Hannah Luchinsky only vaguely. Forman tells him that she was a girl who became pregnant, and they threw stones at her and drove her out of the city. Forman confesses that he was the one who debased her, back in his student days. And now he wants to consult Hirschman, the cabalist, who has delved into the cabala and the forbidden mysteries of numbers.

The other men learn of Forman's trouble and are impressed— except Schlissel. He professes to be an atheist, so if he doesn't believe in God why should he believe in demons? Forman furiously flings open the office door and wildly demands that the dybbuk reveal itself.

With a blood-curdling laugh, the girl (Risa Schwartz) declares that she is Hannah Luchinsky. And how did she possess the grand-daughter's body? She was on a yacht in the sea of Odessa with five wealthy merchants; a storm wrecked the yacht and all were lost. Her soul flew to Belgorod, where the sages rejected her because she was debauched. Next, her soul entered the body of a cow, but the cow became insane and was slaughtered. So now she has entered the body of this girl. It is an eerie recital and the old Jews are so impressed they are almost numb.

The girl sprawls in the Rabbi's chair, talking no more, so the men leave the office and close the door. Schlissel recovers his cynicism, remembering that the last time he saw the girl she said she was Susan Hayward.

What to do now about the dybbuk? The Rabbi here is too young to be experienced in such things. Schlissel suggests the Korpotchniker Rabbi of Williamsburg, a sage among sages. Alper prefers the Bobolobitcher Rabbi of Crown Heights. Zitorsky thinks the Lubanower Rabbi of Brownsville is the man.

The Cabalist, Hirschman, has finished his long prayers and come forward, and is told that Forman's granddaughter is possessed by a dybbuk. This news is of great import to the Cabalist, for, after fasting and praying three days, last night he heard the whimpering of a woman's soul somewhere. He agrees that the rabbi in Williamsburg is the best man to consult—and a cousin of his, too. On the coin phone outside the Rabbi's office he makes an appointment for Forman to see the great man right after morning services, and Forman departs—armed with all manner of conflicting advice from his friends on how to get to Williamsburg from Mineola.

Into the synagogue bustles the Sexton with his tenth Jew in tow— a fine-looking, if troubled young man named Arthur Brooks (Donald Harron). The Sexton gives him a black paper skullcap from a carton of them and hurries out again to round up the Kesslers, for it is only seven minutes to services. Arthur becomes preoccupied with dark thoughts, and the other men have a pleasant time speculating what an exorcism will be like.

Another worshiper, Harris (Martin Garner) arrives and begins doffing his outerclothes. He is more than eighty, and needs a lot to keep warm. Besides an overcoat he removes several sweaters. Then he puts on his phylacteries. (A phylactery is a leather thong; one is wound on the bare left arm and hand, the other on the head, to the accompaniment of incantations.)

Alper moves cordially to the stranger, Arthur, and offers him a set of phylacteries. Arthur, who has a hangover, says rather brusquely that he wouldn't know what to do with them. He also declines a prayer shawl. He says he was brought in off the street by a man who said he'd kill himself if he didn't come, and the man promised that all he would have to do was stand around a few minutes wearing a hat. Arthur further declines a prayer book, saying he can't read Hebrew and anyhow there is nothing he wants to pray about. All he wants is to get away as soon as possible.

Out of Arthur's hearing, Schlissel comments, "Where are all the Orthodox Jews? They have apostated to the Reform Jewish temples, where they sit around like Episcopalians, listening to organ music."

Arthur announces that he wants to make a rather personal phone call and is told there is a telephone in the Rabbi's office. He sits at the desk there and makes his call—and the girl, in a catatonic state, sits in the leather chair and pays him no heed. He gets his connection—his psychiatrist, whom he has waked up. He wants an appointment in an hour or so. He has been drunk for three days, and early this morning he found himself here in Mineola banging on the door of his ex-wife's parents' home, where she now is living.

The girl's presence bothers him and he reminds her that this is a very personal call. Would she mind letting him have the use of the office for a few minutes? In a hollow voice the girl answers, "I am the Whore of Kiev, the companion of sailors."

Finishing his call, he goes out into the synagogue with the information that there is a pretty strange girl in the office—the Whore of Kiev. Schlissel figures that if *this* gets around they'll *all* be put in an asylum. They'd better get her out of the Rabbi's office and hide her somewhere else. Alper offers his basement. Everybody else in the house is still sleeping, and they can sneak her down there now.

Alper goes to the office to get the girl, but she doesn't react when he speaks gently to her. He tries again, and she gives a strange grunt and then emits an electrifying scream. Alper, at wits' end, emerges from the office. Arthur, beginning to get indignant, demands to know what is going on. Schlissel informs him the girl is possessed by a dybbuk; Alper takes a more scientific tack and explains that she is a catatonic schizophrenic, but there is no cause for alarm. Arthur wants to know what a dybbuk is, and Alper says it is a migratory soul which possessed the body of another person in order to return or get into heaven. It traces back to the Essenes, and was popularized by Spanish cabalists in the thirteenth century.

After a while the young stranger cools down. The Sexton comes in with two more recruits, the Kessler boys, making a quorum. On time right to the minute comes the Rabbi (Gene Saks), a modern young churchman. There are "Peace be with you's" around, and the Rabbi heads for his office to get his phylacteries. Schlissel blocks his way and Alper gives him another set, reminding him that it is late.

As each man's voice rises in prayer,

The Curtain Falls

ACT II, *Scene 1*

It is fifteen minutes later. The Jewish prayer service is beautiful and impressive, and it is splendidly done by these actors on the stage. As it proceeds, the girl decides to come out of the office. She moves out a few steps and Arthur hears her and turns to her warily. Completely lucid and gentle, she asks him if they are reading from the Torah now. He thinks they are, he says.

She becomes interested in him and they begin talking in low voices. Soon they move back into the office, where they can *really* talk. It is a sweet, touching scene of self-revelation on the part of both. The girl talks openly, almost clinically, about her mental troubles, about her great love for her grandfather, about the movies. She was in *David and Bathsheba*, not Susan Hayward, and she was the girl who danced in *The Ten Commandments*. He listens with gentle understanding and she is surprised that he doesn't mind her being insane. Why should he? he counters. He is being psychoanalyzed himself, and has tried to commit suicide so many times it has become a family joke. One day, he assures her, he will really make it; he will forget to make a last-minute telephone call and nobody will come to save him.

Life, he says, is dreary, and unbearable if one is sensitive. He considers his own life a meaningless sham. His parents were very poor so he spent twenty years hating the rich. Then he shifted to hating his mother and left home to live alone. Living alone was unbearable, so he married. Marriage was so dull he spent most of his time in the office and thus became a very successful lawyer. He and his wife thought children might save their marriage, but children didn't. So he began drinking, and this has been no salvation either. Having tried everything, he now wants to stop living somehow.

The girl thinks he is wonderful.

And from the synagogue one hears the Rabbi singing out, "Blessed art Thou, O Lord our God . . ."

There now comes one moment, one instant, which I thought was important to the play—the insane trying to cure the sane. The girl says she never met anyone who wanted to know the meaning of life as desperately as he does, and she would like to give him a book which was given her by the Cabalist, called *The Book of Splendor.*

Arthur leaves the office, rejoins the praying men and speaks to Schlissel about the girl. Somebody should call her father or mother. Schlissel asks, complainingly, then what would happen to the exorcism they have planned? Arthur can't believe he is serious.

The front door of the synagogue is flung open and in comes Forman, greatly distraught. He lost his way; couldn't even find the Long Island Rail Road station for the first leg of his trip to Williamsburg. While the men are striking their brows and expressing dismay at this failure, the girl puts on her coat, comes out of the office and goes quietly out the front door without anybody noticing her. Schlissel volunteers to accompany Forman to see the rabbi in Williamsburg.

Prayers over, the Rabbi again makes for his office. Arthur and Alper try to stay him, but he brushes by, goes in and closes the door, and those left on the outside chorus "Oy!" and wait for trouble. Brisk and businesslike at his desk, he telephones an old friend, Harry, to congratulate him on having got his first congregation.

This one-sided conversation is a modern "Cohen on the Telephone," filled with humor, wisdom, and practicality as the Rabbi, speaking from experience, gives Harry some advice. Being scholarly and pious, Harry has no business being a rabbi; he must be a go-getter. He must have a Youth Group, a Young Married People's Club, a Theatre Club, a Little League baseball team, a bazaar with raffles and bingo.

When the Rabbi comes out of his office Arthur braces him, saying he wants to talk about the girl in his office. *What* girl? The Rabbi is puzzled. Soon the others discover that the girl has vanished—but they tell the Rabbi about her anyway—about the dybbuk and the plan for an exorcism. He is not too impressed, and he hurries off to the printer's to arrange for some raffle tickets.

Before anybody can decide what to do about the missing girl, she returns, carrying a beautifully bound book and looking for Arthur —but he is not here. She begins to get panicky, but now Arthur comes through the front door, somewhat breathless. She offers him the book, saying she went home to get it for him. He tells her he just couldn't leave until he knew she was all right. They stare at each other for a moment, then she runs to him and flings herself into his arms.

The Curtain Falls

Scene 2

It is several hours later and quiet has settled. The Cabalist is dozing over a thick tome, the girl is napping in the Rabbi's office and the Sexton, Zitorsky, and Alper are drowsing. Only Arthur moves restlessly. Suddenly the Cabalist, eyes wide, awakens and in an awed whisper says, "Blessed be the Lord. Almost as if in a trance, he recites what has befallen him in his sleep. He has dreamed of his father, who has forgiven him and pronounced for him eternal peace among the righteous. The Cabalist, in a great state of religious ecstasy, calls for a celebration of cakes and wine, which the Sexton distributes. Even Arthur, half amused, partakes. The Cabalist breaks into a religious song and soon they begin to dance, forming a small ring with their arms around each other's shoulders. Round and round they stomp and sing; Arthur is delighted and the noise brings the girl out of the office.

She, too, would dance; but instead of ecstasy her face shows a sullen lasciviousness, and the men watch her with growing horror because the dance is wanton. She stops suddenly and sways with faintness, and the men lead her back to the office where she soon falls into a sleep. The old men are certain that the dybbuk has been at work again; Arthur, believing she is ill and having no truck with the dybbuk nonsense, thinks that someone should call her family, or at least get a doctor. Upon threat of calling the police he obtains from Alper the girl's home phone number and dials it—and there is no answer.

Alper quarrels with the old men over what to do about the girl, and at one point he says he, himself, believes in not a damn thing —no truth, no beauty, no infinity. The Cabalist, branding him a fool, declares it would be wiser to believe in dybbuks than nothing at all. The young man takes up the phone again, this time to call the police, when Forman and Schlissel burst in. After all this time and many voyages—some ending in New Jersey—they have not found Williamsburg and the Korpotchniker Rabbi.

Suddenly, in the Rabbi's office, the girl sits up, eyes clenched in pain, clutches her hands to her throat and begins to scream terribly. The old men are convinced she is dying, and Arthur's own alarm is great. Alper begs the Cabalist to save the girl, for, after all, he has just had a sign from God and is among the righteous. *He* could perform the exorcism. Arthur, more emotional than he knew he could be, begs the old man to perform his exorcism.

The Cabalist is suddenly all business and authoritative; he orders the Sexton to bring forth black candles, the ram's horn, and white prayer shawls.

The Curtain Falls

ACT III

Half an hour later the girl is sitting nervously in the Rabbi's office. The Sexton is by the wall phone, trying once again to round up enough Jews for a quorum of ten, and he is having little luck, what with refusals, one man working and another being in Miami. The Cabalist, hooded in his prayer shawl, approaches the girl and she shrinks from him in terror.

He addresses not her, but the dybbuk, demanding why it possesses this girl's body. In the voice which is not her own the girl answers that her soul was lost at sea, and there is no one to say the prayers for the dead over her. The Cabalist offers a bargain: If the dybbuk will leave the girl's body through her smallest finger, doing no damage, he will sit on wood for it for the First Seven Days of Mourning and will plead for its soul for the First Thirty Days. The bargain is cynically refused; this dybbuk wants vengeance for forty years of limbo.

Beginning to sob, the girl sinks on the couch and speaks in her own voice when the Cabalist orders preparations for the exorcism to proceed. She tells Arthur she is frightened, and he answers that he has telephoned his analyst and this gentleman has said he thinks the exorcism is a good idea—a form of shock treatment. She begs him to stay with her, even though he seems to be running away from love, having some strange dybbuk of his own. She loves him and wants to be his wife. She would be a good wife, even is she *is* a schizophrenic. With an effort he stands off her pleas, but gently.

Staring at him, the girl declares he is possessed by a dybbuk that does not allow him to love. With this, the old Cabalist agrees. Arthur's generation, the venerable one declares, is a faithless one, and love is an act of faith.

The Sexton has been out of the synagogue, prowling for two more Jews, and has encountered two policemen in a prowl car. Big, strapping Cossacks with revolvers, they ask the Sexton if he has seen a man named David Forman and his granddaughter. Their car is outside now.

Arthur makes a practical suggestion: If they start their exorcism right away, the policemen will let it go on, for they will not interrupt a religious ceremony . . . especially if they don't know what it is. The Cabalist agrees, and tells the Sexton to bring one black candle for each man.

The Cabalist declares that the Book of Codes gives no definite procedure for an exorcism, so he has selected passages of prayer which he thinks are most apt. Though they do not have a quorum, God may decide in their favor. Even Arthur submits to being enshrouded in a prayer shawl.

This scene of prayer, so magnificent vocally and so profoundly devout, has been staged with magical effectiveness by Tyrone Guthrie. Some times one man speaks, some times all—even Arthur. Forman leads his granddaughter out into their midst. Just as the Sexton has brought out the ram's horn a big, authoritative policeman enters the synagogue, stands in the doorway and demands to see Rabbi Marks. He is looking for one Evelyn Forman. Is this the girl here?

Alper chides the officer for interrupting a service in a synagogue. The cop apologizes, and says he is Jewish himself. The tenth man! Thinking fast, Alper tells him that the girl is about to be married and they are now performing the Ritual of Shriving. The Rabbi comes in. He is not sure that what is going on is right, but he goes along with it.

The ceremony continues. With ten men holding lighted candles, the Cabalist commands the dybbuk to leave the girl, but she makes no answer. Then, says the Cabalist, he will invoke the curse of excommunication upon the dybbuk. The Sexton begins a series of hollow blasts on the ram's horn, and the girl just stands there slackly. Suddenly Arthur moans softly, then utters a great scream and falls on the floor in a faint.

Says Alper: "I think what has happened is that we have exorcised the wrong dybbuk!"

Arthur recovers and is helped to a chair. Shaking, he tries to tell the others how he feels. He has lost the truth as he once knew it, and now he has desires—a passion for life, the pleasure of work. He begs God to give him the ability to love. Addressing the dybbuk, he vows he will cherish this girl, tend to her needs, possess her soul. All business now, he goes to the office to get the girl's coat. He orders the policeman to telephone the girl's father and tell him she has been found and is being brought to him. His next move, as a lawyer, will be to get her released from the institution to which she has been committed.

Says Alper: "He still doesn't believe in God. He simply wants to love. And when you stop to think of it, gentleman, is there any difference?"

The Curtain Falls

TOYS IN THE ATTIC

By Lillian Hellman

THIS drama, which won the Best Play citation from the New York Drama Critics Circle, is Miss Hellman's eleventh. Twenty-five years ago she had a brilliant start as a playwright with *The Children's Hour*. One can list among her other impressive works *The Little Foxes*, *The Searching Wind*, *Watch on the Rhine*, and a fine adaptation of Anouilh's *The Lark*.

Eleven plays in a quarter century is not a remarkable output numerically, for Miss Hellman is a painstaking writer. It took her three years and three full versions to get *Toys in the Attic* ready for the stage. She has said that she doesn't consider any of her plays "social," in the sense that they comment upon society; she has always written about people as individuals. And, most often, she has written about them profoundly in the sense that she has probed deeply into the characters she has created.

In an interview with Seymour Peck of the New York *Times* during the Boston tryout of her new play, Miss Hellman said she didn't remember clearly the inception of the piece, adding, "I think I wanted to say that not all kinds of love—so-called love—are noble and good, that there's much in love that's destructive, including the love that holds up false notions of success, of the acquisition of money.

"I started out with a man who interested me, his two unmarried sisters who raised him, and his wife. All these women love him and seem to want him to be successful—he never has been—but once he is, they find they don't want him that way. They are scared of losing him to success."

No dramatist could ask for a more careful production than Kermit Bloomgarden has given *Toys in the Attic*. The players are top-flight, including Jason Robards, Jr., Maureen Stapleton, Irene Worth, and Anne Revere, and a young lady, Rochelle Oliver, who made an impressive Broadway debut in the role of Robards' wife. Like Robards, she learned the acting trade off Broadway, and learned it well. For a director, Bloomgarden chose—and chose well—a man who learned *his* trade on television, Arthur Penn. This is the third play Penn has staged and his record is impressive, for the other two were *Two for the Seesaw* and *The Miracle Worker*.

The newspaper reviews of *Toys in the Attic* were uniformly favorable, but John McClain of the *Journal-American* offered a note of protest which is interesting. Said he, "Right off the bat let me say that I am fed up with plays about decadent Southern families, no matter who writes them. But in the same breath I must add that I think Lillian Hellman's play is a solidly constructed drama, acted with excellent effect by a brilliant cast, and will probably be a big hit.

"My quarrel with it is a simple and quite prudish irritation with the people—must they all be so monstrously mixed up? Here we have again all the more complicated frustrations and abnormalities which have served Tennessee Williams throughout his successful career."

My own estimate ended this way: "*Toys in the Attic* offers much to remember in a season in which there has been so much to forget."

THE PLAY: ACT I

The setting, by Howard Bay, is an out-of-date but solid middle-class house in New Orleans. The furniture is heavy and old and, although everything is neat, much repair work should be done. Mainly we see a living room, an entrance porch with two rockers and a small garden with table and chairs. The house belongs to a family named Berniers—two sisters, Anna (Anne Revere) and Carrie (Maureen Stapleton) and their errant brother Julian (Jason Robards, Jr.).

Miss Hellman's estimate of her own work—that she writes about *people*—is a good one. She makes us acquainted with her characters before requiring them to *do* much of anything. In the work of a less perceptive writer this could be tedious exposition; as Miss Hellman does it, it is interesting because we soon become interested in her people ourselves.

The first two we meet are the sisters, Anna and Carrie, as they come separately home from work late on a hot summer day. Anna is about forty-two, spare, tired, and not given to much talk. Being the first one home, she opens up the house, waters a camellia pot and puts it on the porch. Carrie follows her home. She is about thirty-eight, still pretty, but tired-looking and definitely feeling the heat. She is the talkative one, but she isn't a bore; there is firm opinion and down-to-earth humor in whatever she is prompted to say.

These two have inherited this house from their parents, who died years ago. They don't like the house and never did like it particularly, but it is what they have and they accept it. But the house can't stop them from dreaming and planning, and for a long time they have dreamed and planned of a wonderful trip to Europe—a year, maybe seven years. They have been saving for it and until recently had $2843 in the bank. They have had the house up for sale, too, but there have been no takers; the agent says they are asking too much.

They don't believe their brother Julian ever liked the house very much, either; when he was little he preferred eating supper on the porch steps to being inside. But what *about* Julian? They are worried because they have not heard from him in so long a time—two weeks, in fact. Usually he writes often.

Julian got married a year ago to Lily, a very rich girl; rich enough, anyhow, for her mother to give her $10,000 as a wedding present. And Julian has a business. They thought he was in Chicago, but their last two letters to him there have been returned.

Carrie, possibly because she is the younger, is the more energetic of the two, and as she is played by Miss Stapleton she becomes quite a person—full of plans and longings and chat. She would like to go to Europe now, and on the chance that it might happen she has bought a book which is now on the piano—*French Lessons in Songs*. She still likes to play the piano, and she wants to learn French because on their trip they will be going to Strasbourg to eat some *paté* and put flowers on the graves of their mother's people. Yet, for all her longing, Carrie doesn't feel sorry for herself; she is too practical for that. Yet she may not be *too* practical. She tells Anna that they don't have as much money saved as she thought, for yesterday she took out a thousand dollars and sent it to Julian in Chicago, just in case he needed it for his business. And now he's not there.

Anna doesn't quite like this, but is not quarrelsome. It isn't the money which bothers her; it is because wiring it is interfering, and they had promised themselves that they would not interfere with Julian and his marriage.

While the sisters are in the house, two people appear in the garden. One is Albertine Prine (Irene Worth), a handsome, self-possessed woman of forty-five, the mother of Julian's wife. The other is Henry

Simpson (Percy Rodriguez), a handsome, well-dressed Negro. He is carrying a chauffeur's cap, but one senses that the relation between the newcomers is not exactly that of mistress and servant, for they seem to be at ease in each other's company.

She rings the porch bell, and the sisters are flustered by the unexpected visit. Albertine has come by to ask them what time they expect Julian and Lily. She informs the surprised pair that Lily left a message for her mother that they'd be here tonight—and there is no reason for hurrying off to meet the Chicago train because they are *already* in New Orleans. In fact, she saw her daughter two nights ago, but not to speak to; the girl was walking up and down in front of her house, as if debating whether to go in—and she didn't go in.

Albertine and Henry depart, leaving Carrie in a swivet of speculation. What about that nigger? And what about Julian and Lily? Anna has a hunch that Julian has failed again, and doesn't want to tell them. Just in case this is the case, Anna gives the savings bank book to Carrie and tells her to give it to their brother. Carrie takes it gratefully, and declares confidently that if Julian does take the money he will repay it soon, as he had done before.

They hear a car stop outside and Carrie sees from the window that it is her brother and his wife. Suddenly calm, she asks her sister, who can be so cold, to welcome Julian as he should be welcomed, even if he *has* failed again.

The couple reach the porch. Julian (Robards) is handsome, tall, about thirty-four and outgiving; Lily (Miss Oliver) is a pretty, frail blonde about twenty-one. Both Julian and the taxi driver who follows are burdened with luggage and packages of all sorts. The greetings are warm, and Julian overtips the driver so much that even the driver is surprised.

Anna puts food before her ravenous brother, and as he eats with relish she asks how the shoe factory is—the one he bought in Chicago. Lightly he says *that's* gone. The factory was a crooked sell and he never should have bought it. Warmhearted Carrie has no thought for the factory, being happy that her brother is home again; Anna seems to be resigned to making the best of things.

Lily is a very odd girl, timid, even fey; she is timid with her husband—not fearful of him, but fearful of his displeasure. When the couple are alone on the porch among the packages, and Carrie is poking at the piano but eavesdropping, Lily asks Julian who was the lady he talked to on the train—the same one he has been seeing on the streets here in New Orleans. They have been in town a week, and she confesses she has disobeyed his order not to see anybody; she has watched Julian and the lady in the park, at a restaurant and other places. She apologizes, but Julian isn't upset, the way a man thus observed might be; he rather gently tells her never to follow him again.

Carrie gets Julian aside and gives him the bank book. He is profoundly touched and grateful to both his loving sisters—but this time he won't need it.

Now begins a party—and Robards is splendid in the abandon with which he showers gifts on the women—gaudy ball gowns, an evening coat, jewelry, the paid-up mortgage on the house, and tickets for a two-room suite on a boat sailing for Europe day after tomorrow. Moving men appear with a new spinet piano to replace Carrie's beaten antique. He pours champagne and opens caviar for a party. He has been in town a week—and busy! On behalf of his beloved sisters he has resigned their jobs for them, for everybody is rich now. He displays an envelope containing $150,000 in bills—less the small change he has spent on presents; half of this is for him, half for his partner.

Nor has he forgotten Lily. Although she draws back in protest, he takes the wedding ring off her finger—a $20 ring from a pawn shop—and replaces it with one sparkling with a large diamond. Lily declares almost whimperingly that she wants her old ring back because it is her "married ring."

One might think that everybody would be overjoyed at such largess, but a kind of gloom settles over the house. In the first place, where did he get that kind of money? He answers airily but mysteriously that he sold some real estate. Once he liked somebody and she liked him, and she remembered it for years, and now when she hears about a good thing she gives him a tip on it.

The women try to get more detailed information out of Lily, but she has none to give. All she knows is that a lady phoned him in Chicago, and when they came here she was on the train, and since they have been here she has called him every night at six o'clock. It is around that time now, and when the phone in the house rings Lily, happening to be closest, answers. No, she says to somebody, he isn't here, and hangs up.

Carrie is the one who is most profoundly upset; she just doesn't like any of it—the "whore's clothes," being rushed off to Europe, the wrong jewelry—and now owning this awful house. Lily isn't happy, either; she thinks her new ring is vulgar and wants her old one.

Julian has been out getting caviar and champagne when Lily answers the phone, and when he asks her about it she admits it was the lady who calls him every evening. Reproachfully he tells her he had business with that lady, and telling her he was not here was not respectful to him.

Nobody but Julian wants the champagne and caviar. As a party this certainly is a failure.

The Curtain Falls

ACT II

It is early the next morning. Carrie's spinet and the refrigerator Julian bought for Anna loom in the living room. The sisters are alone; Anna is working at a battered suitcase and polishing some shoes, and Carrie is rattling on about everybody being crazy. That Lily is a queer one, moving about half the night. And Julian doesn't treat her right—pampers her like a child instead of treating her like a wife. Moreover, even if Anna *is* packing, she doesn't want to rush off to Europe day after tomorrow; she wants to get the eight-thirty streetcar and go to the office and retrieve Julian's letter of resignation before the boss sees it. She reminds her sister that it is not good to be without a job at their age. She just doesn't believe in Julian's richness.

In this act we explore further than we have been. We have come to know Julian and his two sisters quite well, and now it is time to take a look at Julian's wife and her mother. Perhaps all parenthood is incredible, but this particular mother-and-daughter combination has an extraordinary disparity. The mother, Albertine, is intelligent, cool in her judgments, sure of what she wants and knows; yet she is understanding rather than dictatorial. It seems one of nature's quirks that she should be the mother of Lily.

We come to know them better when the mother comes this morning to visit her daughter. She has come forearmed with a check for five thousand dollars, for she senses that Lily is in some kind of trouble—and trouble to her means money. She learns that Lily's trouble is *having* money, not needing it.

This girl is an oddball. She cannot tell anything straight because after she begins even a simple, declarative sentence she gets off on some tangent. But she is not insane—just wispy around the edges. This morning, when her mother sees her, she is wearing a nightgown over her dress and is barefoot.

This is not as odd as it looks, once we learn more about Lily. The girl is as full of yearning as she is of shyness, and in her is a suspicion that Julian doesn't love her—and she is profoundly in love with him. She thinks that perhaps her mother *sold* her to Julian by paying him to marry her, and that her only hold on him is the sex relationship. This is why, so much of the time during the play, we see her in a slip or nightgown, barefoot and ready for bed.

What with her tangents, it takes Lily quite a time to explain to her mother what the trouble is. It is money, all right: she hates it, and now she and her husband suddenly are rich. She remembers happier times in Chicago, when the shoe factory failed and their money vanished and they had to live in cheap lodgings and eat very little. These were the happy times for Lily. Often, with nothing to do, Julian would stay in bed with her all day long, just talking and day-dreaming.

Like her mother, Lily is a night-prowler. Last night Julian went to bed in another room of the house, claiming that he had too much champagne and was in no mood for husbandly behavior. So she went out and walked and walked and came to a place where there was noise upstairs. So she went up, and here were people taking turns about talking about themselves from the top of a box. One woman said she had lost a leg but it was growing back. A man confessed that he used to drink and use a gun. And the main lady on the box told everybody that the only way to life was Truth, and the way to Truth was to open their hearts with a knife and throw them up here.

This woman held up a knife as she talked, and kissed it. Finally everybody went away but Lily. Lily had tarried because she hoped to buy this wonderful Knife of Truth. The woman said the knife was not for sale, but it could be swapped for something. So Lily swapped her big new diamond ring for it and fell asleep in this strange place and dreamed of struggling up the mountain path toward Truth.

Awakening at two in the morning, she telephoned her mother—

but Henry answered, and Henry came and brought her back here instead of to her mother.

And now Lily, so completely and unquestioningly in love, is in mortal fear that her husband will leave her now that he has some money. She hates money, she repeats.

The telephone rings and Lily dashes to answer it; but Anna, still packing her valise, is nearest and she gets the call. It is for Julian. He comes down with his big envelope of money in the pocket of his dressing robe and takes the call. It is from The Woman, of course. He assures her that everything is all right and he has the money right here with him. He will meet her at the time and place they had agreed on.

Julian fishes around among the packages and brings forth a present for Albertine—a flaming red Spanish mantilla. A silly present. She assures him that she thinks silly presents are the best, and he is momentarily happy, for everything he has brought for everybody else seems to have made everybody else unhappy.

Albertine seems so understanding that Julian tells her something of his good fortune. There is a man in town he has always hated, from the time this fellow teased him as a boy. And recently Julian got something this man wanted, so he went boldly to him and declared he wanted in payment one hundred and fifty thousand dollars cash in one week. It was two acres of swamp land which this man needed, but Julian had got to it first.

Carrie returns from her streetcar expedition to the office, bitter toward her brother. The boss had read the letter before she got there; he not only accepted the resignation but suspects that Carrie herself wrote the letter. Julian *must* come down and save her job by saying the letter was just a joke.

The act moves to a swift close when some unpleasant truths become known. Albertine and her shadowy shadow, Henry, have figured out Julian's real estate deal. He has sold the swamp land to Cy Warkins, a tough old businessman who needs it for a real estate deal, and he has acquired the land on a tip from Cy's wife. Once, ten years ago, Julian had made love to Mrs. Warkins; she is still grateful and she also hates her husband and needs money to get away from him.

Silly Lily, in a desperate bid for attention from her husband, inflicts a deep wound in a hand with her Knife of Truth and is over-

joyed when he essays to kiss the wound well and carries her up to
her bed.

Carrie cannot believe what Anna has been telling her—that Julian
slept with Charlotte Warkins ten years ago. Not her brother; not
that innocent boy; not the one who is now lost to them because he
has married a crazy little whore. . . .

Coldly, incisively, Anna shocks Carrie by telling her that Carrie
always wanted to sleep with Julian and still does.

The Curtain Falls

(Some protests have been made that Miss Hellman's sudden voic-
ing of the subject of incest at this point has been gratuitous and
dramatically cheap. I do not agree, for the moment has been handled
well dramatically. As Miss Stapleton plays Carrie, Carrie is shocked
and incredulous. Anna may have brutally spoken the truth, but it
is something that had never before entered Carrie's conscious mind.)

ACT III

The scene continues. Anna still is packing suitcases for the trip
to Europe—alone. Julian comes downstairs, whistling and singing
buoyantly after some time above with his wife. With forced casual-
ness he tells his sisters he and Lily will be leaving today, for a camping
trip of New York or who knows where, or for how long. But before
he goes he will make sure his sisters will be all right. Taking out the
bank book Carrie has given him, he pats it and announces that he
is putting twenty thousand dollars into it this morning.

Today is his big day. In his pocket he has money for another
good lady, too. He is going to meet her in Sailor's Lane and give it
to her, put her on a train and say "Have a good life." Then he
will go around and bank their share. A great day. The best of his
life . . . and Lily is childishly happy at being told that afterward
they will go somewhere together and alone.

Up to now we have had interchanges in the play between this
one and that one except for two persons—Carrie and Lily, the two
who love Julian the most. It is implicit in playmaking that they
should reveal themselves to themselves and the audience, too, and
Miss Hellman does an adroit job of it. Carrie, who fears loneliness
and old age; Lily, who craves only the possession of her husband.

But can she possess him, alone? Carrie, with some spite, suggests that she ask Mrs. Cyrus Warkins about *that*, for they were together years ago and now he has gone to meet her again and put her on a train.

All of Lily's uncertainty floods upon her. She knows Cyrus Warkins, for he is her mother's lawyer. Carrie adds that he is a tough and tricky man with plenty of riffraff friends to do his dirty work.

Desperately bent upon saving Julian for herself, Lily telephones Warkins and spills the beans in one of the most interesting one-sided telephone conversations since George Jessel first called his mother from the stage apron of the Palace Theatre and Luise Rainer won a movie Oscar for a bit in a filmed show about Ziegfeld.

Lily, in her childish innocence, begs Mr. Warkins to ask his wife to let Lily have her husband just one more year. . . . They are meeting now, she thinks, in Sailor's Lane. . . . Would Mrs. Warkins please let Julian alone just for one year?

There is another short and biting scene between the two sisters, with Anna still preparing to shove off for Europe alone and Carrie doubting that she is serious about the move. It would kill Julian to know that there was something wrong between her and Anna— but there has been: long years of spinsterhood and boredom. Carrie urges Anna to stay, for she has a hunch that their brother will be needing them.

The time comes to wrap up the drama, and it is wrapped up quickly and stirringly. Lily's mother and Henry reappear, having bought back the diamond ring from the woman who swapped it for the Knife of Truth, and the fact that Albertine and Henry have long been lovers is clearly established.

Julian returns, and he does indeed need his sisters, his wife, and anybody else handy. When he met Mrs. Warkins to give her her share of the real estate money, two thugs set upon them. He has been brutally cut, bruised and torn and he gasps that Mrs. Warkins' face has been slashed into disfigurement. He cannot understand who tipped Cyrus Warkins off to the rendezvous, which had been strictly for business.

And, of course, all of Julian's money is gone.

Oddly, Carrie and Anna are not violently upset by this brutal tragedy, which is so magnificently related by Robards. They have their brother back again, dependent as always. Of course, there is

Lily too, now. But Albertine guesses that sooner or later one of them will tell Julian about Lily's phone call to Mr. Warkins. Then there will be three of them. Albertine will come and pick up Lily and take her back home.

The Curtain Falls

BYE BYE BIRDIE

Book by MICHAEL STEWART, *music by* CHARLES STROUSE, *lyrics by* LEE ADAMS

THE theater is always a gamble, but there are two ways of at least trying to play safe in the music-show business. One is to adapt a well-known novel; the other is to have a star like Ethel Merman, Mary Martin, or Jackie Gleason to bolster the box office. And it also is safe-playing to have the show written by Rodgers and Hammerstein or Irving Berlin.

It is refreshing to find an entertainment which contains none of these elements but which is good even so, and *Bye Bye Birdie* is such a one. The producer, Edward Padula, was an unknown, having been that anonymous theatrical worker, a stage manager. The cast has many excellent members, but the best known of them, Chita Rivera and Kay Medford, are not big box-office names. Michael Stewart, the librettist, has written some revue sketches and TV scripts, but this is his first musical comedy book. Charles Strouse and Lee Adams have written songs for revues and night clubs, but this is their first full-length show. (Adams supports himself by being assistant article editor of *This Week* magazine.) The director, Gower Champion, is well known as a dancer and choreographer, but this is his first attempt at staging an entire musical. Dick Gautier, who plays Birdie, makes his Broadway debut, having heretofore sung in night clubs. Dick Van Dyke, who plays Birdie's agent, is a television and night club comedian who made his first Broadway appearance—a brief one—earlier in the season in the revue, *The Girls Against the Boys*.

My own reasoning concerning the success of *Bye Bye Birdie* is this: Instead of trying to satirize such phenomena as Elvis Presley, rock-and-roll and teen-age hysteria, it regards them with a kind heart. My recollection of thirty-five years of seeing bad comedies as well as good ones leads to the conclusion that it is difficult almost to the point of impossibility to satirize something which is a satire to begin with—like Hollywood, radio, television, and advertising.

Six of the seven next-day reviews of the *Birdie* premiere were enthusiastic. The *Times* man, Atkinson, said it was neither fish, fowl nor good musical comedy. He reported, "Last evening the audience was beside itself with pleasure. This department was able to contain itself." My own report began, "It is the funniest, most captivating and most expert musical comedy one could hope to see in several seasons of showgoing. And one of the best things about it is that practically nobody is connected with it."

THE LIBRETTO: ACT I

The subject and the central character of the musical are almost instantaneously established by the projection of a film clip on a screen. It is a montage of shots of Conrad Birdie (Dick Gautier), with sideburns, wild hairdo, half-closed eyes and pouting lower lip, and glimpses of boys and girls reacting ecstatically. Any resemblance between Birdie and Elvis Presley may be coincidental, but it is intentional.

The first scene is the New York office of the Almaelou Music Corp., headed by a pleasant but now worried young man, Albert Peterson (Dick Van Dyke). He is just learning on the telephone that, disaster though it may be to the morale of the American teen-ager, his client and sole dish of bread and butter, Conrad Birdie, must report for Army induction in two weeks.

Al's troubles mount when his secretary, Rose Grant (Chita Rivera), flounces in and figuratively slaps her resignation on his desk. She has worked here for eight years and has been more than a secretary to Al, and all the appreciation she ever got was a $5 raise in 1954 and a bottle of perfume last Christmas.

He warns the girl that is she's after a piece of the company she can't have it. "Almaelou" was named for himself, his mother Mae and his dog, Lou, which departed this life six years ago. Any division of the corporation would kill his mother. Rosie counters that *nothing* could kill his mother except maybe a silver bullet.

When Al moans that he is up to his ears in debt and is losing his client, Rosie says, in song, that Birdie's going into the Army is the best thing that could happen; now Al will be free to stop being a music-business bum and go back to college, even though he now is thirty. She'd love it if he became an English teacher and they could have a little apartment in Queens.

But Rosie hasn't stopped working for Al just because she has quit. She orders her puzzled employer to pick a name from a list of members of Birdie Fan Club 2748 of Sweet Apple, Ohio. He does, and the name is Kim MacAfee, age fifteen, sophomore at Sweet Apple High. This girl, Rose informs Al, will make Conrad Birdie the hottest soldier since Joan of Arc. Birdie will give his last kiss as a civilian to this girl and then will sing a number called "One Last Kiss," which Al will now write. Sale of this record will make him enough money to get *three* college degrees if he wants that many. Hope springs anew in Al's troubled breast.

The following scene, "The Telephone Hour," is a gem of imagination and humor. The setting is stacked ceiling-high with fragments of rooms, each big enough to reveal a teen-ager, indescribably contorted, talking on a telephone. Girls are talking to girls, boys are talking to girls, boys are talking to boys. It is a funny and affectionate glimpse of American youth. The burden of the song is the gossip that Kim MacAfee has "got pinned" by Hugo Peabody and will consequently be going steady.

The scene dissolves into something simpler—Kim and her bubbling friend, Ursula Merkle (Barbara Doherty), in their respective abodes and jabbering on the telephone. Ursula thinks it is awful that Kim has resigned from the fan club because now she must devote herself to one man. Kim counters that, since she is fifteen, it is time she settled down. With the phone call ended at parental request, the girls talk some more from their respective windows—for they live next door.

Now in her room Kim (Susan Watson) sings about how lovely it is to be a woman—to have a female, grown-up feeling and to have a figure that's round. And as she sings this paean of self-appreciation she puts on the most outrageously unfeminine attire—jeans, a bulky sweater, thick, drooping socks, and a baseball cap.

Kim gets another telephone call which puts her in a daze. She announces to her parents (Marijane Maricle and Paul Lynde), who don't understand her very clearly at any time, that Conrad Birdie is coming here to Sweet Apple to kiss her goodbye.

At Pennsylvania Station, New York, Al is rehearsing three sad-looking girls in a farewell song to Conrad Birdie. One of the lasses is so deeply sunk that Al sings her a cheer-up song, "Put on a Happy

Face"—if she's feeling cross and bickerish she should think of banana splits and licorice.

Rosie appears at the station to help with Conrad's departure for Sweet Apple. She asks Al if he has told his mother yet about dissolving the Almaelou Corporation. Not yet, he says, because yesterday was the anniversary. Six years ago the dog Lou was hit at 181st Street and Broadway by a *Journal-American* truck.

Al's mother appears, too. The stage directions say she "is a present-day Mamma in every sense of the word." And in the person of Kay Medford, an actress who can maintain an unbelievably discouraged and discouraging attitude, she is extraordinarily funny—blonde, tough, besequinned, and wearing a mink coat.

When Mrs. Peterson sees Rose she makes out that she doesn't know her, for she has changed so much—from a sudden shock or something. When Rose makes off for the train platform Mamma tells her son that it's a wonder some older man doesn't snatch Rose off —a personable matron like that. Obviously, Mamma is determined to hang onto her little boy.

Mamma has come down to see her son off. Al gets no farther toward breaking the news about the corporation than telling her that Rose thinks he should give up Almaelou, and Mamma protests that this is killing her.

There is a great flurry as Conrad Birdie arrives, followed by kids, reporters, cops, and a guitar-bearer. He won't permit a picture to be made until he fixes his pompadour with a pocket comb. Dick Gautier, playing Conrad, is a big and talented young man, son of a Metro-Goldwyn-Mayer cameraman. His great charm and his fine theatrical effect lies in the fact that he plays his role straight, as if he believed every moment of it. This is no doubt due to the influence of George Abbott. In all the farces he used to stage—*Room Service* and *Three Men on a Horse*, for example—he has never permitted a comedian to "act funny." All have been in sober earnest, which makes them just that much funnier to an audience.

Conrad gets a rousing musical sendoff from the youth of New York—and adults, too—who chorus that he is a fine, upstanding, patriotic, Normal American Boy.

Conrad gets a rousing and similar musical reception at the railroad station in Sweet Apple. As the crowd drifts away two youngsters are left—Kim and Hugo. Kim is in an awful hurry, but Hugo says it's important to talk to her. He's upset because the day after she gets his pin she goes around kissing someone else. Kim soothes his wounded and worried vanity by saying she is constant to him in a song, "One Boy." Rosie, sitting on some luggage and worrying about the man *she* wants, Albert, has her own refrain, "One Guy."

And now we see the populace of Sweet Apple headed for the Courthouse to look at Conrad Birdie—including an eager old lady in a wheel chair.

The Mayor is delivering a nice dull speech of welcome, but the kids scream him down. They want to hear from Conrad. Ursula wants to know how he makes those sounds that reduce her to a jungle beast. Conrad, plucking his guitar, sings the answer: "You gotta be sincere." It's pandemonium.

Next morning at his home Kim's father is eating a hurried breakfast on a small TV table. The dining table is elaborately set for a breakfast for one—for Conrad Birdie is a guest of the MacAfees and may come downstairs any minute. Kim's mother is in as great a tizzy as Kim is, and they want to get Daddy out of the way. The poor man doesn't stand a chance of enjoying his breakfast. With mounting anger he delivers himself of a speech about his rights as head of a household—and as played by Paul Lynde he is a fine example of a put-upon American husband and father.

At last Conrad appears in the momentarily empty dining room. It may be empty, but people are covertly watching. He takes a nonchalant look at the table so beautifully set for one, takes a can of beer out of the pocket of his wild dressing gown, pushes his way to the sink in the kitchen, finds a can opener, punches the beer open and drains the can in a gulp. He hands the empty container to Mrs. MacAfee and says "Call me for lunch." Seeing his host, he calls out a "Hi, Fats"—and goes back upstairs.

Daddy is sputtering with outrage and the family is in a lively fuss when Albert appears on the upper landing and announces excitedly that the whole family is going to be on television with Conrad—on Ed Sullivan's show! He urges them to put aside their petty differences for this great event.

The remote telecast for the Sullivan show is set up at the Central Movie Theatre. The manager says they ain't had real actors here since vaudeville went out and they brung in that darn silver screen.

Rosie and Albert are in the manager's office, where Albert tells his secretary that he has told his mother all about Almaelou. He wrote her three days ago, and is confident that his mother knows about it by now. And indeed she does—for in she comes, wearied by three days on a Trailways bus. Always the martyr, she takes a bus when others take trains and planes. And now she is here, for this letter obviously was written when her son was under the influence of drugs. She says she is a sick old woman and will die soon, and she wants a stone with "Albert's Mother" on it.

On the bus Mother has met and engaged the ideal secretary for her son, whom she brings in—a big, very sexy young female named Gloria Rasputin (Norma Richardson). When Al protests that he already *has* a secretary, Mother counters that there is work enough for two—and, besides, Gloria can do other things besides sec. On command, Miss Rasputin goes into a Ruby Keeler-type tap dance, ending in a split. Al is definitely interested, and he takes the sizable siren off to test her on her typing ability.

Rosie, alone, says to herself that she could just kill Albert. She falls into a murderous reverie which turns into a ballet. (Chita Rivera, as Rosie, is a highly skilled dancer.) This ballet of imagination involves several ways of doing away with Albert—leading him to a guillotine on a tumbrel, splitting his skull with a hatchet, stabbing him, bombing him and setting a gang mob on him.

And now the Sullivan show! In the blackout following the ballet one hears Ed Sullivan's voice, just finishing a Kodak commercial and leading into the "One Last Kiss" performance in Sweet Apple.

The lights rise on a setting like a TV screen, and the telecast itself makes a hilarious first-act ending. Conrad Birdie, elaborately costumed, singing his song. Kim nearby, waiting for her cue to get bussed. Soon teen-agers and townfolk are in the act—and in the act most of all is Mr. MacAfee, who changes from an indignant paterfamilias to the hammiest and muggingest of hams, breaking up the carefully set routine in order to get in front of the camera as often as possible. Comes the climax, when, on cue, Kim approaches to be kissed. Conrad takes her in his arms—whereupon Hugo steps up and belts Conrad a good one, knocking him out. In front of the camera Hugo denounces Conrad as a thief of love.

As if this weren't enough of a disaster, another one falls upon the hapless Albert. Still in a fury over Gloria Rasputin, Rosie walks out on him.

The Curtain Falls

ACT II

Another film montage begins the act. It is a wild hodgepodge of all means of communication—newsboys selling extras, phone operators plugging in wires, tickers spewing Wall Street tape, Greek runners, natives beating jungle drums, a lover leaving a note in a hollow tree . . .

Rosie is in Kim's bedroom, disconsolate at first but increasingly angry as she sings "What Did I Ever See in Him?"—meaning Albert, her six-foot tower of Jello. Kim comes in and joins her in the song, for she is mad at Hugo F. Peabody.

Into the MacAfee living room come Conrad, Albert, and Mother, all babbling. Conrad insists he is all right and doesn't feel like going to bed. Rosie comes down, on her way out and leaving for good again, but Albert bars her way. He tells her she may have let Hugo onto the TV stage to sock Conrad, but Albert will have the last word. The kiss *will* take place tomorrow morning at the station just as Conrad leaves. Rosie bangs him with her suitcase and makes her getaway.

Mr. and Mrs. MacAfee come into the house just as their daughter comes downstairs with *her* suitcase, for she intends to leave too—to go out into the world and *live* with Rosie. Daddy chases her upstairs. Albert, vowing that he loves Rosie and wants her back, says he is going out to look for her—whereupon Mother goes to the kitchen, turns on the gas and sticks her head in the oven, with a request to her son that he turn off the gas when he comes back. He turns it off now.

Conrad now adds to Albert's mounting woes. Coming downstairs, dressed in tight jeans, a leather jacket and boots—and also wearing a large black eye—he announces he is fed up with the routine. He wants to have some *fun*—go out and meet a couple of young chicks. Sings he, "There are chicks just ripe for some kissin'."

As he sings he moves into a street of Sweet Apple, spots three chicks and asks them where one goes to have a ball in this town. They suggest the church basement, the Sweet Shoppe or the ice house. The ice house is where people go when they want to be alone. He spies Kim, who has escaped from home and is lugging her luggage. He grabs her arm, saying there are things to do and places to go. All the teen-agers in Sweet Apple seem to gather to help Conrad sing, "Oh, life's a ball!"

Mr. MacAfee comes out of his house looking for his daughter, and the jilted Hugo informs him Kim is with Conrad Birdie somewhere. Daddy breaks into his own furious song, "What's the matter with kids today?" His wife, also coming out, joins him.

Hugo, bent on drinking himself to death, finds his way to what passes for a dive in Sweet Apple. Ignoring a sign in Maude's Roadside Retreat which says no minors will be served, he deepens his voice and tells the bartender he will have "a double rocks on the scotch." The bartender gruffly orders him to beat it. As he leaves, in comes Rosie, with luggage. She orders double bourbon, scotch on the side with three cherries. It's the Spanish coming out in her, she tells the bartender.

The phone on the bar rings—and one can see Albert on the other end of the wire in the MacAfee house. He has tracked Rosie down by telephone. When she takes the instrument he pleads with her in song, "Talk to me." Soon this becomes a duet . . . and then four customers at the bar pick up the melody in a male quartet obbligato. Albert can hear the noise and fears that Rosie is not alone.

Rosie notices that a number of men are coming in and going directly to another room. It's a private party in a private dining room, the bartender warns her—so Rosie pushes her way right in.

This scene, in the private room, is Miss Rivera's dancing highlight of the show. She finds she has crashed, not a party, but a very solemn meeting of red-fezzed Shriners. Beginning to dance, she breaks it up, but good, and the finale comes with all the Shriners hiding from her under the long table.

The dance over, Rosie, wearing a fez, comes limply out the back door of the Roadside Retreat. Here she meets Hugo, who asks plaintively if she will go back in and get him some grain alcohol. She wouldn't go back in there for a million—but the Shriners come piling out and *carry* her back in. Albert appears, in pursuit of Rosie, and so does Mother, in pursuit of her son. Firmly, he tells her to go home, and she puts on a fine, whimpering Unwanted Mother act.

Next to appear are Mr. and Mrs. MacAfee, looking for Kim and Conrad. A neighbor arrives, looking for *her* daughter. Another parent appears, looking for three daughters, two of them twins. They all reprise the song about not knowing what's wrong with these kids today.

Rosie makes her escape from the Roadside Retreat, pursued by a Shriner. She informs Albert that Conrad and Kim have gone to the ice house. Mr. MacAfee bellows for his wife to call the Mounted Police.

Conrad and Kim are alone in the ice house. She is choking over a cigarette, trying desperately to be abandoned and appalling Conrad by talking about jail bait. He, being a nice young man, wants to escape—but before he can get away the twosome are joined by Ursula and a whole posse of teen-agers, who sing that they've got a lot of livin' to do. It is a fast dance number, interrupted by the arrival of Albert, Mr. MacAfee, and two policemen. Kim's father orders the cops to arrest Conrad, and Conrad, putting an arm around Mr. MacAfee, voices thanks to Heaven that he has come. The cops lead the teen-agers' dream out.

Since·it's getting near curtain time, a few small things have to be resolved. Hugo arrives in the ice house and Kim runs to him. Rosie turns up and Albert declares he loves her. Mother shows and is stricken when Rosie calls her "Mother." Happy at last at the prospect of being Mrs. Albert Peterson, Rosie does an exultant Latin-American number, "Spanish Rose."

Albert is at the Sweet Apple railroad station early next morning, and so is Conrad, whom Albert has bailed out, disguised in a big coat and a veil. Mother isn't far behind, nor is Rose. Mother, grieving to the last, lies down on the tracks—and Miss Medford utters in her gravelly voice one of the funniest lines in *Bye Bye Birdie:* "Don't worry about the coat. You'll have three mink stoles as soon as the train passes over me."

Albert—a new and dominant Albert—sharply orders his parent to get aboard the train. The train begins to move and Conrad appears on the rear platform, yelling for Albert and Rosie to get aboard. But Albert has other ideas. He and Rosie will take another train to Pumpkin Falls, Iowa, where they will get married, and they will answer an ad for two people, preferably married, to teach English and domestic science in the junior high school there.

The Curtain Falls

DUEL OF ANGELS

By JEAN GIRAUDOUX, *translated by* CHRISTOPHER FRY

THIS was Jean Giraudoux' last comedy. It does not, to me, measure
up to his *The Madwoman of Chaillot*, being more cerebral than
emotional, but it is a work of adult wit. The translation, lucid and
graceful, is one of the best things Christopher Fry has done for the
theater. The production, as imported by Roger L. Stevens and S.
Hurok, seemed without a flaw. There were three elegant 1860-period
settings by Roger Furse and three spectacular gowns designed for
two spectacular women by the late Christian Dior—the last garments
he made. And the style of acting, cool, carefully studied, and almost without movement, was set by the director, Robert Helpmann. Helpmann, an actor and director—or producer, as they say
on the English stage—has also been one of the fine dancers of
the Sadler's Wells Ballet (now the Royal Ballet), and he knows the
effectiveness of perfectly controlled motion.

THE PLAY: ACT I

This could be called a modern morality play in which the dueling
angels of the title are Virtue and Vice. The time could be any time,
then or now, and the place could be any in France. But the time
and place chosen are 1868 and Aix-en-Provence. First we come upon
the terrace of a tea shop under the lime trees, and here we meet
Count Marcellus, an elegant rakehell played with suave charm and
disarming frankness about himself by Peter Wyngarde. He soon is
joined by two friends, Paola (played by Vivien Leigh, whose dark
allure is heightened by her vivid red costume) and her husband,
Armand (John Merivale).

These two have come from Court, where they have heard Mr. Justice Blanchard denounce Count Marcellus most severely. The occasion was the sentencing by Blanchard of a girl who "used to visit"

Marcellus and who had killed her baby. The real culprit—but an unpunishable one under the law—was Marcellus, according to Blanchard, and this righteous man has consecrated himself to seeing to it that vice and debauchery must be driven from Aix.

The waiter politely asks Marcellus to take another table, for the one he has is reserved. It is reserved for the wife of Justice Lionel Blanchard, who comes here at this time every day to eat an ice with hot chocolate sauce. Marcellus, obliging, speaks ironically of this woman, a really virtuous wife who, despite her seemly conduct, seems to know frailty when she encounters it, by instinct.

The wife, Lucile, appears. As played by Mary Ure, she is blonde, pale, dressed in white and cool—if not cold. With her has come a friend, Eugénie (Ludi Claire). Eugénie is a woman of wit and opinion, and as she sits with Lucile she has some witty opinions. There is beginning to be talk in the town about Lucile's likes and dislikes; she can tolerate thieves and drunkards and has even been pleasant to a murderer; but if someone in love so much as passes by, Lucile freezes. Aix, says Eugénie, was a town of love before she came here with her husband.

To Lucile, love is love, purely and simply, like the love between herself and her husband, Lionel. But there are other kinds of regard which pass for love, and Lucile can detect by instinct the impure from the pure, and when she does she freezes. It's as though she saw slimy, crawling things on people's bodies or coming out of their mouths. She can see their senses lying transparent under their skins.

When Eugénie comments that her friend's morality seems to be uncommonly physical, Lucile replies with cool conviction that God takes care of our souls Himself, but has entrusted our bodies to our keeping. She thinks her own body is all right—healthy, loyal, and sensible.

Eugénie sees Paola and her husband, Armand, and nods a greeting. She suggests that Lucile do likewise, for Armand is smiling over to them most insistently. The virtuous woman flatly refuses to nod, for her instinct tells her that Paola has taken a lover. This deliberate lack of cordiality is so disturbing to Armand that he comes to the women's table. If Lucile won't talk, he can at least talk to Eugénie.

Lucile's pointed refusal to acknowledge Paola's presence on the terrace—and his own—disturbs Armand because it means, if Lucile doesn't speak, that she thinks he is either an unfaithful husband or a deceived one. And he knows *he* is faithful to his gorgeous wife. He speaks lyrically of her—how to him she is every minute on the clock. Although Lucile sits without reacting, Armand can't stop talking. He *knows* his wife is faithful. Why, at least once a day he returns to his house unexpectedly, and all he has ever found is complete innocence on the part of Paola. Before he returns in defeat to his wife's table he makes a suggestion: If Lucile won't talk or even nod to Paola, perhaps she can signify recognition by lifting her glass of water to her lips in a kind of toast of recognition? There is no move by Lucile, and the disturbed young husband returns to his wife. Then, absently, Lucile lifts her glass—and Armand beams across at her joyfully.

Eugénie chides her friend for what she has done—putting a confident husband on guard against his wife. In a flash, she predicts, he is going to imagine that he sees every one of Paola's lovers.

And so it turns out. Purposely having left his gloves at Lucile's table, Armand returns to retrieve them—a different Armand. He tells Eugénie that he notices now that his wife's voice is hard, that her eyes are steel, that the lips he thought so lovely twist and snap, that her smooth skin also is slightly sweaty. What a change has come over him so suddenly! Now he has taken a different view of those midnight visits she used to make without disturbing him, to a church where the incense had the smell of tobacco and where they gave red roses to the faithful . . . He knows now that Paola has lied to him.

This change, wrought by Lucile's magical silence, is more than Eugénie can bear—for she, too, is frail enough to have a lover. She says good-by, leaving Armand and Lucile alone. Armand denounces her, saying he had come to this place with a young, faithful, beautiful wife—and now he is leaving with a graceless one. Lucile's eyes surprisingly fill with tears and she tries to explain her silence by saying that she had heard that Armand had spoken ill of her husband.

In a comedy like this, any slight pretext to move characters about is good enough, and in this case Paola comes to her husband beside Lucile's table and asks him to slip back to the house and bring her wrap. And so it is that the Duel of Angels begins.

This is not—yet—a physical duel. It is a duel of ideas and ideals and it is spoken with *politesse*. Paola seizes the offensive by saying that Lucile, in spite of or perhaps because of her air of virtue, loves men—physical men. She is a rare type—a woman who never gets used to living among millions of male bodies and souls. This is because she has never been able to take her own sex for granted; she is still astonished at being a woman.

Paola is equally frank about herself, the complete opposite of Lucile. She has had many lovers, probably will have many more—but she still clings to her husband as someone she wants—someone who has her everyday life in his keeping. She does not intend to let Lucile separate her and Armand. She, Paola, is the one who loves her husband, not Lucile hers. If Lucile were in love, she wouldn't let him go away every week on his judicial circuit, while she lives contented and comfortable alone in bed. She is suffering the worst thing that can happen to any woman in love—the absence of the lover.

By now Lucile has got up enough steam beneath her calm to declare that she hates Paola, and Paola gets up more steam, too. She warns Lucile that "we"—meaning Womankind—are not going to tolerate her behavior much longer. She must accept deception as an ingredient of life. And, to begin with, she must speak decently to Armand, who has returned with his wife's wrap.

Lucile, back up now, *does* speak to Armand—but not as Paola expected. She tells him his wife is a monster who has been unfaithful to him countless times. Leave her, she advises. And Armand, agreeing, takes bitter leave of his wife.

In a comedy such as this, any simple dramatic device, no matter how silly it may seem, will serve to further events. In this case, Paola drops a powder in Lucile's glass of water, and soon after she drinks it the virtuous woman falls into a faint. Paola takes charge, ordering the flustered tea shop staff away and sending one of them for a woman named Barbette, who lives across the street.

Barbette crosses the street quickly, as people do in plays. As portrayed by Margaret Braidwood, she is a witch out of folklore. What would Paola like to have done to this unconscious woman? Give her a drug to make her come out in sores?

No, Paola orders. Take her to Barbette's house and put her in bed—but first rumple the clean sheets. Undo her bodice, let down her hair, overturn the vase of flowers on the table. She will sleep for two hours, says Paola.

Should Barbette bring a "client" when Lucile is in this condition? Not at all, says Paola. It will be enough if Lucile *thinks* something happened—and with the most handsome and corrupting man possible, Count Marcellus. What evidence will there be? The Count's handkerchief, which Paola has lifted from his pocket. She gives the kerchief to Barbette to put in Lucile's hand.

The Curtain Falls

ACT II

It is the next morning in Count Marcellus' luxurious home, and Paola has come to see him—an odd time of day for her, for she usually comes here at night. She tells him, with mocking mysteriousness, that the virtuous Lucile has been ravished. He bemoans his lot at not having been the ravisher, for he has been dreaming about this unapproachable woman ever since she came to Aix, and trying to figure a means of trapping her.

Paola springs her surprise: He *is* the ravisher; Barbette saw it all last night at her house—and here is circumstantial evidence, the Count's kerchief. When Lucile awoke from her spell of unconsciousness in disarray in a strange bedroom, Barbette told her a man had brought her there—Count Marcellus. "Madame Blanchard is yours if you want her," Paola announces. "So now, Marcellus, to work. Her husband won't be back today."

He is ready to depart for Mme. Blanchard's house to press his fictitious advantage when Lucile turns up at *his*, and Paola hides in his bedroom.

Lucile is reproachful, contemptuous—and *désolée*. With the air of a South of France Don Juan, Marcellus tells her he doesn't feel one twinge of remorse.

From here on, this act could have been written and played like an old-fashioned French sex farce, but it isn't. It maintains its decorum amidst the improbabilities, and Gallicisms, aphorisms, and witticisms flow unabated.

Lucile's rigid concept of virtue in a woman gives an interesting twist to the play. Accepting the fact of last night's betrayal, she now considers herself Marcellus' wife—and she loathes him. She wants to consider herself the wife of her first husband when he comes home tomorrow, but Marcellus stands in the way. Her only out is to become a widow, so the Count must kill himself. He doesn't feel like suicide, but he promises to kill himself—or at least disappear—if she will give herself to him, consciously this time, once more. The suggestion is repugnant.

A further farcical development ensues. Armand, filled with jealous rage since Lucile opened his eyes to his wife's faithlessness, has figured that Marcellus is the one Paola has been visiting. So now, having found the Count's door unlatched, he breaks in upon Marcellus and Lucile. He has been listening to them from the hallway for some time. He has not come in pursuit of Paola, for this is not her time of day; he has come to kill Marcellus in a duel. Since Lucile would like the man dead, would Lucile accept Armand as her champion? Indeed she would.

A French duel usually takes time and much formal arrangement, like a State dinner; but Giraudoux, needing to get on with his second act, cut the red tape. Armand, in a hurry to have at his betrayer, has already alerted seconds for himself and Marcellus and everybody is waiting—so off the men go to the field of honor and their pistols.

Paola emerges from the bedroom and the two enemies confront each other once again. Paola pretending that she drugged Lucile for her own good and made a woman of her; Lucile accusing Paola of having committed this deed out of fear—fear of the power of virtue. Being sure of God's power on her behalf, Lucile defies the other woman to drag her down to her level.

A manservant appears to announce somebody. Ah, hopes the blonde, Armand has returned alive! But it isn't Armand, it is Mr. Justice Lionel Blanchard downstairs inquiring for his wife.

Paola certainly does not like Lucile, but in a case like this, women against men, women must stand together. She sends Lucile home by a back stair and promises to keep the Justice here long enough for her to get home. She will tell Blanchard that Lucile has come here to help Paola through an ordeal, and has already left.

The Curtain Falls

ACT III

The setting is the Blanchard house, showing the Justice's private office, which leads to his bedroom and his wife's. The Justice, working on some papers at his desk, is what one might expect—rather pompous, opinionated, and humorless, in a good performance by Alan

MacNaughtan. A clerk is fetching papers concerning the Thomasse case, in which one Thomasse is accused of poisoning his wife.

Blanchard is surprised when the clerk tells him his wife has come home. He goes to her door and finds it locked. He knocks and there is no answer. Fearing she may be ill, he shouts that if she doesn't open the door he will force it—so she comes out and he greets her with endearments and flowers.

But she acts so strangely, fending off his embrace! Why, oh why, didn't he stay away until tomorrow, when everything would be all right? Doesn't he see that she is a different woman today? He doesn't. She begs him to let her alone and go away until the morrow—or at least until they have had news of the duel. He assures her there will be no duel, for Paola has told him about it and he has dispatched police to stop it.

Lucile puts him a hypothetical question: Suppose she had been married before, and widowed, and he has just found it out. Would he take her back again? If another man had touched his wife, he declares, he wouldn't see her again, ever. But why such a foolish question?

Lucile tells him of the events of the night and of her visit to Marcellus to ask him to kill himself and thus purify her. Outraged, Blanchard leaves the room, and as he goes a hurrying clerk bumps into him with the news that the most important evidence in the Thomasse case, the phial of poison, has disappeared.

Armand appears. The duelists have eluded the police and he comes to tell Lucile that Marcellus is wounded and dying. It is too late, she moans. Why did she insist on considering herself Marcellus' wife, instead of remaining the dishonored wife of a loving, if unhappy, husband? And it is too late now, for she has just seen in Lionel a husband she never knew and couldn't love.

The deadly Paola comes in with Barbette in tow; she is here to have vengeance for Marcellus' death—vengeance on Lucile, the woman who sent Armand away from her. Her vengeance is hellish, for she prompts Barbette to tell the truth about the hoax that was played last night. Lucile is as pure as she ever was. She taunts, "What a disaster it is, to lie down a martyr and rise a virgin!"

Lionel reappears, running up the stairs, filled with outrage. He has seen Marcellus die—die with the name of Lucile on his lips. He orders his wife out of the house.

Armand tries to explain the hoax to Lionel, but, unaccountably,

Lucile commands him to be still. Armand suggests that the Justice question Barbette if he wants to learn the truth, and Lionel does so. Blandly the woman repeats the original lie—that she saw Marcellus undress Lucile and ravish her, and, unconscious though she may have been, Lucile smiled and thanked him. Lionel storms out again, and Paola's revenge seems complete. How does the pure-in-heart Lucile stand now?

Still pure in heart, and she will keep herself so, thus gaining the final revenge. She drains the Thomasse poison bottle, which she has filched. Dying, very gently and prettily, she makes a last request of Armand—that Lionel must keep on believing Barbette's lie. A final taunt to Paola: The world *does* have purity, beauty and light. She dies in Barbette's arms—a modern Lucrece.

The lights go down a moment, and when they come up Barbette is alone with the corpse. In a long and touching apostrophe to Lucile, beautifully written and beautifully spoken by Miss Braidwood, she wraps up the play. Purity is not for this world, but it is men, not women, who make it impure. Many a saint has been canonized for less than has befallen Lucile.

The Curtain Falls

THE DEADLY GAME

Adapted by JAMES YAFFE *from a novelette by* FRIEDRICH DUERREN-
MATT

FRIEDRICH DUERRENMATT, a Swiss fictioneer and dramatist
who writes in German, came forcefully to the attention of American
theatergoers with *The Visit*, a baleful fantasy in which Lynn
Fontanne wreaked an implacable vengeance upon Alfred Lunt. *The
Deadly Game* is more cynical than baleful—a courtroom drama set
in a living room which begins without a crime. Duerrenmatt wrote
this weird tale of suspense and surprise as a long short story called
Trapp, after the name of the Swiss traveling salesman who is the
central character.

In making the American play adaptation, Yaffe has made a few
changes in the tale but has not altered its essence. He makes the
central character an American salesman selling in Switzerland, which
is not illogical; and he has his three old men living more elegantly
than they did in the original.

The next-day reviews were generally favorable but not at the pitch
of enthusiasm engendered by *The Visit*. One of the good things
about the production was the return of Pat Hingle to the stage in the
role of the salesman. Hingle, while playing the title role in *J. B.*, was
severely injured in a fall down an apartment elevator shaft and was
hospitalized for months. In the new play he walked with a cane, but
the simple device of having him say he hurt his leg took care of *that*.

THE PLAY: ACT I

The curtain rises on a dark stage and one hears a clock strike seven.
When the lights come up they reveal the Judge's living room, and a
mountain snowstorm is swirling outside. A dinner table is elaborately
set in an alcove. At a table in the center two men are deep in a chess
game, and an old man is deep asleep in a nearby armchair. They are
in evening clothes.

One of the chess players, the Judge, is the owner of the house. The Judge (Ludwig Donath) is a benign, cheerful man in his late sixties, now retired from the bench. His opponent, the Defense Attorney, (Claude Dauphin), is in his late sixties. He seems unassuming, but he has an emotional nature and his moods range from despair to boyish enthusiasm. As the men go on with their game, a manservant, Pierre (Frank Campanella), brings in two bottles of wine so that his master may choose one of them to go with the roast goose. Pierre is a Boris Karloff type, and he is mute.

The Old Man (Pat Malone) shakes off his sleep and asks where Gustave is. He is in his seventies, mild and slightly senile. He is assured that Gustave will be here; probably delayed by the storm—and when they hear the doorbell they are certain that Gustave has arrived to complete this festive dinner group. Pierre opens the front door—and here is a stranger. He is Howard Trapp, a typical American salesman—friendly, frank, and pleasant. He explains that his car has bogged in snowdrift, and asks if he can be put up for the night. With warm cordiality the Judge invites him in—and tells him he is a lucky man, for this road is treacherous and the house is built on the edge of a mountain. Better to have struck a snowdrift than to have gone over. The Judge introduces the newcomer to his companions, and the Old Man's eyes brighten oddly as he says, "We have been waiting such a long time."

Trapp is surprised when the Judge quickly pegs him as a salesman. The Defense Attorney explains that they are all retired lawyers and experienced students of human nature. Brandy is poured and drunk and Pierre leads the young American upstairs to a guest room to freshen up for dinner. Trapp *would* like to tell his wife, who is on top of the mountain at a ski resort, what has happened, but there is no telephone. After he has gone up, the others talk about him with odd speculation—is he possible?

The bell sounds again and this must be Gustave. The Judge suggests that they don't say anything about the stranger and see how long it takes Gustave to guess what has happened. Gustave, the Prosecutor (Max Adrian), is in his late sixties, silkily formal, coldly logical, and forcefully eloquent. He astonishes his friends by asking where the stranger is—the American. His deduction is Holmesian: he has seen an American overcoat dripping water in the hall.

Trapp comes down, having exchanged his wet trousers for a pair he found in the guest-room closet.

The conversation flows as tastefully as the wine during the excellent dinner, and the American learns that these old cronies foregather periodically to play a game of their own devising after their dinners— they play at their former jobs. They re-enact famous trials—Socrates, Dreyfus, Joan of Arc—with the Prosecutor prosecuting, the Defense Attorney defending, and the Judge finding the verdict and pronouncing sentence. Often they disagree with history, as when the Prosecutor proved that Caesar was murdered by his wife and not by political enemies. The Defense Attorney chimes in that he got Judas Iscariot off.

And this is more than a game to the men, each of whom lives alone in his own house. They meet three or four times a week in one house or another for their make-believe, because their lives depend on it. When age limits forced them to retire they became physical wrecks, but now that they have found something to do they are healthy and hungry.

They suggest that Trapp join them, and he accepts with wine-warmed enthusiasm. It will be much better, they tell him, if they have live material to work with instead of history. Once in a while they *do* get a live case, like a former mayor of the province who became snowbound a month ago. After dinner they convicted him of poisoning his wife and he was sentenced to hang. Trapp happens to be wearing the mayor's trousers, they tell him, for the mayor neglected to take them with him.

Trapp happily volunteers to be the defendant—but, he adds, he is a pretty respectable citizen. No crimes, no secret vices, a good credit rating; his past is an open book.

The Judge, the Prosecutor, and the Old Man go into the kitchen to supervise Pierre's making of the dessert, so that this volunteer defendant may confer with his attorney. The Defense Attorney tells Trapp he must plead not guilty to something—embezzlement, wife-beating, or whatever—and then stand trial. It would be well if he told his lawyer all the details of his crime now. The American protests in astonishment that he hasn't *committed* any crime. No one, his lawyer says intently, is completely innocent. He suggests that Trapp stand trial, say, for swindling an insurance company in order to help a poor widow. When Trapp still protests innocence, counsel warns him to be wary of the Prosecutor, who is sure to discover *something*.

The others come from the kitchen, with Pierre bearing the *flambé* dessert. The Prosecutor tells Trapp that from now on they will be deadly enemies in the game, but nothing personal will be intended. Trapp genially suggests that, if they are so serious about their game, why not make it a *good* one?

The mock trial begins, with the crime not specified. The prosecutor elicits from the defendant that he is married, has a son, seven and a half—here's his picture—who is in New York with a governess. His wife insisted on coming abroad with him on this trip because she is crazy about skiing.

Wasn't his wife fearful of his setting out today from the ski resort to Geneva with a storm brewing? She was, but when he told her a five-thousand-dollar commission was at stake she let him go. Commission on what? A new miracle textile he represents.

The Prosecutor continues probing, and the Defense Attorney worriedly cautions Trapp to be careful of his answers. Trapp is successful now, but he *was* a poor boy, with a father who never made as much in his life as he makes in a year now. He tells his success story. Left second year high school. Went to work for a sharp real estate dealer who snapped up pieces of property the city was planning to buy. He got to doing the buying for the dealer because he looked young and innocent.

His attorney suggests that he might stand trial on this, and Trapp genially agrees. But the Prosecutor snaps that the decision about the crime is no longer in Trapp's hands, for he is already on trial. The Judge concurs.

Trapp's father died. His mother, too, a couple of years ago. But he set her up in a nice apartment on Central Park South and supported her to the end, even when he knew she was slipping money to his two no-account brothers, who never *could* earn a living. His conscience is clear and he is enjoying the game. And the cognac which the Prosecutor offers him.

The Prosecutor flatteringly suggests that Trapp has bulldozed his way up rather quickly. Damned right he has. Ten years ago he was just another salesman—chief assistant to a Mr. Foster, the European sales agent, stuck in the New York office without even an expense account. He'd never have got around Foster, but Foster died five years ago and this was his great break.

The Prosecutor pounces. Now they have their crime! He formally charges the incredulous Trapp with the murder of his boss. In a flutter, the Defense Attorney objects, but the Judge overrules him. Trapp protests that they are carrying their joke a little too far.

The three lawyers retire to put on their robes of office, leaving Pierre to clear the dinner table and Trapp with the Old Man. Trapp asks the venerable one why *he* doesn't have a robe of office, too, and the Old Man says it wouldn't be in good taste. For twenty-five years, he explains, he was the municipality's official hangman.

The Curtain Falls

ACT II

The furnishings of the room have been moved about and now it has a sinister courtroom effect. Pierre has finished the rearrangement and Trapp is getting uneasy. He tries questioning Pierre, but all the man can do is nod or shake his head. How about the time they tried the mayor—everybody came down for breakfast in a good mood? Nod. Mayor in a good mood when he left the house? Shake. But he *did* leave the house? Nod—and Pierre laughs to himself at some private joke.

The Prosecutor, robed, comes down for a private talk with Trapp. He offers him the opportunity to plead guilty of murder in the second degree, thus avoiding the supreme penalty. Trapp, by now figuring that these old boys are off their rockers, scornfully refuses to plead guilty, for that would spoil the game.

Court resumes. The Defense Attorney moves for a mistrial on the grounds that the Prosecutor has been tampering with the witness. The Prosecutor maintains that Trapp talked voluntarily. The two fall into a vehement legal argument which Trapp enjoys hugely. The Judge cuts in by asking Trapp if he feels that the Prosecutor used undue pressure on him—because if this is so he will dismiss the case. Trapp doesn't want the game to end, so he says there was no undue influence. The Defense Attorney sighs.

Trapp, cheerfully drunk, carries a brandy bottle and a glass. Defense suggests that he has had enough, and the Judge orders Pierre to take the liquor from the astonished salesman.

The Prosecutor gets going on the witness. How did he kill Foster and thus get his job? Poison? Strangulation? Trapp pretends to break down and volunteers to Tell All in a mock confession. He went to Foster's office and the boss pointed out an error in his report. So Trapp thanked him for doing part of his work and announced that he would turn over this week's salary check to Foster—and Foster dropped dead of the shock! Trapp thinks it is hilarious but the others don't. The Judge warns him against levity in the court.

All kidding aside, says the defendant, Foster *did* die of a heart attack. He had had two or three attacks before this last one in the last few years, but he had hidden this from everybody in the office. But Trapp found out—from Foster's wife.

Ah, he and Mrs. Foster were friends? The Prosecutor proceeds relentlessly. They met at a party and she made a play for him. She was alone because her husband had gone off to Europe, and Trapp was alone because his wife was running around with some poet in Greenwich Village. Mrs. Trapp is the type of woman who raises hell when her husband plays around, but thinks *she* has a right to play around as much as she likes. Why—how does it happen Trapp is here now? Would he have been on his way to see a little girl in Geneva if his wife hadn't been making eyes at a ski instructor all week?

How about Foster—did he know of his wife's playing around? No indeed. She was the only thing in the world the "old gangster" loved—besides making money and getting his way.

Did Trapp ever think that he might hurt Foster through his wife? Hell, no, says the American. You don't think of the husband when you're sleeping with a woman.

Wouldn't it have hurt Foster gravely if he had found out about this affair when he came home from his business trip a year ago?

Trapp laughingly denies that he had any idea of hurting Foster, and Foster *didn't* find out about the affair when he got back. As a matter of fact, he didn't find out about it until the day he died.

The fat is in the fire and the Defense Attorney groans helplessly.

Trapp didn't tell Foster, either. It was Joe Wilson who did. Joe always had his eye on Trapp's job, and he peached to gain favor with the boss. And *who* told Joe Wilson? Trapp did, over a couple of beers. He didn't think Wilson would ever have the guts to go to the boss with the story.

Implacably the Prosecutor wraps up his case—the psychological murder of an admitted enemy—as Trapp flounders helplessly and in disbelief. The Defense Attorney sums up as urgently and persuasively as he can, but his approach is an emotional one rather than logical. The prosecution reaches its summation: Naturally Trapp was unconscious of any purpose in his actions and naturally has no pangs of guilt, but nevertheless he murdered, and must pay for his crime with his life.

Horror grows in Trapp as he realizes that the Prosecutor means every word of what he has said. He wildly declares he is through with the game these lunatics have been playing. He makes for the door, but Pierre seizes him and leads him back to the witness chair. The Judge sentences him to death by hanging.

The Prosecutor and the Defense Attorney genially congratulate each other on a game well played. The Judge brings drinks, and then suggests that the Old Man escort Trapp upstairs. Frightened, Trapp refuses to go. When Pierre approaches him he loses all control and shouts in a frenzy that they were right—he wanted Foster dead and he made sure of it. Before anybody can move he dashes out the door into the storm. The Judge hurries to the window, looks out and cries, "Not that way!" The Attorney yells, "The precipice, Mr. Trapp!" Then they all freeze in horror.

The lights dim out. When they come up it is several days later, and the scene is like the one at the opening of the play, including the chess game. The doorbell rings, and Pierre admits a woman wearing only a chic touch of mourning. She is Mrs. Trapp.

Helen Trapp (Frances Helm) tells the Judge she is flying back to America tomorrow, and has come here to learn what she can of her husband's last moments. They had had a quarrel. Had he—? The judge assures her that her husband's death was an accident and that, indeed, he had spoken very interestingly of her that evening. Since it is getting late, why doesn't she have dinner and spend the night here? Perhaps, after dinner, they can think of some little parlor game to take her mind off her troubles. She accepts.

The Curtain Falls

THE ANDERSONVILLE TRIAL

By Saul Levitt

IN a foreword to his drama, Mr. Levitt says, "The basic source material is the official record of the actual trial of Henry Wirz, which took place in Washington, D.C., in the summer of 1865. The play may be considered 'documentary' to the following extent: that it is set in the time and place circumstance of the historical trial; that the formal roles and names of its characters repeat those of the historical participants; and that some of the dialogue derives from the trial record. It might be added that the theme expressed in the play inheres in the trial record. Essentially, however, the play expresses the author's conception of the personalities and the occasion, and it is to be read as 'drama' and not 'documentary.'"

And so it is with any good dramatic history or biography. A literal transcript of any notable trial or the purely factual account of the life of a great man would be extremely dull on a stage—and it would take a day or a week to perform. Here is where the dramatist does his work—shortening, highlighting, and adding his own creative skill to the established record.

A courtroom drama is difficult to write and stage, for little of its excitement can come from physical action. A play without sex also is difficult to write and stage, and here we have one which makes no mention of romance and has not one feminine character. It was most admirably carried off by the author, the players, and the director.

The reviews of *The Andersonville Trial* the day after it opened ranged from approval with reservations as to some details to solid enthusiasm, with the exception of Robert Coleman's estimate in the *Mirror*. He called it "a worthy attempt that doesn't come off." The *World-Telegram*'s Frank Aston summed up Levitt's intent thus: "The playwright points his thesis: An individual who surrenders his conscience to any person, power or authority is imperiling the hope of mankind: he who would remain free with honor speaks only for himself. Mr. Levitt has turned up a hell-raising heart-searcher." My own estimate was, "It is an adroit courtroom drama which, instead of being neatly wrapped up at its conclusion, leaves in one's mind the question, 'Was justice done?' "

There was nothing but admiration for José Ferrer's direction and for the performances, chief of which were those of Herbert Berghof as the defendant, Albert Dekker as his attorney, and George C. Scott as the prosecutor. Also singled out for critical mention was Russell Hardie in the role of the general who presided at this military trial—none other than Lew Wallace, who subsequently won fame, not as a fighting man, but as the author of *Ben-Hur*.

THE PLAY: ACT I, *Scene 1*

The setting, designed with impressively ugly severity by Will Steven Armstrong, is the United States Court of Claims in Washington, and the time is a sweltering morning in August 1865. Everything in the room—the chairs, desks, and tables—is functional, except for a chaise longue. This luxury is permitted the defendant, who is an invalid. Behind the judges' table are an American flag and a large plan of the Confederate prison stockade at Andersonville, Georgia.

As the curtain rises almost everybody is in the courtroom and almost everybody is in the uniform of the Union Army; two defense lawyers and three newspapermen are in civilian attire. Normally, a military trial such as this one would be secret; but so great is the public passion over the case of Confederate Captain Henry Wirz that the trial has been opened to the public—which is why the Court of Claims is being used.

People have been waiting for the Court itself, and now it comes—eight finely uniformed Union officers headed by Major General Lew Wallace, age thirty-seven, who reveals a chill authority which he will maintain through the play. He is not, however, the martinet type; he speaks formally but gently, and as Russell Hardie portrays him he senses deeply the obligation to be what any head of any court of justice should be—impartial. Sitting at a long table amongst his colleagues, he checks over those present. They include Lieutenant Colonel N. P. Chipman, who will prosecute on behalf of the War Department. As George C. Scott plays him, he is rather pale and intense. Also present is Otis H. Baker for the defense. In the person of Albert Dekker he is a big man with longish hair, a longish mustache, good summer clothes and the easy, quiet air of a Southern gentleman.

But where, asks the general, is the defendant, Henry Wirz? He is told that Wirz will be here shortly. This morning Wirz attempted suicide by breaking a brandy bottle—the brandy a prescription from the prison surgeon, Dr. C. M. Ford—and slashing a wrist. A guard stopped him before he did too great damage to himself.

In a moment Captain Henry Wirz is brought in. He is a foreigner, he is ill, he is excitable, and he feels that he will get the short end of a trial for his life. As he is played by Herbert Berghof he is an example of bravura acting which is not often seen in our theater, which has devoted itself to understatement since World War I.

The indictment against Wirz charges criminal conspiracy to destroy the lives of soldiers of the United States in violation of the laws and customs of war. As commandant of a Confederate prison at Andersonville, he had as many as forty thousand Federal prisoners, who were not given adequate shelter, food, clothing, or medical care, with the result that more than fourteen thousand died. Moreover, he established within the prison stockade a deadline, and if a prisoner ventured beyond it he could be shot by a guard. He also used bloodhounds to hunt down, seize, and mangle escaped prisoners, of whom about fifty died. He also personally ordered the deaths of thirteen others.

The Civil War is over, but Abraham Lincoln was killed four months ago and Northern feeling against the South runs high. The defense attorney, Baker, tries to make the point that Wirz is being made the goat—the single target of the mood of vengeance—and his military superiors have been left out of the indictment.

Wirz is obviously suffering when he is brought in, but he is proud almost to the point of arrogance. He has suffered ever since he was wounded in battle. Talking with a slight Germanic accent, he tells General Wallace that he tried to take his life this morning, not from a sense of guilt, but from a feeling that he has been condemned in advance.

Any courtroom play—and any real courtroom—obviously pits the prosecution against the defense and vice versa. The defense man, Baker, explains himself. He is a Baltimorean. Some in this divided city thought him an enemy of the Confederacy because he thought slavery was unworkable and not worth dying for. Others thought him opposed to the North because he did not believe in the glorious future a Northern victory was predicted to bring. He is being paid by a committee organized in defense of Wirz.

The prosecutor, or Judge Advocate, Chipman, lays himself on the line as a man who was brought up to believe slavery was evil and who answered Lincoln's second call for volunteers.

It is Chipman's turn to present evidence. Before the first witness can be presented, Wirz breaks in with the first of many emotional interruptions, shouting that the real crime he committed was choosing the losing side. The first witness, D. T. Chandler, is a former Confederate lieutenant colonel, and on the witness stand he is caught between loyalty to the Southern cause and his own essential humanity and good breeding.

Under Chipman's questioning, the case against Wirz is filled with horrifying detail. Chandler knows about Andersonville, for he was assigned to inspect the prison camp and spent two weeks there. Using the chart behind the judges as an illustration, he described the camp as a stockade a thousand feet long and eight hundred feet wide. The timber wall of the stockade was fifteen to twenty feet high, with a platform running along the top and sentry boxes at intervals. Within this enclosure was nothing but bare ground, except for a line of posts set twenty-five feet inside. This was the deadline. A stream, about a yard wide and a foot deep, meandered through the enclosure. The weather here could range from more than a hundred degrees in July and August to near freezing and rainy in winter.

When Chandler made his fortnight's inspection the camp was "tightly crowded," so that each prisoner had thirty-five and a half square feet of bare ground—comparable to a cell six feet by six. The little stream was used for everything—drinking, washing, cooking, and sewage disposal. Except for new ones who had come clothed, the prisoners were in rags or almost naked. Some had dug burrows in the ground to escape sun and rain, heat and cold. Their food was meal so coarsely ground as to be undigestible, maggoty meat, rats for a delicacy and sometimes the corpse of a departed comrade.

After his horrifying inspection, Chandler officially recommended the closing of Andersonville as a blot on the Confederacy and the transfer of prisoners to other camps, but his superior, General Winder, turned him down, saying that if half the prisoners died there would be twice as much room for the rest.

Chandler made a second report to the Confederate War Office, this time recommending the removal of General Winder. But he had *not* recommended the removal of Winder's commandant at Andersonville, Captain Wirz, because during his time there he had seen nothing in Wirz's conduct of a malignant disposition toward the prisoners.

The next witness is a country-doctor type, Dr. John C. Bates (Ian Keith), who was a medical man at Andersonville for eight months in 1864. He describes his duties as writing prescriptions for drugs that were not available, removing gangrenous limbs, and writing death certificates. In the spring he would write fifty, sixty, seventy certificates a day; in July, August, and September, the deaths averaged three thousand men a month. He figures that if the camp had medical supplies and was sanitary, seventy-five to eighty per cent of these mortals could have been saved.

Up to now, the defense has not acted strenuously, although Wirz has made some emotional interruptions . . . as, for example, to say he cannot help laughing when he hears how he killed all those men. But now the defense lawyer, Baker, makes some pointed inquiries from the witness Bates, and establishes the fact that Captain Wirz was not responsible for the medical supplies or the amount of food per prisoner. Such things were decreed by the Surgeon General and the Commissary General at Richmond. Even so, Dr. Bates thinks that Wirz had a calloused attitude toward his prisoners. One other telling line of testimony, resulting from a question by the prosecutor, is that Dr. Bates does not remember one instance in which Wirz offered any criticism of the orders of his superior officer.

Another witness, Ambrose Spencer, a glib, unctuous country-squire type, adds more evidence to the pile Chipman is building. Crops were good all around Andersonville in '63 and '64 and plenty of food was available. One time, a group of women, including Mrs. Spencer, arranged to have twenty tons of food delivered to the stockade, but the four big farm wagons were turned back at the gate by Wirz. Wirz, says Spencer, cursed the women foully and said they were giving aid and comfort to the enemy. The effect of this evidence is somewhat blunted by Baker, the defense lawyer, drawing a reluctant admission from the witness that Wirz's superior, General Winder, was present at the gate.

Emotional tension in the courtroom mounts. Wirz, breaking in with voluble protests, finally faints on his chaise longue and has to be revived with brandy. General Wallace declines to postpone the trial, saying Wirz will be tried *in absentia* if he is too ill to remain. Wallace and Baker get into a warm discussion of national ethics, and Wallace judges him in contempt and orders him removed from the trial. Only a plea by Chipman that the defendant should be represented by counsel saves the moment for Baker. As Baker makes an ironic apology to the court,

The Curtain Falls

ACT I, *Scene 2*

The trial has now been going on for a week in stifling weather. On the stand is the last of a long list of Andersonville prisoners who have testified to suffering and cruelty. This man, James H. Davidson (James Greene), tells how he and a companion tunneled out of the stockade and were fifteen miles toward freedom when they were treed by dogs. Prison guards ordered the men down, and when Davidson's companion went down he was leaped upon and torn by the dogs. Wirz rode up and saw this and cursed the victim like a madman.

Wallace has become irritated by the Judge Advocate's long parade of witnesses telling the same story. He wants Chipman to conclude his case this afternoon—but first Baker must have his opportunity to cross-examine Davidson, who is only nineteen and whose physical frailty is becoming more apparent. Baker relentlessly breaks down the young man's story. Davidson can't explain why the dogs didn't attack *him*, too; yet he, too, was bruised and bleeding—from stumbling through brush and against rocks. Davidson's positiveness falters and he begs General Wallace to be allowed to go home. Chipman, angry that this witness has become less certain of his story, tries to get him to restate it positively—but the boy has had enough and is close to breaking. General Wallace gently excuses him.

Chipman calls as his final witness one Jasper Culver (Robert Gerringer), another alumnus of Andersonville. This one has his story down so pat that Baker suspects he has recited it many times, adding imagined details now and then. It is a seemingly brutal tale about a one-legged, half-demented prisoner called Chickamauga who begged to be let out of the stockade just for a few minutes so he could lie under a pine tree. He was shot and killed at Wirz's order, according to Culver.

This cross-examination is one of actor Albert Dekker's best scenes, as he leads Culver from positiveness into confusion. At the end of this testimony General Wallace adjourns court and reluctantly permits Chipman to bring in more witnesses tomorrow—but these must be witnesses supplying *new* criminal evidence.

When the officers of the court have left, Baker and Chipman have a profoundly interesting private conversation. Baker shakes Chipman by suggesting that, as a Union officer following orders to prosecute the case, he is morally the same as Captain Wirz, who was following orders in his management of the stockade.

At the end of the act Chipman and his legal assistant, a major named Hosmer, talk the whole case over and figure where they stand. Hosmer figures that Wirz is already convicted beyond hope. This may be, Chipman agrees—but, even so, he hasn't yet *proved* against Wirz the charges of conspiracy and criminal acts.

Chipman, who has grown increasingly nervous and irritable, is now wrestling with his conscience more than he has been with the defense attorney. He begins to think a moral issue is involved. If he and Hosmer feel that Wirz should have disobeyed the orders of his general, and if they are afraid to raise this point, are they any better than Wirz was at Andersonville? Are they, as prosecutors, carrying out orders from their superiors and setting conscience aside? Just like Wirz?

The Curtain Falls

ACT II, *Scene 1*

It is the following morning at the trial. Chipman has been obligated by General Wallace to present new criminal evidence, and the Judge Advocate proposes to do this by bringing as a witness one Sergeant George W. Gray (Frank Sutton), still active in the Union Army at Nashville, who will testify to a murder committed by Wirz himself.

Calmly and easily, Gray declares that while he was imprisoned at Andersonville he saw Wirz knock down and then shoot a private named William Stewart, while he and Stewart were outside the stockade on an assignment to carry a body to the dead house. This is so factual a story, with the name of the victim and his regiment, that it is impressive. But when Baker gets at Gray he learns that the soldier cannot *describe* the victim, nor can he name any others who saw the shooting. Gray, a professional soldier, seems to have told a story he cannot substantiate.

Gray has been a surprise witness, so Baker knows nothing about him—but he begins learning. Before he joined the Army he farmed some, and ran dogs. Ran dogs hunting, in Illinois, Indiana, and Virginia. Virginia? Was he running dogs there to bring back runaway slaves? Gray admits he was.

Chipman, at once furious and uneasy, rests his case. Baker makes the astonishing announcement that the defense will call only one witness—Dr. Ford, who has been caring for Wirz since the trial began. Ford's testimony, though medically complex, is simple: Wirz's right arm is swollen and ulcerated, and his right hand is somewhat crippled. His left shoulder is partially dead, for most of the muscle has been shot away. He is unable to raise his left arm. Moreover, Dr. Ford has spoken with Dr. Bates, who examined Wirz at Andersonville in 1864, and his condition was the same at that time.

In other words, Wirz was physically incapable of knocking a man down or pulling a trigger. Having thus disposed of the murder charge, Baker dramatically rests his case.

Both sides have wrapped up their evidence, but Chipman is strangely and increasingly uneasy. He asks General Wallace for more time to consider the situation at Andersonville; struggling to keep the trial going, he makes the astonishing suggestion that Wirz himself take the stand. Wirz is eager to do so, even though his attorney is appalled. Baker tells him he may likely be convicted, but on tainted evidence. The case must then go to the President of the United States for review, and if he chooses the President may issue a pardon.

But Wirz, fever building within him, insists on speaking, and is sworn. Baker does the questioning and tries to hold his man down to short answers. He elicits the information that Wirz was born in Zurich, arrived in Massachusetts in 1849, worked in textile mills, then moved with his family to various parts of the United States. When the Civil War broke out he was in Louisville, Kentucky. There he enlisted as a private in the Confederate Army. Having had military training in Switzerland, he was promoted to a lieutenancy. He was wounded in the Battle of Seven Pines, and was given an invalid's job by General Winder—the command of the Andersonville prison camp.

The camp was sufficiently provided in January 1864, but in March conditions worsened when prisoners came in by the thousands without a proportionate increase in rations. He wrote a letter of protest to General Winder, and the general himself came to the camp. It was *his* opinion that the prisoners were being taken care of as well as

Confederate prisoners were being cared for in the North—at Elmira, New York, for example.

The drama is building to its biggest scene and to a supercharged performance by Berghof as Wirz which set the first-night audience cheering some minutes before the end.

The deadline? Wirz feared so many prisoners might rush the stockade and asked for more guards but was given none. So he set up the deadline—as common a military procedure as a sentry outpost—as a substitute for more manpower.

The food the women brought? General Winder at first graciously consented to let it be brought in, but then he got news that Sheridan was burning farmhouses and crops in the Shenandoah Valley, and in a rage he ordered the food turned back.

Shooting down one William Stewart or killing any other prisoner? Lies!

Baker tries to close his examination, but Wirz shouts, "Am I not to be asked my conception of my duty?" With growing bitterness, and with the conviction that he will be condemned, he describes duty as doing what one is ordered. His duty was to keep prisoners alive so far as possible and to keep them from escaping so far as possible. He hated Andersonville, for it was hell, but General Winder refused to transfer him.

In his cross-examination, Chipman goes at the captain savagely and coldly. Wirz maintains that he was not authorized to enlarge the stockade, permit shelters to be built, or send out foragers to commandeer food supplies.

But how about the *morality* of his deeds—or rather the lack of them. Wirz insists that the situation was General Winder's responsibility, not his.

General Wallace becomes uneasy at his Judge Advocate's pursuit of ethics, and points out that Chipman is on delicate ground in discussing the circumstances under which officers may disobey their military superiors. It may be philosophically true that a man has a human right to judge the commands of his military superior—but in practice he would do so at his peril. This, Wallace reminds Chipman, is still a military tribunal.

The change which has been working in Chipman since the trial began now becomes complete. He admits to General Wallace that he entered this case with vengeance in mind, but now he wants to go deeper than the circumstantial surface and probe the moral issues involved. Turning to Wirz, he expresses the belief that General Winder was the captain's military superior but certainly not his *moral* superior. Andersonville was a grossly immoral situation; why, then, did Wirz obey?

The captain insists that this was, to him, a military situation, plain and simple. Chipman prods him by asking where his conscience was— in General Winder's pocket? Wirz shouts in fury that the victors here are making up a morality for the losers. He repeats in a proud but touching speech that he did his duty as he saw it. Chipman closes his case.

The Curtain Falls

Scene 2

A week later General Wallace and his seven officer colleagues find Wirz guilty as charged and sentence him to be hanged. (And he *was* hanged; the President issued no pardon.) Chipman is not elated by his victory.

The drama ends with a question which Baker puts to Chipman: Men have always been subject to powers and authorities, and how are we to change *that* slavery? Chipman can offer no answer, except to say, "We try."

The Curtain Falls

A DISTANT BELL

By Katherine Morrill

ONE of the season's quickest failures was one of its most interesting plays, A Distant Bell, a first play by Katherine Morrill, a Canadian who is a copy writer in a large New York advertising agency. Public apathy was not to blame in this case; it was critical antipathy. I was in the minority in my admiring estimate of this work, so it had no chance at the box office; there is no time on Broadway any more for a play to find a public.

While one of my colleagues opined that the drama was written in the manner of Laura Jean Libbey, I felt that it contained some of the best writing of the season—imaginative, lucid, unhackneyed, and very often beautiful. Except for an occasional work by Christopher Fry or Robert Anderson, and one play by Archibald MacLeish, there is little literary quality in the contemporary theater. Directness of expression, rather than felicity, seems to be the goal. This reminds me of the advice Nunnally Johnson once gave an aspiring film script writer. "It's easy to write a scenario," said Johnson. "You just put down a series of ten-word telegrams."

The principal complaint about the play seemed to be that it was "confusing," but I found no trouble in discerning what Mrs. Morrill was telling. On the first night I reported, "This is a play which cannot be given a label, for some of it is whimsical, some of it glows with human warmth and some of it is tragic. I recommend it because of these varied qualities, which somehow come and fit together." Under the direction of Norman Twain, the producer, there were fine performances by Martha Scott, Patricia Roe, Evans Evans and other members of the company—and a particularly winning one by Andrew Prine, a newcomer, in the role of a young reporter gifted with understanding and whimsey.

THE PLAY: ACT I, Scene 1

It is April in a New England town and we are in Lucy Greer's house (skillfully designed and interestingly lighted by Mordecai Gore-lik). It is early morning and first we see Lucy Greer (Martha Scott), a frail woman with a sweet face, in her little upstairs bedroom. Cards are spread on her bed and she flips more from a pack in her hand. She isn't playing solitaire and it isn't exactly fortune telling, either. When she turns up the king of clubs she says, "That would be you, James." James, her husband, died recently, and she muses about him, not mournfully—talks to him, and how he tricked her into that trip to Burlington to play golf with Mabel Farrow. . . .

The scene fades and the light reveals the house below—the living room, the front door, an archway framing a wide staircase. And here are The Relatives—Lucy's brother-in-law, Burton Greer (Richard Nicholls), a rather silent and dominating man about sixty; his plump, gentle wife, Dora (Nydia Westman), and Keene Stanfield (Frieda Altman), who has a keen mind and a hard heart. They seem anxious to get out of the house before Lucy comes down. They can leave now, for Burton has completed all arrangements by engaging a house-keeper. Lucy doesn't know about the housekeeper yet, for they sneaked her in last night.

Burton gives the housekeeper, Mrs. Brighton (Mabel Cochran), some instructions. He will send household money every month, and she might give Mrs. Greer a little spending money. The three girls will be sent their allowances out of their father's estate direct. Keene isn't so sure this arrangement will work out. True, Lucy would walk out if they sent her back to that rest home in Burlington—but there are asylums where she *couldn't* get out . . . Keene has been at the stairway, eavesdropping on Lucy's card game, and laughs at hearing that she is the ace of spades upside down and Burton is Benedict Arnold.

The relatives have gone by the time Lucy comes down for break-fast, clad in a soft pastel cotton dress with a pretty white apron. She plans so much to do, after ten years in a rest home. Now she can run her own house—let some dust accumulate, straighten the pictures, let the garden grow . . . and take care of her three daughters, Barrett, Waverly, and Flagg. Last night she gave a shampoo to the bust of Beethoven on the piano and then put a veil over it to keep it clean, but somebody has removed the veil.

She isn't taken aback when Mrs. Brighton, an Englishwoman who drops her h's, comes from the kitchen with a tray of breakfast for her. She regards the woman sweetly and cordially, figuring her to be the guest of one of the girls. She declines the breakfast tray, for one of the first pleasures of her new life will be to cook breakfast herself, with popovers. Her husband never felt she was strong enough to do that. She notices that a clock is ticking and Mrs. Brighton says she wound it. Lucy tells her to let it run down again, for she thinks time has no right to hound the human race the way it does.

She is a most interesting person, Lucy Greer. She does and says odd things, but there is logic in everything, like wanting dust to accumulate because she wants to see what it looks like. Her mother-in-law, now dead, never let any dust gather when *she* was running this house.

Lucy's daughters come down one by one, and they, too are almost immediately interesting—fully drawn characters. Barret, (Patricia Roe), twenty, looks pleasant but seems stiff and restrained. Not in Lucy's hearing, of course, she advises the new housekeeper to treat her mother as one would a child. The second daughter, Waverly, nineteen (Phyllis Love), is a dreamy, bookish, inward-looking lass, who starts reading Santayana before breakfast. The third daughter, Flagg, seventeen (Evans Evans), looks like Waverly but is her opposite in temperament—cheerful and bouncy.

Lucy urges the girls to the dining room, where her popovers are ready, and now she learns that the stranger in the house is nobody's guest, but the housekeeper Uncle Burton has hired. Lucy is very sweetly but firmly opposed to any housekeeping but her own. After first inquiring if Mrs. Brighton has a home to go to, she tells her sweetly she can go as soon as she finishes breakfast. Then, full of happy plans, she dismays the girls by telling them she has invited twenty people here for a party Saturday afternoon. Twenty will make a good start; later they can have larger parties. Barrett wonders privately what her mother will wear—the bedroom or the living-room curtains.

The Curtain Falls

Scene 2

The party, Saturday afternoon at sundown. Lucy has rearranged the living room, making it artistically fascinating, and now she is presiding over the tea table in a charming dress made from the living room undercurtains. She and the girls have had just one guest—Mr. Wilbur, the undertaker (Louis Girard). When this poor man has been stuffed to capacity with tea, sandwiches, and brownies—eleven cups of tea—he departs most politely. Lucy is puzzled, but not exactly hurt, that nineteen invitees failed to come or even send regrets. A bit tired from preparing and serving the party, Lucy goes to her room, leaving the girls to talk over the fiasco. Waverly and Barrett think what their mother has done to the room is terrible, but Flagg likes it—likes the way different-sized pictures have been jumbled together in an arrangement which somehow seems "right." Flagg cheerfully tells her sisters that they love little dark corners where they can hide from life.

As the evening grows, Lucy calls down to her daughters that she has locked up for the night—and has purposely locked Mrs. Brighton out. She dismissed the woman again this morning. What happens, of course, is that when the housekeeper returns from her afternoon off one of the girls lets her in. Hearing her, Lucy comes down barefoot, in a flannel nightgown, and for the first time she is pitiable in her frustration. She is still gentle-spoken, though, as she tells the intruder that she must be the reincarnation of her mother-in-law, if there *is* any reincarnation, and she does not want her cooking, her tea and the money she doles out. She simply must unbarnacle herself—go. When Barrett protests that Uncle Burton *wants* Mrs. Brighton here, Lucy opines that he is a reincarnated Benedict Arnold —and the housekeeper might be a spy dating back to the French Revolution. Why the housekeeper, and why did nobody come to the party? Why do people play these games with her?

The Scene Fades

Scene 3

It is late on another afternoon. Mrs. Brighton has stuck, though she has been dismissed several times and has even been generously told to collect three months' pay in advance from wherever she gets it. The two older daughters, Barrett and Waverly, are ashamed of their mother, and Waverly, who has met an interesting new young man, talks to him on the porch to keep him from meeting her mother. But on this afternoon he appears at the door and is admitted by the housekeeper. Waverly has seen him coming and in fear and mortification has hidden outside. She often hides—like the time they found her in the cellar after she got a 72 in algebra.

So Barrett tries to hold the fort with the caller. He is John Creighton, and the author describes him as a young man of twenty-four, with quiet assurance, who can appreciate a good book and dig a good ditch. He also has artistic sensibility, which is revealed when he admires a piece of cloth Lucy Greer has framed. Barrett is dismayed when her mother comes downstairs, but she introduces John —and this is the beginning of a delightful, imaginative scene in which Lucy and John hit it off perfectly. While Barrett writhes inwardly, John matches her mother book for book, quote for quote, fancy for fancy.

He seems not at all surprised to hear that many years ago Lucy played golf, but she gave it up after a trip she took to Burlington to play golf with Mabel Farrow. And in their hotel there were her husband, his brother Burton, her sister-in-law Keene, and a doctor— and it was six months before she got home from the rest home they put her in.

If it hadn't been for books, life in the home would have been dull. They wanted her to read Ellery Queen or something else light, but she preferred Shaw, Tolstoy, and such. John knows them all, and Shelley too, and music. He tells Lucy he was brought up in Chicago and recently came here after being a reporter in Chicago. He has dropped by to leave word for Waverly that he will be a bit late for their date tonight because of an assignment.

Barrett tries to get rid of her mother by making her take tea with Mrs. Brighton, but Lucy is having too good a time. She talks of the good times she had, too, when she was in Vienna at the time of Strauss, and a courtesan in the court of Louis XIV with five illegitimate babies. It has all come out of reading, of course, and John enjoys going along with her. He remembers that, about five thousand years ago, he was a king in Mesopotamia. They get on evolution, and he exclaims how exciting it would have been to be the first fish to grow feet.

Barrett firmly tells her mother to go for her tea. Before leaving, Lucy remarks that the Journal failed to print an item she sent about the "at home" she gave Saturday afternoon. John offers to help if she wants something in the paper again. He asks Barrett to give Waverly his message, and when he has gone Waverly comes out of hiding.

It was delightful to watch Miss Scott play this scene so lightly, so charmingly. Lucy has imagined herself to be many people, and as I watched on the opening night there came to my mind somebody she forgot to mention—Elwood P. Dowd and his friend Harvey. But, of course, Dowd was a man, and Lucy has only been women.

The Curtain Falls

ACT II, *Scene* 1

It is about 11:30 in the evening of this same day, and in the living room John and Waverly have been listening, enthralled, to a recorded selection from *Tristan und Isolde*. John, definitely interested, probes beneath the girl's habitual, lonely reticence—and succeeds, for she tells him he is the only person she ever could talk to. This bookish lass thinks she knows all the ways of the world through her reading. John, with affection in his amusement, tells the girl that books are not all there is to life—that experiencing a kiss is vastly different from reading about one.

This might become a romantic scene, but Flagg skips in with some cronies she has met at the movies and invited over to share a bottle of wine she found in her late father's golf bag. These friends are Arthur Wilson, "handsome, hep, and dumb" (Dale Helward); Clara Hurd, who has sex appeal but no sophistication (Lynda Carr), and Jackson Dunne, a bespectacled studious type who is Clara's intended (Mark Fleishman).

The author of *A Distant Bell*, Mrs. Morrill, has an unusual gift for establishing characters, even minor ones, in no time at all, and this scene is an interesting contrast between Waverly's sensitive reticence and the simple outgoing qualities of the others, with John, in the middle, being able to understand and appreciate both. During these moments John learns how Mrs. Greer's three daughters got their names. Barrett, the first, was named for Elizabeth Barrett Browning because her mother was intent upon Browning poetry during her time of expectancy. Waverly was the result of reading Walter Scott. Flagg would have been named Pickwick, but her father asserted himself and insisted that she be given some name that really belongs to the family.

This scene is a warm and kindly look at ebullient youth, with dancing to one of Flagg's popular records and Flagg pretending to be woozy from one small glass of wine. Flagg, the flirt, aims herself at John, and at one moment when they are alone offers her face so temptingly that he must kiss her—and feel disloyal to Waverly in so doing. There was a particularly amusing "bit" performance by Dale Helward as the school athlete-hero who must go home at midnight because he is in training for the shot put.

When the party is over and all have gone, Waverly stands alone, sobbing silently and shivering. Her mother comes downstairs and discovers her thus. She brings the girl a coat and would like to make her a hot drink; but Waverly fends off her mother's solicitude and runs sobbing up the stairs.

The Curtain Falls

Scene 2

This is the beginning of the tragedy of Waverly, and the change of mood in the play is skillfully wrought. It is three o'clock in the morning, a few days later, and Flagg and John come into the quiet house after a long night of walking and talking.

Flagg, as forthright and enthusiastic about sex as she is, say, about dance music or the movies, offers herself to John—begs him to possess her. An honorable young man, John declines to take advantage of the girl's youthful abandon—and he has a deep twinge of regret over Waverly. He *likes* Waverly, yes; but the happy, forthright Flagg has aroused in him a deeper affection. How he wishes that these two weren't sisters, so he wouldn't feel so much like a traitor!

And all this while Waverly has been listening from the head of the stairs.

The Curtain Falls

Scene 3

It is the following afternoon. It is interesting to see that the red outer drapes in the living room windows have been cut about half way up. Barrett is plunking at the piano in her untalented style when Waverly comes wearily in from the garden and sinks on the couch. She hasn't slept all night, she tells her sister. She keeps thinking of John, imagining that he is hers and has proclaimed undying love.

The girls' mother comes down, wearing a good-looking dress made from the curtains. She wishes the afternoon paper would come, but it is late today. And she is genuinely worried about Waverly, who has not eaten and slept properly since John Creighton first came here. She warns her daughter that once *she* had the same experience; one morning she awoke and felt there was nothing worth getting up for. There was nobody there to tell her that her husband and children loved her and needed her, so she turned her face to the wall. And this was when they tricked her into the golf date in Burlington . . . and when she got back her whole family were strangers.

Still the paper doesn't come, but Aunt Keene does—and Aunt Keene has read the *Journal*. In it is an item stating that Mrs. Greer has announced the engagement of her daughter Waverly to John Creighton and has set the wedding date. Keene is certain that this is just one of Lucy's tricks and there isn't a word of truth in it. She tells the shocked Waverly she knew it couldn't be true because the girl has never been much for boy friends.

When Aunt Keene has gone, Waverly tells her sister it *might* be true, and they could invite everybody to the wedding and have the wedding in five churches of different denominations just to please Mother. In a waking fantasy she dreams aloud of such a wedding. The paper arrives and Lucy seizes it—but Waverly already knows what it contains. Why did she do such a thing? Because, says Lucy with utmost seriousness, she has been so worried about Waverly. The girl has always been so alone, living among her fantasies. Perhaps just *printing* this announcement might make it come true. "Take care," she warns her daughter, "or *they* will move in and swallow up your whole life."

Mrs. Greer discharges the housekeeper again and invites her to stay on as a guest. They go out together for some shopping and Barrett leaves, too, even though Waverly pleads that she is afraid to be alone.

Alone, she finds someone to talk to—herself, in the mirror on the back of the closet door. She is repeating what she heard Flagg say to John that night when Flagg comes in, unnerved at finding her sister talking to herself. Waverly wonders aloud what Flagg will say when she hears about the engagement—and Flagg is enormously upset when she sees the announcement in the paper.

Waverly taunts Flagg by repeating things she overheard that night on the stairs, and Flagg slaps her face. When Waverly keeps talking into the mirror—about her forthcoming wedding now—Flagg, in a desperate fury, shoves her sister into the closet and locks the door. Flagg eases herself out of the house, leaving Waverly screaming to be let out.

The Curtain Falls

ACT III, *Scene 1*

It is nine o'clock the same evening. Waverly is in her room, gravely ill from the horror of being locked in a dark closet for so long a time before somebody let her out. Flagg is profoundly remorseful. And Lucy is profoundly worried, for she sees her daughter now as she herself once was—alone, with nobody to talk to. Who shall save Waverly from the ten years of agony Lucy once had? Lucy is determined to do the saving.

The rest of the family has been summoned, and when they arrive Uncle Burton makes the firm decision that Waverly must be taken away to some place where she can be cared for, even if they have to use force. When they try to mount the stairs to get the girl, Lucy, a tigress defending her young, stands at bay, threatening to bombard the intruders with all the vases on the piano. If they are not out of the house by the time she counts to ten, she will let fly. Burton, Dora, and Keene make an uneasy exit, and Lucy is going upstairs to her daughter as

The Curtain Falls

Scene 2

It is one A.M. Barrett has persuaded Lucy to take a nap after her long sickbed vigil, saying she will look after Waverly. This is a ruse. Keene and Dora come in, and Uncle Burton is outside in the car with the motor running. Barrett brings her faltering sister, clad in dressing gown and slippers, down the stairs, and the relatives, deaf to her pleas, kidnap her. In vain does Waverly protest that she shouted to herself at the closet door because nobody else would listen, and it was the same kind of shouting her mother used to do—not because she was crazy but because nobody would listen. The kidnaping takes place in spite of Flagg's pleas that it was *her* fault, not her sister's, that Waverly became upset.

The Curtain Falls

Scene 3

It is early the next morning, and Lucy becomes increasingly distraught as she searches the house in vain for her ailing daughter. Flagg and Barrett make a miserable pretense of not knowing what happened, and the conviction grows in Lucy's mind that the relatives have spirited Waverly away. Mrs. Brighton, who has been in on the conspiracy, cannot bear Lucy's agony any longer, and she tells the truth—that "they" were here and took the girl away. But nobody knows where they took her.

The Curtain Falls

Scene 4

This morning Lucy is alone against the world; but an ally turns up —John Creighton. He has heard about Waverly being taken away and has come to help. He is, he affirms, Waverly's fiancé, because it was in the paper. He had told a girl in the office to run Lucy's announcement, but he hadn't looked at it to see what it said.

He knows the family would never tell Lucy where they took her daughter—but as a fiancé and as a newspaper man he has a different standing. He calls Uncle Burton's home, asks a question or two and listens at length. The call finished, he tells Lucy, Barrett, and Flagg that they took her to a rest home called the Pines, about five miles from here.

Lucy immediately prepares to go there to retrieve her daughter, saying that she has got out of places like that, so she ought to be able to get into one. But, says John, Waverly isn't there now. She slipped out, in her nightgown, about five o'clock on this rainy morning when her nurse dozed a moment.

The wheel upon which Lucy once was torn has come full circle; she knows what Waverly is doing because often she did it herself: her daughter is trying to get home. Flagg sees something white flutter in the garden—a rabbit, perhaps. It is Waverly and John hurries into the garden to carry her in. Her bare feet are battered, her night-

dress is soaked with rain and she is shivering desperately. But she is
home! Ever since she was a little girl, she says, she knew they would
spirit her away one day; but now she is back and they didn't bring
her here in a coffin. But they will come after her, she is sure, to take
her away again. . . .

In the crisis Lucy is all business. She orders the housekeeper to
bring blankets and hot-water bottles, asks John to carry the girl up
to her bed and telephones a doctor.

The lights fade to indicate the passing of an hour. Mrs. Greer and
a doctor come slowly down the stairs. Waverly has died because she
didn't seem to want to live. Lucy remembers the day the child was
born . . . and now it is forever finished for her.

Flagg sobs that it is all her fault, but the mother says it is her own.
How could *she* save her daughter when she couldn't save herself?
And, in a savage outburst of passion, Barrett agrees. The mother's
poison, she shouts, is in their blood and her curse hangs over their
heads. Waverly lies dead upstairs simply because her mother is
crazy. After some moments of paralyzing shock, Lucy manages to walk
out of the room with an air of dignity.

The housekeeper answers the doorbell and in come the relatives,
who figure that the missing Waverly most likely is here. She is, says
John. She is upstairs—dead. The relatives stand frozen in shock as
the lights fade. The sound of china crashing on the terrace outside is heard.

The lights come up on Waverly's room, and Lucy Greer is by
the window, speaking to nothing and nobody outside. It is a touching soliloquy about her unhappy life—the life of a woman who had
only love to give and nobody to give it to.

She goes to a bureau, pours a number of pills from a bottle into
a glass, and fills the glass with water. Holding it up for a last look
at it, she comments with the humor which has always been hers,
"Oblivion looks exactly like cream of mushroom soup."

But this is not the end of Lucy Greer or quite the end of the
play. Firmly she puts down the glass and announces to herself that
she will play out the hand of cards which fate has dealt her.
"There have been many moments worth living for," she muses.
"Wherever I go surely there'll be a window . . . Is there anything
more beautiful than dust in a stream of sunlight? . . ."

Lucy takes her daughter in her arms and sings her a farewell lullaby,
then comes down to those waiting apprehensively below. She kisses

the housekeeper and Flagg gently, avoids Barrett and without rancor tells the relatives they can have what is left of Waverly. Out the door she goes, saying that if anyone should inquire where she is, the housekeeper can say she has gone to Burlington to play golf with Mabel Farrow.

The Curtain Falls

THE BEST MAN

By Gore Vidal

THERE were two plays about national politics during the season, and by coincidence Melvyn Douglas had a leading role in both. The first was *The Gang's All Here*, a drama by Jerome Lawrence and Robert E. Lee which was a deliberately fictionized version of the betrayal of President Warren G. Harding by his poker-playing cronies. Douglas had the role of the President—an affable small-town publisher who found himself miraculously thrust into the White House. This play was respectfully reviewed, but it had only a moderate run.

Then Douglas reappeared in the role of a candidate for his party's nomination for the Presidency at a national political convention. Vidal, author of *The Best Man*, had had one other play on Broadway and it, too, was a success—the whimsical *Visit to a Small Planet*. Grandson of the late and noted blind Senator Thomas P. Gore of Oklahoma, Vidal has enough politics in his blood to make *The Best Man* an interesting comedy-melodrama about our First National Sport, and it was particularly timely because real Presidential nominations and an election were forthcoming in the summer and fall. Most astutely, Vidal chose no party in his play. It was admirably cast, its scenery was skillfully designed by Jo Mielziner, and the director, Joseph Anthony, maintained a heartening pace. One of the pleasures of first-nighting at this one was to see Lee Tracy on the stage once again—the Lee Tracy who, years gone by, played the madcap reporter, Hildy Johnson, in *The Front Page*.

All the newspaper reviews of *The Best Man* were enthusiastic, and my own began, "The flagging spirits of this playgoer were lifted several notches last evening . . . After a long, dreary round of failures, it was a pleasure to attend an excellent performance of a well-made, keen-witted play of contemporary interest. The Morosco Theatre box office has just the ticket for an election year."

THE PLAY ACT I, *Scene* 1

The setting is a hotel suite in Philadelphia—a bedroom, sitting room, and doors leading to the hallway, the bathroom and a third room which is provided as an office. Says the author, "The décor is early Conrad Hilton." On a wall is a poster advising WILLIAM RUSSELL FOR PRESIDENT, and there are various campaign placards here and there, indicating that Russell has been a great governor, a great Secretary of State, and will be a great President. Later on, we shall see the opposite number of this suite—a duplicate set of rooms, except that the layout is from right to left instead of left to right, picturing the temporary residence of another candidate, Joe Cantwell. The poster and the placards will be equally enthusiastic about Joe.

Right from the beginning there is great movement and bustle in the drama, but the director, Joseph Anthony, has avoided making it look pointlessly or farcically frantic. At the rise of the curtain there is a flashing of many camera bulbs as their suite is entered by William Russell (Melvyn Douglas) and his wife, Alice (Leora Dana). With them is Bill's campaign manager, Dick Jensen (Karl Weber), an intense man who is apprehensive by nature. Alice, in her early forties, is very much a lady and seems diffident and shy.

Russell, whom the reporters address as Mr. Secretary, is a handsome, poised man who is unusual for a politician; he is well-spoken, well-read and has wit at the tip of his tongue. What the reporters want to know now is, has Russell got ex-President Hockstader's endorsement yet? The answer is "No." Another reporter, who has talked to Hockstader in his own suite, volunteers the information that the ex-President has narrowed his choice down to two men, Russell and Joe Cantwell, and plans to make a statement about his selection tonight.

At last Jensen herds the press out and Alice has a chance to unpack. On the phone, Jensen learns that Mrs. Gamadge, the national committeewoman, is on her way up, and Russell describes her in an oft-quoted line, "The only known link between the NAACP and the Ku-Klux Klan." As she is played by Ruth McDevitt she is quite a formidable party, "serene in the knowledge that she is the Voice of the American Woman, by default." Right off the bat she puts a nosy question to Russell—his wife *is* here with him, isn't she? Then she turns her fire on Jensen, whom she calls an egghead and a professor. She doesn't mind professors, she admits, but a great many women are suspicious of them.

The committeewoman feels certain that Russell will win the nomination on the first ballot, and she wants to talk turkey. He is not the ideal candidate for women, because he is trying to be funny all the time. They are *very* suspicious of a man who doesn't take things seriously. He must not talk over their heads. Blandly, Russell thanks her for the tip. And, Mrs. Gamadge goes on, they want to see a lot more of Mrs. Russell and their two sons; women must feel that there is a woman behind him. She opines that it did Adlai Stevenson great harm, not having a wife—and trying to be funny all the time, too.

Alice comes warily from the bedroom to meet Mrs. Gamadge, and she passes muster. Naturally gray hair is an asset. Mabel Cantwell dyes *her* hair, but she gets away with it because it is such a bad job women feel sorry for her, says the lady politician. As First Lady, Alice should not do too much like Mrs. Roosevelt or too little like Mrs. Eisenhower; a Grace Coolidge type would be best. Mrs. Gamadge departs, and at the door throws her harpoon—she has heard that Joe Cantwell is going to smear Russell with something.

When the Russells are alone for a moment we get a briefing on their domestic situation. They have been separated for years, but now Alice is with him for appearance's sake. She doesn't mind; she philosophizes that politics makes strange bedfellows. Even so, they seem to like being together again. Perhaps Dr. Artinian was right when, after Russell had his breakdown, he said that Alice was good for him. But she has no romantic illusions now, and she lightly asks him what he will do about women if he is elected—smuggle them into the White House or have a special place on K Street?

The former President of the United States, Arthur Hockstader, makes a very odd entrance into the suite by coming in from the *bathroom*. He explains that he found a connecting door in the suite next door. As he is played by Lee Tracy, Hockstader speaks simply and directly with a dry twang. He is frank and friendly and the Russells are happy to see him, for he looks so well after his operation. He dismisses the operation lightly, saying it was nothing but a hernia he got from bouncing his grandson too hard.

Hockstader accepts the bourbon and branch water offered him, saying he will "strike a blow for liberty." (I remember that Vice-

President Jack Garner, who liked corn liquor, often said he would "settle the dust.")

Talking easily, Hockstader recalls that he was bitten by the political bug when he was a boy and heard William Jennings Bryan's "cross of gold" speech.

Russell would like definite assurance of Hockstader's support, but the wily old man evades commitment. He does have a fatherly feeling—for, after all, he made Russell his Secretary of State, and before that Bill had been a good governor of Rhode Island. But people don't give a damn about Secretaries of State; they think such an official is a foreigner by definition.

Russell asks Hockstader's opinion of Joe Cantwell, and the answer is, "Just plain naked ambition." To get elected he would lie, cheat, and destroy the reputations of others. But this doesn't mean he wouldn't make a good candidate or even a good President. Russell begs his former chief not to support Cantwell—not because of Russell but for the good of the country.

They talk politics for a while, and then Hockstader stuns Russell by announcing that he is dying. He got the doctors to announce that his operation was a success, but it wasn't; he has cancer and may live just long enough to attend the next inaugural. He shows no self-pity, but he admits he is scared—and he pledges Russell to secrecy. Just before he leaves—through the bathroom again—Hockstader drops the comment that those rumors about Russell and his lady friends won't do him a bit of harm.

Jensen comes in to Russell, eager to know if the ex-President has promised his support. "He won't let us know until tonight," says the candidate—and then he adds, slowly and assuredly, that Hockstader is going to support Cantwell.

The Curtain Falls

Scene 2

The Cantwell suite—same kind of hotel layout, except in reverse. Mabel Cantwell (Kathleen Maguire), blond, pretty, and in a dressing gown, lies on a sofa, sips a martini and watches television. She is alarmed when she sees herself in a newsreel shot because she doesn't like her hat.

Joe Cantwell arrives with his manager, Bill Blades (Joseph Sullivan). As played by Frank Lovejoy, Cantwell has a warm manner which suggests ease, even though he is under great tension. He has a habit of not listening when he is preoccupied. In the living room, Joe calls out to his wife, who is in the bathroom trying on the offending hat, and when she comes out they embrace warmly. Mabel chatters on about a women's tea she has attended, and what a chilly looking woman Alice Russell is on television.

They have only thirty minutes in which to dress and go to the dinner, but suddenly Cantwell announces that he must see Hockstader right now and tell him everything—the works. Hockstader may not come out for Cantwell, but he surely will drop Russell.

We have time now for an intimate look at the Cantwells, who are effusively and genuinely affectionate, calling themselves Momma Bear and Poppa Bear. Mabel is certain she will be the First Lady, after Joe springs his stuff about Bill Russell tomorrow.

Blades had got through to Hockstader and asked him to come down, which he does. He strikes another blow for liberty at the bar in the room, then thoughtfully contemplates Cantwell as a man who doesn't smoke, doesn't drink, and doesn't philander—the purest young man in politics. Also, he has done right most of the time as a Senator—much brighter and more ruthless than Senator McCarthy was. He made quite a national case out of charging that the Mafia was running the country, even though it wasn't so. Hockstader is frank to say that it disturbs him that Joe takes himself so seriously. Cantwell, in a burst of anger, admits that he *does* take things seriously, and in his view Hockstader's record as President is one of the heaviest loads the party has to carry. Hockstader springs out of his chair in a fury, but subsides when Mabel comes in from the bedroom with a friendly greeting. Cantwell shoos her back, and she listens behind the door as she hears the two men lay it on the line. Hockstader admits that he never liked Cantwell—but this doesn't necessarily mean that he won't endorse him; he has often endorsed men he disliked because he thought they'd do the job.

Hockstader, suffering a spasm of pain, goes to the bar for another drink. Cantwell brings from his desk a file—a complete set of reports on what he has on Russell, and is so intent on his purpose that he doesn't seem to hear the ex-President's announcement that he is dying. His file contains evidence that Russell's nervous breakdown was more than that: he was raving mad for a year. Moreover, he deserted his wife and is merely using his marriage as a political front. The psychiatrists say Russell had suicidal tendencies.

Hockstader shrugs it off, saying there are rumors about every public man. When he was in the White House he was supposed to have paresis and to be keeping a colored girl in Alexandria.

Cantwell drives ahead. No manic-depressive, apt to crack up under stress, should be President—and if Russell doesn't withdraw by Wednesday he, Cantwell, is going to give a copy of this file to every delegate at the convention. Hockstader observes that *after* his breakdown Russell was Secretary of State in a rough period and showed no signs of strain. And, speaking of records, Cantwell is leaving himself open to a similar kind of attack. Joe confidently declares that there is nothing to hide in his private or public life.

As he leaves the suite, Hockstader explodes a bomb. He contemptuously tosses at Cantwell the copy of the speech he had intended to make at dinner tonight—a speech endorsing Cantwell. But now, he vows, he is going to get Cantwell's political scalp. It isn't that he minds Joe being a bastard—it's his being such a *stupid* bastard he objects to.

The Curtain Falls

ACT II, *Scene 1*

Back in the Russell suite the next afternoon. A group of delegates, just leaving, assure Russell he will be nominated on the first ballot. After the group leaves, Russell, Jensen, and a pompous prairie Senator talk practical politics for a while. They have been puzzled by Hockstader's speech last evening—for he didn't endorse *anybody*. The Senator asks Russell if he would consider a ticket with Cantwell running for Vice-President, and he gets a flat "No." Then, says the Senator in another quotable line, "I suppose we better try for a Catholic. That seems to be the big thing this year."

When the Senator has left, Russell and Jensen talk over their problems. What to do after Cantwell springs his evidence? Russell's psychiatrist, Dr. Artinian, whose file Cantwell has filched, is on his way to Philadelphia to testify that Russell is sane. And, meanwhile, Jensen has uncovered some dirt about Cantwell . . . Jensen is not sure Russell will have clear sailing, and says, "Bill, you may have to pull a Nixon. Go on television. And cry on the nation's shoulder. With *two* cocker spaniels."

Dr. Artinian (Hugh Franklin) appears, ready to testify on Russell's behalf and also to sue Cantwell for theft from his files. Hockstader appears, bouncing with enthusiasm at the prospect of a good, dirty political fight. He still won't endorse Russell, but he is off Cantwell because Cantwell lost his head—and a man shouldn't get flustered like that. So, he supposes, Russell will be President by default.

Jensen brings in a man named Sheldon Marcus (Graham Jarvis), a rumpled and reluctantly talkative man. Hockstader in particular listens with growing fascination as Jensen's questions pull Marcus's story out of him. The story is this: Marcus and Joe Cantwell served in the Army together, in the Quartermaster Corps on the island of Adak in the Aleutians. They both were captains. It was very lonely up there, what with no women, and Cantwell. . . . Marcus hedges nervously until Hockstader puts a blunt question: Was Cantwell a "de-generate?" He was, says Marcus, and Army records will show a case involving a lieutenant named Bob Fenn.

Hockstader and Jensen are overjoyed by this piece of political dynamite—and stunned when Russell announces that he will not use it—not even if Cantwell springs the insanity charge on him. Russell flatly refuses to join a smear campaign.

The Curtain Falls

Scene 2

The beginning of this scene is an amusing sidelight on the women's side of politics, with Mabel Cantwell, Alice Russell, and Mrs. Gamadge in the Cantwell suite. The wives of the two candidates are just finishing up a joint press conference, with Mrs. Gamadge giving all the answers. When the three women are alone a natural antipathy—well, no, a dissimilarity—begins to show between Mabel and Alice. Mabel is a prattler, Alice is coolly controlled. When Mabel asks pointedly how Bill Russell is feeling, Alice says he is in splendid health. Privately, Mabel thinks now would be a good time to begin building up a not-feeling-too-well story, so it would seem more natural when Russell withdraws from the race.

Cantwell, his man Blades and the pompous Senator, Carlin (Gordon B. Clarke), come into the suite. Blades assures Cantwell that everything is all set; six hundred photostats of the medical report are ready and will be distributed to delegates at three-thirty this afternoon.

There is a phone call for Cantwell—Jensen, Russell's man, on the wire. Pretending cordiality, Cantwell says he can't see how he can hold up his release any longer. . . . Does he know who? . . . A Sheldon Marcus? He doesn't think so—but something Jensen says brings a startling change over him. He says harshly that he wants to see Russell right now.

Frowning as he hangs up, he orders the puzzled Blades to hold up that stuff on Russell—to stop it, in fact. He sits on the bed, thinking.

Mabel's wifely intuition is working hard as she goes to Joe and puts her arms about him. Is it—? she asks fearfully. He nods.

The Curtain Falls

Scene 3

It is a few minutes later, and in the Cantwell suite Hockstader—who seems to be grimly fighting pain—has listened with Russell and Jensen to all of Sheldon Marcus's story, including the court-martial, and they have it all down on paper. Blades appears, saying it would be better if Russell met Cantwell in *his* suite because there are not so many reporters around.

But Russell doesn't want to go, and he again refuses to make use of the dirty information on Cantwell. Hockstader, an experienced and unprincipled political fighter, turns on Russell in great anger, saying he isn't *strong* enough to be President; he, Hockstader, will do everything he can to get Cantwell into the White House—and he insists that Russell see Cantwell as Jensen had arranged by phone.

The old man orders the two managers, Jensen and Blades, to make a dry run through his bathroom passageway and see if they can get to Cantwell without being observed. They try it, going through a suite occupied by some salesman and a woman not his wife, and it works. Eying Russell coldly, Hockstader says this is his *last* chance —so Bill follows the two men on the second trip.

Alice and Hockstader are left alone in the suite. She tells the ex-President she is not sure this is the right thing for her husband to do . . . and she seems unaware of the look of agony on the man's face. He tries to take a pill but cannot lift his hand. Quietly, he tells Alice to telephone Dr. Latham here in the hotel and tell him

to come quickly through the back way. And to bring a stretcher because he can't move. "I'm afraid the old man is just about dead,"
he announces.

The Curtain Falls

ACT III, *Scene 1*

It is a moment later in the Cantwell suite and Mabel and Joe are
waiting. Cantwell has been vainly trying to long distance a General
Conyers, who can back him up in his story of what happened
on Adak. Mabel, in a panic, is beginning to hate politics, and Joe
comforts her with some Momma Bear-Poppa Bear talk. Alice Russell
phones, wanting to get word to her husband that Hockstader has
been taken to a hospital and is dying. Cantwell warns his wife to
say nothing of this to Russell.

When Russell, Blades, and Jensen arrive, Cantwell asks if he can
talk to Sheldon Marcus himself, and Jensen goes to fetch him. Mabel
and Blades retire to the bedroom, and the two candidates take each
other's measure in a scene of complete conflict between two vastly
different kinds of men. Cantwell boldly suggests that Russell step
aside, and promises him an ambassadorship or Cabinet post in return.
Russell, the man of intelligence and principle, can't seem to get
through to Joe that he has come here to tell him he cannot bring
himself to using the Marcus testimony, and thinks Joe should drop
his evidence, too. Cantwell cannot see it this way, for it would
be tantamount to giving Russell the Presidency. *He* wants the post
because he thinks he is the better and stronger man for it.

The fearful Marcus is brought in, and Cantwell, after a smooth,
buddy-boy, long-time-no-see, you've-taken-on-weight warmup, goes
after Marcus like a district attorney. Marcus, he announces, has come
to Philadelphia with his story in the hope of harming Cantwell, because on Adak Cantwell turned him down for a promotion and a
transfer.

Nor is this all. A Lieutenant Fenn had shared a Quonset hut with
Cantwell for some months. Cantwell learned he was a degenerate
and set a trap for him. At a court-martial Fenn confessed improper
acts with twenty-eight men, including Cantwell—but he had added
Cantwell's name to the list out of revenge, says Joe. The records,
says he, will bear him out. What did the military court do? It dropped

twenty-seven men from the service—but the twenty-eighth, Cantwell, was promoted for uncovering the mess. But, to Russell's disgust, he leaves the impression that he was not innocent with Fenn.

To Russell, Cantwell is a man with no sense of right or wrong— only what will work. He changes his mind and determines to make use of the Marcus evidence.

When the visitor has gone, Cantwell orders Blades to go ahead and release the medical testimony.

The Curtain Falls

Scene 2

It is the next morning in the Russell suite. Band music from the convention hall can be heard. Alice is packing. Jensen is watching TV, but takes the phone when it rings. Russell comes in from a fruitless attempt to visit Hockstader. It's Senator Joseph on the wire, says Jensen. There have been five ballots, the score being Cantwell 474, Russell 386, and a third candidate, Merwin 214. Merwin wants the best possible terms before deciding if he should give his votes to Cantwell or Russell. Russell has been hurt by Cantwell's smear, but not fatally—and Senator Joseph, on the phone, is begging for Russell to release his Sheldon Marcus story. With that out, he'd win on the next ballot.

Cantwell has played his own cards cleverly by pretending to be outraged at the maliciously exaggerated rumors about his opponent's help. And now he wants to come up and see Russell!

When Joe comes in, Russell greets him almost gaily and banteringly suggests that he should be working on his acceptance speech. Cantwell bluntly announces that Hockstader is dead—but this isn't his purpose in coming here. He wants to solve the convention deadlock by putting Russell on his ticket for the Vice-Presidency!

Sensing that they have Cantwell over a barrel, Jensen begs for permission to get Senator Joseph back on the phone. Now is the time to spring the Marcus story! After thinking a moment, Russell tells Jensen to get the Senator on the wire. Desperately, Cantwell's manager asks Russell not to make the call.

But Russell has the Senator on the line. To the blank astonishment of everybody, he tells Joseph to have some chairman of a State delegation pledged to Russell to announce that he has withdrawn from the race. "And," he adds, "that I am releasing my

384 delegates with instructions to support Governor John Merwin."
When Jensen protests that Merwin is nobody, Russell chuckles that
he's somebody now. Joe Cantwell, he says coldly, is through in
politics. Cantwell, on leaving, says without rancor that Russell is a
fool.

The TV is turned up again. The Utah delegation switches to Merwin. The deadlock is breaking. Alice and Bill are alone. "I like the
way you won," she says proudly. And she makes a decision of her
own. The convention may be over for them now—but she is going
to *stay* with her husband.

The Curtain Falls

FIVE FINGER EXERCISE

By Peter Shaffer

PETER SHAFFER, whose drama won the New York Drama Critics Circle citation as the best foreign play of the year, was born in Liverpool and, moving to London, won a scholarship to Trinity College, Cambridge. During World War II, when boys could be conscripted to work in the coal mines, he spent two and a half years as a miner; then, after three years at Cambridge, he came to New York, twenty-five years old (he is now thirty-four), and got a job with the Public Library. Returning to Britain, he was employed by the music publishing firm of Boosey & Hawkes as a publicity and advertising assistant. He wrote one play while he was in New York and another when he had his music job, and both of these were produced on TV by B.B.C. His first play to be done in a theater was *Five Finger Exercise*, which opened at the Comedy Theatre in London in July 1958. When four of the five actors involved came to New York to do the play at the Music Box, another cast was recruited for London.

Five Finger Exercise is an exercise in playwriting which is more interested in character than event, and in which five characters are induced to bounce off, or react to, each other. There are no "leads" and there is little theatrical plot. In the *Times*, Brooks Atkinson wrote, "As writing and acting it represents a theatrical genre that is thoroughly British. Admirably British, in fact. Mr. Shaffer seldom raises his voice in the writing. The prose is precise. There are no gaudy phrases. The characterizations are subtle."

My own first-night view of the drama was less approving than the others, calling the play a stylish example of theatrical doodling. My conclusion was, "Well, they (the five characters) all have their say, and when they have finished the curtain comes down and what they have said has been intelligently written and gracefully spoken. But, adroit though it is, *Five Finger Exercise* is less than satisfying because it fails to strike a major chord."

Major or minor, Shaffer's drama became a solid box-office success.

THE PLAY: ACT 1, *Scene 1*

The rise in cost of scenery construction and the expense of backstage labor has resulted during the last twenty-five years in a clever development by playwrights and scenic artists. In times before, a "one-set" play was just that—usually a living room which sat on the stage all evening. There came into use what is called the unit set—still one piece of scenery which remains unchanged except in detail but consists of a group of scenes which can be blacked out or highlighted as the action moves about. This is a time-saver as well as a labor-saver. An early example of this design was the setting of *Grand Hotel*.

The setting here, designed by Oliver Smith, enables us to see a fair amount of the Harrington family's weekend cottage in Suffolk, England—the living room, the hall, the stair landing on the upper floor and the upstairs schoolroom where the young daughter, Pamela, has her lessons. For a country place, the living room is too modish and expensive. It expresses Mrs. Harrington's aggressively tasteful personality, and in it her husband feels uncomfortable.

It is a bright Saturday morning early in September, and as the curtain rises we find Stanley Harrington (Roland Culver) and his wife, Louise (Jessica Tandy), in the living room. (Culver, London-born, has made one other New York appearance, in *The Little Hut*, in which he also played a typical Englishman. Miss Tandy also is from London, but has spent most of her time on the American stage since 1930.)

Stanley and Louise are joined in a moment by their son, Clive (Brian Bedford, who is making his New York debut). Clive is nineteen, quick, nervous, and likable. His father is forceful and self-possessed, but the author psychoanalyzes him by saying "there is something deeply insecure about his assertiveness." Louise is described as very good-looking, with a manner bespeaking a constant preoccupation with style; but even so she doesn't show any insincerity or lack of affection.

Clive, being served a late breakfast by his mother, asks where his sister, Pamela, is, and is told she is out walking with her tutor—the German boy Louise has engaged to give Pamela her lessons and to live with them as part of the family. He came last night and has "the most divine manners." This arrangement is a surprise to Clive and he doesn't like it. His father shrugs it off as one of his wife's whims. As Best People, they aren't going to do anything common like sending their daughter to school. Oh, well, Stanley can afford it. His bluff view is that all this culture stuff is fine for those who can afford it—but he doesn't think his son's plan to study poetry at Cambridge next month is practical; sooner or later he is going to have to stand on his own two feet, without his father being alive to pay the bills. He doesn't like the pansy, arty-tarty set of young men he has seen Clive with.

Louise has *her* say. Unfortunately, she comments, her son is not like his father—an orphan who built up a furniture factory by sheer will-power. Stanley goes off to play golf. He doesn't understand Clive, but Louise adores the boy and the adoration is mutual.

While Louise and Clive are in the kitchen doing the breakfast dishes, the fourth member of the family comes into the house at a run. Pamela (Juliet Mills, young daughter of actor John Mills) is fourteen, as quick as her brother and without his melancholy. Having been made to follow her at a run, her new tutor, Walter Langer, is not far behind. Walter (Michael Bryant, making his initial New York appearance) is a slim German of twenty-two, "handsome, secret, diffident, but happily at ease with his young student."

Reluctantly, Pamela goes up to her schoolroom and begins her French lesson with Walter. She is not fond of French and would much rather learn American. Walter, replying to one of her girlish questions, says he was born in Mühlback and used to like skating alone for miles on the river at night, and then meeting a torchlit crowd of happy people celebrating the new year. His memory is so vivid that Pamela would like to learn German and spend the Christmas holidays with him at home—and then she remembers that Walter doesn't *teach* German. Why? He won't answer—but he points out that he has been in England five years and soon will have his citizenship.

Having set Pamela boning on French, Walter comes down for an introductory scene with Clive. The young tutor expresses his pleasure over the elegance of the house, and his good fortune in living with this, his first family. Clive warns him it isn't a family, but a tribe of wild cannibals; he thinks Walter is lucky not having a family of his own. The cannibalism, he adds, is not practiced on outsiders; only on one another.

Louise hauls Walter off to the music room—an addition she has had put on the house because she bought a piano—to give her *her* lesson on the piano, and Pamela, fleeing French, bounces down to the brother she adores. He is supposed to quiz her on history, but she doesn't know any history; she'd rather have him make up one of his wonderful stories. So he begins with a tale about a little girl who lived all by herself in a prison and wore only blankets. Walter comes in to fetch Louise her purse, and when he goes back to the music room Clive's mood of light whimsey turns dark. It wasn't a girl, he says rather bitterly. It was a little German boy with blond hair who plays the piano and walked into the prison of his own free will.

The Curtain Falls

Scene 2

It is a Saturday night in late October, after dinner. Stanley is smoking a cigar and reading a golf magazine. Clive is pouring himself a drink. Pamela can be heard practicing on the piano. Louise is clearing up the coffee things. Walter goes up to his room and puts a record on his portable phonograph.

Under these conditions we learn more about Stanley. He would like to get out of the house and go see the Bentons. He cannot stand his daughter's practicing or Walter's highbrow music.

The playwright arranges for Louise to do the dishes alone this time, clearing the way for a father-and-son scene in which Clive is wary and his father is bluff. Clive angered his father when he went to the factory to get his first allowance for Cambridge and told the manager there that the furniture they made was shoddy and vulgar. This furniture, says Stanley, is what people want, and Stanley gives it to them because he is in business to make money.

How is Clive settling down at Cambridge? What does he do apart from lessons? Well, Clive has joined the Dramatic Society as an actor. No cricket or football, but he might take up fencing. Stanley can't see that his son is getting anywhere with his education, which is what his mother insisted on. Clive protests that he can't tell his father definitely where he is going, because education is like setting off on an expedition into the jungle; all the things you know disappear and suddenly you find new ones. Education, argues the boy, is simply the process of being taken by surprise.

Stanley doesn't know what his son is talking about. What Clive should do, he pronounces, is make the right friends—not drifters and arty boys, but people who will be useful to him later on. He will see to it that Clive has enough money to hold up his end. He is friendly enough to suggest that they walk over to see the Bentons and have a quick one at the Red Lion, but Clive protests that he must do some reading—so Stanley goes alone.

Clive has been drinking a bit, and says perhaps more than he should to a stranger when next he encounters Walter. He shocks the German by speaking bitterly of his father—of his whole family, indeed. And he makes his mother uneasy by announcing that he is going to the pub. Why is he going there *now* when he declined his father's invitation?

Over coffee and cakes with Louise, Walter makes the observation that Clive is not very happy, and he wishes he could help somehow. He is such a receptive young man that Louise confides that she isn't a very happy person, either.

The story or her marriage as a very young girl comes out. Her French mother was a helplessly extravagant aristocrat and her father was an English lawyer who lost more money than he made. When Stanley Harrington came into view Louise was taken by his rugged charm and blind to the fact that he had no time for the things she was interested in, like art, music, and poetry. It was later that this gulf appeared—and she tells Walter outright that these past few years have been intolerable. She has stayed only because of the children.

Louise would like to know more about Walter, but when she asks him to tell about his family in Germany he stiffens and says there is nothing to tell. He was an orphan, and brought up by an uncle. As for his people, he tells Louise she is too good to understand Germans. She thinks of them as kind and quaint—but they can be monsters. England is Paradise to the young tutor, where people want to do good and don't want power.

She looks on him with great, gentle sympathy and takes his hand, and impulsively he bends and kisses both her hands. Tenderly she takes his head and holds it close to her—just as Clive comes through the garden door and stares at them. Louise beats a flustered retreat to her room, and the rest of the act is Clive's—Clive, who talks so beautifully and with such imagery and is so miserable. He does not seem to object to the scene he encountered, but is appallingly brutal about his mother's pretensions to aristocracy.

Walter tries to get away from the boy, but Clive continues on a new note—a note of sympathy for Walter for having been taken in. Why doesn't Walter get away by joining him during his Christmas holidays? They could go somewhere, anywhere. But Walter fends him off, saying he has an obligation to the family here. Clive pleads in vain that he needs a friend so badly.

Walter escapes to his room and Clive is pouring himself a drink he doesn't need when his father comes home. Instead of drinking alone, the boy should have been having a good time with him and the Bentons at the golf club. Jolly nice crowd—the sort of fellows Clive ought to be mixing with.

There ensues another scene of an overwrought youth protesting that his father doesn't understand him, and his father admitting he doesn't. But Stanley is no sitting duck for a playwright's potshots; he does have sympathy in him and he can win it from an audience. Clive works himself into a rage at being patronized. Stanley is genuinely worried—worried that he may have failed his son. He tries to get the drunken boy to go to bed, and when Clive refuses he starts up himself. Clive, on the sofa, begins to weep uncontrollably, and his father comes to him, helpless in his sympathy. What is wrong? Did something happen while he was out? Did his mother say something? Or is it Walter? It *must* be Walter, he decides, and demands what happened with Walter.

Clive tells him he came in here and Walter was kissing his mother on the mouth. She was half undressed. On the breasts . . .

Stanley knocks his son down.

The Curtain Falls

ACT II, *Scene* 1

It is the next morning, Sunday, bright and cold. Pamela and Walter have finished the cereal, eggs, and kippers Louise has fixed, but Stanley and Clive haven't come down yet. Pamela, dressed for riding, chatters gaily with Walter—but all her talk isn't thoughtless girlishness. She can think and she can understand. She tries to analyze the gulf between her father and her mother, with Mother trying to keep him out of her life with the weapon of Culture. But whose fault is it? It could be his, for he made Louise keep out of things when they were first married—even threw a modern picture she had bought into the dustbin. She has equal sympathy for both.

Stanley comes down, tired, strained, and monosyllabic. He gives his wife a good-morning kiss, stares oddly at Walter, refuses all offers of breakfast, takes up the paper. Pamela observes that her father and Clive must have been having a man-to-man talk last night, for she could hear their voices. She makes a shrewd guess that Clive must have been drunk, or he wouldn't have had the courage to talk so long with his parent.

Her mother urges the girl not to be late for riding, and Pamela asks if she can borrow her father's lumber jacket against the cold, even if it *is* too big for her. She goes upstairs to get the jacket and finish dressing, and on the way calls to Clive to get up. Stanley goes silently into the garden and sits there in the cold.

Clive comes down and surprises his mother by also declining breakfast. Worrying about Stanley outside, she asks Clive to go tell him to come in—and she gets another shock when her son, the loving mother's boy, tells her sharply to leave Stanley alone. Figuring that Clive may be jealous of the presence of another young candidate for her motherly affections, Walter, she mothers her son almost with baby talk and draws his head close to her. The boy finally agrees to accept a little breakfast.

Stanley comes in from the garden and without a word crosses the room and goes out the front door, banging it. Pamela, wearing her father's jacket and laden with riding crop and picnic basket, starts downstairs, misses her footing and lands in a heap on the landing. Walter, who has gone to his room to play some phonograph music, dashes out and picks the girl up like a baby—which enrages Pamela because he has made her lose dignity. The girl puts herself together again and goes off for her ride.

Clive and Walter have a brief colloquy in which Walter apologizes for having run out last night. He'd be honored to listen to Clive's troubles. But Clive has changed since last night; now he wants Walter to go—for Walter's own sake. He has a crush on this family and the family doesn't deserve it. He should have had a family of his own.

He *did* have a family, Walter answers—and still does. His father and mother live in Mühlbach. His father was a Nazi and the town regarded him as a war hero. Even after the war he would make Walter recite Nazi slogans. And then he found out; found out that his father was one of the executioners at the Auschwitz concentration camp. Oh, yes, says Walter, as he speaks of his father with loathing, *he* knows what it is to have a family. Clive seems unmoved by the story and repeats his request that the young tutor get the hell away from here.

Clive bangs out the door like his father, thus setting the stage for another tête-à-tête between Walter and Louise—and this is a scene of profound misunderstanding. When the tutor tries to tell his employer he is worried that something inside Clive will explode, she puts it down to jealousy. Clive will realize that a woman's love cannot be rationed, and that there is room in her heart for more than one boy. Last night, she says, held one of the most beautiful moments she has known in years. She felt then that she and Walter could have a really warm friendship.

Walter, misunderstanding completely, says something that is close to his own heart. Would it be possible for someone to find a new mother? The expression of eagerness on Louise's face fades swiftly, and she refuses to discuss her son's problems any more. With false sweetness she reminds Walter that he is only a newcomer to the family. He looks bewildered when she suggests that he go upstairs and play some of his nice music. He goes up, and Louise picks up a tray of dishes and silverware—then puts it down with a big crash.

The Curtain Falls

Scene 2

After supper that night. There is a charming, humorous scene in Pamela's schoolroom, with the girl trying to avoid learning French from her tutor. Clive hasn't come home, and his little sister thinks it would be wonderful if he were giving babies to all the schoolgirls in Ipswich . . .

We move downstairs to a big scene. Louise has been out in the garden and Stanley comes in the front, taking off his overcoat. The subject is Clive, to begin with. Stanley has found no trace of him in the pubs—where he would most likely be, because he is turning into a drunkard. Louise counters by saying that Stanley treats his son abominably, not having the faintest idea how to deal with sensitive people. Stanley throws another punch by saying his wonderful, understanding wife has turned her son into a sniveling neurotice, a mother's boy, a looney.

Louise lays it on the line. She can't stand her life any more. When he offers her a divorce—not angrily, but helpfully—she replies that a divorce would be vulgar and there is Pamela to think about besides.

He suggests that they take a trip alone together—to Monte Carlo, say; and she knocks this down by declaring she hates Monte Carlo. Fighting down his anger, Stanley is attempting to get Louise to give their marriage another try.

Louise seems willing—and the first thing she wants Stanley to do is rather difficult. She wants him to let Walter go; tactfully, but the sooner the better. It's because of Pamela. The girl seems to have developed a crush on Walter, says Louise.

Clive blunders through the front door, drunk again, but coherent as always. A big father-and-son row is in the making, but Louise heads it off by reminding her husband that he agreed to go up to Walter's room and say something. Louise goes to the kitchen to fix her son some food, and Clive, weary, turns out the lights in the room and relaxes on the sofa.

Stanley has gone up to Walter with one purpose in mind, but Walter is a strange catalyst and soon the head of the household is telling him *his* troubles—and they are profound. Stanley knows his son hates him. Why? Walter, speaking with difficulty, says he thinks this is because Clive feels his father does not love him. Talking almost to himself, Stanley recites the frustrations of many years—the expectation of a family which somehow never materialized. "Sensitive" people all around him. One realizes, of course, that Stanley is as sensitive as anybody else, and as eager for love.

Walter, unwilling to hear more, politely excuses himself and goes downstairs, where he sees Clive lying in the dark, turns on a light and awakens him. When Clive begs to know what is wrong with himself, Walter says there is nothing wrong but what is in his mind. He must realize that everything his parents have done to him stems from love, and he must stop pitying himself. He must go away from this house—leave Cambridge at term's end, get a job and be his own self on his own terms.

Stanley, coming from Walter's room and standing on the landing, has heard some of this and he hears Clive agree to go away. He comes down and suggests that Clive go up to bed, which the young man does. (He has to be got rid of somehow so there can be a showdown scene between Stanley and Walter.)

Stanley is raging. How dare Walter tell his own son to leave? And how about his friendship with Pamela? Walter is bewildered at hearing that Mrs. Harrington wants him dismissed on the girl's account. It isn't true, he protests—and Stanley doesn't think it is true, either.

Could it be because Walter has been trying to make love to his wife? He has a witness—Clive himself. The dismayed Walter tries to protest, but Stanley continues at high pitch. He is going to fix it so that this filthy German bastard never gets his citizenship and is deported immediately.

With his wonderful new British world falling away beneath him, the young German has a pitiful scene in which he grasps Louise's hands and, on his knees, pleads emotionally for her intercession. With her husband looking on, she is embarrassed rather than touched. She breaks away from him and tells him that both her children have been considerably disturbed by his presence, and that he must go, with an extra month's wages by way of balm. Numbly he finds his way up to his room, shaking off Clive on the landing as he goes.

Clive wants to know what his parents have done to the young man, and his father says he told Walter what Clive said last night about him and his mother. Clive confesses to his mother that he *did* say what Stanley reported—why, he doesn't know, but it is something which always will make him sick when he thinks of it. It was a lie, he admits, but beneath the lie may have been truth. Between them, he tells his mother bitterly, they have broken his father in bits. For the first time in his life Clive is on his father's side. If there is any vulgarity in the house, it has been Louise's, he cries.

Upstairs, Walter has put on his favorite record, the third movement of Mahler's Fourth Symphony. As always happens, the needle fails to take a groove at a certain point and a phrase is repeated until the needle is moved by hand. This time, Walter doesn't move it. Clive, his outburst against his mother spent, now tenderly asks her to stop all her pretenses and be herself, and he embraces her lovingly.

Something is very strange about the phonograph upstairs repeating itself, and Louise hurries up, finds Walter's door barred and smells gas. At her outcry Stanley runs up, forces the door and drags the unconscious tutor onto the landing. He orders his wife to call a doctor and his son to open a window. Kneeling before the inert Walter, Stanley prays to God to let him live.

Walter comes round, and is beginning to get up as the play ends. He has earned this recovery, for he has given Stanley, Louise, and Clive a new insight into each other.

The Curtain Falls

A LOSS OF ROSES

By William Inge

THIS, like Peter Shaffer's *Five Finger Exercise*, is another example of the me-and-sympathy genre of dramaturgy. I reported on the first night of a *Loss of Roses*, "While his friend Tennessee Williams has been becoming more violent, William Inge seems to be gentling down . . . Inge has become more interested in character than event, and he has probed gently and with sympathy into the characters of three people. Since he writes with skill and clarity, Inge has transferred this sympathy to me. These three want something they haven't got, and it isn't material; they have the simple and universal yearning for understanding and love."

My view of the drama was gentler than most. In the New York *Post* Richard Watts, Jr., reported, "William Inge has finally written a very bad play." In the *World-Telegram* Frank Aston summed up with "The whole deal is unreal." In the *Herald Tribune* Walter Kerr confessed, "I found myself feeling deeply sorry for each of his characters, and it didn't help me to like any of them."

Nevertheless and even so, *A Loss of Roses* is a well-made sample of the drama of frustration and complexes which has been explored so fully in recent years and now shows signs of having been written out.

THE PLAY: ACT I, *Scene* 1

The setting (by Boris Aronson) is of various rooms in and parts of the exterior of a small, now shabby house which has seen better times in a small Kansas town. The time is late summer of 1933. A mother and son are eating their supper in the kitchen. The mother, Mrs. Helen Baird (Betty Field), is in her middle forties and she works as a day nurse in the hospital. Hers is a tired and rather tragic face. The son, Kenny (Warren Beatty), is twenty-one, works as a filling station attendant, and much of the time seems to be resenting something. Offstage, we will learn, is a lot next to the Baird bungalow which is used by various traveling attractions, and which now contains a roller-skating rink.

Kenny and his mother eat in a businesslike way as though the meal was simply something to be got out of the way. Kenny has heard some news and he doesn't like it. Somebody is coming to stay here, and he will have to move out of his room tonight and sleep on the davenport. "She," the one who is going to stay, called from Pennant Junction just before Kenny got home from work, said her show had closed and she had no money and no place to go.

So naturally Helen Baird asked her to come here and she is on her way now by car. Who is "She"? Lila Green, now an actress, who used to help the Bairds with the housework when times were better and Kenny was a little boy, and Kenny used to call her Aunt Lila.

Kenny puts up a petulant fuss about being dispossessed by somebody he can't even remember, and his mother soothes him somewhat by promising that if Lila stays longer than one week then *she* can sleep on the davenport and he can repossess his room.

Helen tells her son a bit about Lila—how her parents were poor and quarrelsome to boot, and when Lila, who was very good-looking, had a chance to get away by joining a traveling tent show, Helen advised her to do it.

The only thing about Lila which interests Kenny is that she is coming by car. If it is her car, maybe she will let him use it. He *craves* an automobile—and has found a secondhand coupé which he can get for a fifty-dollar down payment. If his mother would put up the fifty, he could handle the rest. Trying the affectionate approach, he tells her how he could take her riding in it, and to the movies. His mother says "No," reminding him that there is a serious depression on and they should be thankful for having a home and good jobs.

Rising from the table, Helen goes to get the dessert—Kenny's favorite, lemon meringue pie. She brought it home from the bakery on the way from work. Kenny samples it and pronounces it awful— not like the pies *she* bakes. He is indeed a petulant young man.

His mother protests that he isn't a baby any more and shouldn't want her to wait on him hand and foot. He's got a lot to learn before he gets married and settles down with a wife.

Kenny announces that he isn't thinking of getting married, and there's not a girl in town he'd look at. Helen suggests the little

Caswell girl down the street, so pretty, and working in her father's law office instead of going away to school. Kenny bangs his fist and protests that he hates the Caswell girl because she acts so darn superior. She *is* superior, the mother counters—much superior to the girls at the drugstore and the skating rink who seem to get all her son's attentions.

Kenny resents his mother's always trying to talk him into getting married. Does she want to get rid of him? Hasn't he always tried to help her since Dad died? He could look after her now, and she wouldn't have to work in order to share the expenses of the house. Softening some, he puts an arm around her and tries to kiss her, but she pulls away, protesting that he is too old now to be making love to her like a baby. (A hint of an Oedipus relationship.)

Helen repeats that she doesn't want her son to take the place of his father. She may be *afraid* of needing him—for one day he will marry, and how would his wife feel about having a mother-in-law to support? She'd rather see him married than picking up cheap girls at the drugstore.

Kenny has had enough, and he huffs out onto the porch. Here appears Jelly Beamis (most amusingly played by Michael J. Pollard). Jelly—real name Geoffrey—is all for sampling some home brew at the pool hall, then picking up some girls at the skating rink. Jelly is a moocher by necessity, for his mother takes in washing and his father doesn't work and he usually depends on Kenny for the loan of a cigarette.

Jelly is full of youthful and wishful sin. He has heard tales of "Kanz City," where they have naked waitresses and dirty pictures and you can pick up all the girls you want. He wishes he were like Kenny, who is attractive to girls and could even have Miriam Caswell if he wanted to. Kenny remains diffident—and Jelly drags his way home upon hearing the insistent summons of his mother.

Having finished dishes in the kitchen, Helen comes out on the porch in the dusk. Her watch has stopped again, so she asks her son for the time, which is seven-thirty. And no sign of Lila yet. From her apron pocket she takes a small leather coin purse which she has found in the pocket of one of Kenny's soiled garage uniforms—a woman's purse. Kenny evasively answers that he found it in the filling station, where it must have fallen out of somebody's car. The purse isn't worth anything, and there was no money in it—but his mother thinks he should take it back to the station and try to find the owner.

They hear a car stop and a voice inviting, "Come on in, kids, and meet Helen." It is Lila. Lila (Carol Haney, a superb musical comedy dancer who proved herself an actress in this play) is beautiful, blond, voluptuous, sincere, and generous of spirit. Not in keeping with the season, she is wearing a leopard-skin coat. She and Helen embrace warmly after all these years apart.

Lila is followed by some strange companions, all of whom want to drive on to Kanz City but who don't mind stopping to go to the bathroom. They are part of Lila's stranded theatrical troupe, and with their theatrical exaggerations they make an amusing, cynical interlude in the play. One is Mme. Olga St. Valentine (Margaret Braidwood), a tent-show actress of fifty who is very much the Leading Lady. Another is Ronny Cavendish, an aging and obviously effeminate juvenile lead (James O'Rear). The third is Ricky Powers (played with increasing menace by Robert Webber) a sleek, black-haired, handsome man about Lila's age who played all the heavies in the stranded tent show.

After a few moments of relief and chatter, the show folk drive on to Kanz City, where Ricky has already got a job as a bellhop. Ricky has promised to find a job for Lila in Kanz City, and these two manage a few private words before he departs. He warns Lila not to pull anything funny while she is staying here—with that kid Kenny, for instance. She assures him that she will lead a whole new life of not drinking, going to bed early and reading some of Shakespeare. She reminds him that, if he loves her as he says he does, they should be married by now; and he orders her never to mention marriage again.

Kenny has drifted off, bent on a Saturday night's amusement, and Helen and Lila catch up on times past. Lila has heard of Helen's widowhood and learns the details—how Kenneth Baird, a member of the school board, was drowned while saving a girl student from drowning at a school picnic.

As for Lila: Her marriage after she left home for show business was a disappointment, and now this Ricky, who joined the show a couple of years ago, is somebody to lean on and gives her a good time—even though he has an awful temper. She implies that she took him away from Madame Olga.

Helen, a working woman, has to turn in. She explains to Lila how she can reach the bath down the hall from her own bedroom. Lila offers sincere gratitude and promises to cook and clean and help

around the house. Helen goes to bed, leaving Lila smoking a cigarette and looking extremely sad. She goes to a window and hears the
hurdy-gurdy music from the skating rink and brightens somewhat.

The Curtain Falls

Scene 2

It is about two hours later. Lila has unpacked and is asleep in bed.
The music from the skating rink stopped an hour ago. Kenny and
his pal Jelly weave up to the house, boisterously drunk. Jelly goes on
to *his* house and Kenny staggers into the living room, turns off the
table lamp by the davenport his mother has left lighted for him,
stumbles into his room and begins to undress. He has forgotten the
new house guest.

When he falls on the floor trying to take off a shoe, Lila awakens,
startled at first, then concerned over Kenny. He makes his way to his
new bed, in shirt and drawers as is his sleeping custom, and falls in.
But he has forgotten to remove his shoes, which stick out from under
the covers. Lila takes them off for him, and Kenny dreamily begins to
get ideas. He remembers that Lila used to kiss him good night when
he was a kid. Would she now? She wouldn't, and she hurries to her
own room and closes the door.

The Curtain Falls

Scene 3

It is rather late the next morning, Sunday, Kenny is still asleep on
the davenport, and Helen and Lila are on the porch having another
cup of coffee, catching up and confiding. Lila's story is a seedy one
indeed, but she is too cheerful to think of it this way. When she left
home to join the Comiskey Brothers Comedians she married Ed
Comiskey. Ed was sweet to her, but weak. His brother, Vincent, began making advances—only he wasn't Ed's brother, he was his *father*,
who dyed his hair and kept on playing the leading man. Vincent's
wife didn't mind what he did, because she was in love with the
xylophone player. And the xylophone player's wife didn't mind because *she* was in love with the crew boss.

So Lila ran away from the show one day, boarded a train and
found herself in Bismarck, North Dakota, in midwinter. She locked
herself in a hotel room and sort of half-heartedly tried to kill herself

with some sleeping medicine. They found her in time, and sent her to a mental institution for three months. It wasn't a bad place, and she wouldn't mind being back there. The doctor there was a big help, explaining that only emotionally immature people expect the world to be rosy. Lila is no longer emotionally immature, so she no longer expects much out of life—and she isn't going to try to kill herself again.

Helen's story is one of devotion to and disappointment in her son. She could have married another nice man once, but Kenny hated him so she let him go. Kenny worries her, with his drinking and going with trashy girls. And he "takes" things, too, pretending he has found them, like a pair of woman's gloves or a coin purse—nothing of value, like jewelry. He had a chance to start a career in a promising industry when an aircraft factory in Wichita offered him a job and schooling at the same time, but he turned it down because he wanted to stay home. He just doesn't seem to want to make anything of his life.

Helen intends to go to church and wants her son to go with her, but when she tries to rouse him he plays possum. When his mother goes off to her devotions Kenny opens one eye and cocks it at Lila. He cannot remember what happened last night, but hopes he did nothing amiss. She assures him he didn't, and brings him a cup of coffee for his hangover.

He asks her about the shows she has been in, and she tells him—everything from dancing to the lead in *Smilin' Through*. At his urging, she demonstrates some of her dance steps (and with Carol Haney doing the dancing they are enticing). Kenny brightens perceptibly and thinks about breakfast. Could she, an actress, fix him some tomato juice, pancakes, and sausage? She could and she will . . . and Kenny, lounging luxuriously in his davenport bed, allows that he is going to *like* having Lila here.

The Curtain Falls

ACT II, *Scene* 1

It is a month later, and the trees around the house are turning. In this late afternoon Lila, becomingly dressed, sits on the porch steps sipping a cocktail out of a cheese glass and enjoying the twilight. Home from work comes Kenny. The occasion for the pretty dress and a pitcher of rum-and-pineapple cocktails is Helen's wedding anniversary—the only anniversary she observes. Lila has also cooked a fine dinner for it.

Lila gives a sweet smile and a melodious greeting to Kenny when he comes home from work, and the first thing he does is proudly show her a present he has bought his mother—a prettily wrapped package. In it, he says—and he shows the receipt—is a $55.80 wrist watch. He confesses he always felt he owed Mom something, for she could have married again if it hadn't been for him. He has been saving for this gift since June. He asks her for one of her drinks, samples it and switches to a bottle of beer.

Inside the house, the boy makes a grab for Lila and kisses her hard, to her shocked surprise. When he asks what is wrong with it, she protests that she is a lot older than he is, and he softens her by declaring she doesn't look it; doesn't seem any older than the girls he went to school with. It has been hard, living in the same house and trying to keep from making love to her. He is lonely and she is the one he wants, because he feels at home with her.

Lila protests that he shouldn't talk like this if he doesn't mean it, because things like this raise a woman's hopes—and when she finds out the man doesn't mean it a woman even prays to die. She knows, for it has happened to her several times.

Now thoroughly believing himself, Kenny says they could get married, and if Mom didn't like it they could have a place of their own. Lila's emotional tizzy is heightened when the boy suggests that they be together tonight, while Mom is on night duty at the hospital; but she knows it wouldn't be right and tells him so.

Helen agrees to sip an anniversary cocktail, but doesn't take much because she plans to attend the revival meeting tonight before going back to the hospital. Kenny hurries in to take his bath, and Helen, with a vague suspicion that something is up between her son and her old friend, asks pointedly if Lila has heard from Ricky yet—Ricky, who was going to find her a job in Kansas City. It has been four weeks, and no word yet. Helen suggests that Lila might find a job in town—in one of the stores, perhaps, pretty as she is; and she can stay on here. Lila protests that she couldn't hold any job except on the stage.

Kenny comes out, all cleaned up and wearing new slacks and white shoes. Proudly he gives his mother his present, and she opens it hesitantly. When she sees what it is she almost begins to weep and tell her son she can't take it. He must get his money back and get her some *little* present if he wants to—and she will take the watch her husband gave her to be fixed again.

The boy is at first profoundly hurt, then furious. He announces he is getting out of here right now; he is sick of women looking after him, and he will move to Jelly's house. He stalks out, leaving his mother in tears.

Lila can't understand why Helen refused the present, when Kenny was just trying to make up for his father's being gone; every boy wants to be like his father. And Helen answers that there are some ways he can't be allowed. The anniversary dinner goes untouched.

People pass by the house on their way to the revival meeting, and organ music can be heard distantly. Helen goes to her room to get ready for the meeting, and when the phone rings Lila takes it. It is Ricky. He is here in town, he has got her a job, and is coming right over. She calls out the good news to Helen, and says Ricky will take her back with him tomorrow.

Helen starts for the door and says she will see Lila in the morning— adding, gently, that she thought Lila would like to spend the night with Ricky somewhere. She knew Ricky was her lover the minute she saw him. Lila, wanting to confess to somebody, says the doctor in Bismarck told her she was emotionally immature. When she is afraid, she admits, she wants someone close and doesn't care who it is. Sometimes men take advantage of this . . . and that's when she hates herself.

Helen goes off to the meeting, and soon one can hear the evangelist talking about the depression and offering spiritual help.

Ricky arrives and Lila's happiness is complete. When she asks what kind of job she'll have he puts her off. He has a bottle of gin and some reefers in the car and suggests that they go for a ride and get tanked up first. The excited Lila wants to know *now* about the job, and he answers vaguely that they'll play a couple of road houses and some conventions and make some movies. It dawns on her that his plans are for a sex act and some filthy films, and, recoiling, she orders Ricky to get out.

But this evil man is not so easily disposed of; seizing her wrist and twisting it, he tells her she *has* to take the job because without her he won't have one. Kenny appears down the street, gives Lila and Ricky a casual "Hi" and goes into the house to pack up for moving. Ricky tries blackmail, suggesting that Lila's friends might like to see the pictures he made of her one time in Grand Rapids when she was drunk. When Lila refuses to scare, he grabs her wrist roughly and orders her to pack up. They will spend the night at the tourist camp and go to Kaycee in the morning. Go on, he urges, before he knocks her teeth out.

Lila screams to Kenny to help her, and the boy comes running to the porch and orders Ricky to leave. When he has gone, Lila, sobbing, clings to Kenny—as she always clings to somebody when she is frightened. Kenny holds her comfortingly in his arms and Lila sighs in relief. This is his chance.

The Curtain Falls

Scene 2

It is a little after seven next morning. Kenny is in bed—*his* bed— and Lila, deliriously happy, is fixing breakfast. She urges the boy to get up so she can make the bed before his mother gets home.

Lila's happiness is not shared by Kenny, for it is the same old story of remorse and a subsidence of interest. Trying to be gentle, he clumsily points out to Lila that, after all, he didn't *promise* to marry her, and maybe his marrying an older woman isn't such a good idea.

Jelly arrives, looking for Kenny. He was supposed to come to his house last night and he didn't, even after his mother had the room all made up for him. Jelly can guess what happened last night, and he blackmails Lila out of some cigarettes.

She was so happy this morning, so glad to be alive and planning a wedding . . . And when the blow falls the life goes out of her. She hurries to the bathroom to dress. When Helen arrives it doesn't take too long for her to put one and one together—for Lila *didn't* go with Ricky last night. Before she can question Kenny, Lila comes out of the bathroom, screaming and bleeding and afraid to die now. She has cut her wrist with Kenny's razor. The hospital nurse takes immediate charge, examines the wound and tells Lila she will be all right, for she missed the vein. Kenny brings a first-aid kit and the would-be suicide is patched up. She asks Helen to call Ricky at the tourist camp and tell him she will be ready to go by the time he gets here.

Kenny is frightened by Lila's decision, for Ricky is no good. He tells her, while his mother is phoning, that maybe their getting married wouldn't be such a bad idea, but she bravely tells him to forget it. Helen puts her on the bed for a rest and closes the bedroom door. Kenny, weeping now, tells his mother what he has done, and Helen accuses him of having done it to spite her. Kenny does some accusing of his own, saying his father was the only man she ever loved, and is amazed when his mother tells him she has loved him as much as she dared—and if she had loved him any more she'd have destroyed him.

After sobbing on the sofa a bit, the boy goes to a drawer, takes out his mother's present, taps softly on Lila's door, enters the bedroom and gives her the watch. She accepts it with sweet understanding.

Lila is ready for Ricky—and Kenny has made up his mind to leave, too. To leave and be on his own. Perhaps the Wichita job is still open. Helen understands his urge for self-assertion, and tells him this is all right. He embraces her warmly.

Bag packed, Lila stands on the porch waiting for Ricky and contemplating the life ahead. Maybe, she says, she *will* be happy. Who knows?

A neighbor and her small child pass by, on the way to the girl's first day in school. Lila remembers *her* first day in school. She carried a bouquet of roses and gave them to the teacher. Then, on this her first day and not knowing the rules, she talked to a boy across the aisle and the teacher slapped her. Lila cried and wanted her roses back, but the teacher shook her finger and said that when you give lovely presents you can't expect them back. It was a lesson she never learned very well, Lila muses. There are so many things she still wants back. . . .

Ricky arrives.

The Curtain Falls

PRIZE PLAYS

A plurality of members of the New York Drama Critics Circle voted Lillian Hellman's *Toys in the Attic* the best American play of the season. The Pulitzer drama judges declared the season's best to be *Fiorello!* This was an unusual but not unprecedented selection, for two other musicals, *Of Thee I Sing* (1931–32) and *South Pacific* (1949–50) have been given Pulitzer awards.

PULITZER PRIZE AWARDS

1917–18   *Why Marry?* by Jesse Lynch Williams
1918–19   No award.
1919–20   *Beyond the Horizon*, by Eugene O'Neill
1920–21   *Miss Lulu Bett*, by Zona Gale
1921–22   *Anna Christie*, by Eugene O'Neill
1922–23   *Icebound*, by Owen Davis
1923–24   *Hell-bent fer Heaven*, by Hatcher Hughes
1924–25   *They Knew What They Wanted*, by Sidney Howard
1925–26   *Craig's Wife*, by George Kelly
1926–27   *In Abraham's Bosom*, by Paul Green
1927–28   *Strange Interlude*, by Eugene O'Neill
1928–29   *Street Scene*, by Elmer Rice
1929–30   *The Green Pastures*, by Marc Connelly
1930–31   *Alison's House*, by Susan Glaspell
1931–32   *Of Thee I Sing*, by George S. Kaufman, Morrie Ryskind, Ira and George Gershwin
1932–33   *Both Your Houses*, by Maxwell Anderson
1933–34   *Men in White*, by Sidney Kingsley
1934–35   *The Old Maid*, by Zoë Akins
1935–36   *Idiot's Delight*, by Robert E. Sherwood
1936–37   *You Can't Take It with You*, by Moss Hart and George S. Kaufman
1937–38   *Our Town*, by Thornton Wilder
1938–39   *Abe Lincoln in Illinois*, by Robert E. Sherwood
1939–40   *The Time of Your Life*, by William Saroyan

1940–41 *There Shall Be No Night*, by Robert E. Sherwood
1941–42 No award.
1942–43 *The Skin of Our Teeth*, by Thornton Wilder
1943–44 No award.
1944–45 *Harvey*, by Mary Coyle Chase
1945–46 *State of the Union*, by Howard Lindsay and Russel Crouse
1946–47 No award.
1947–48 *A Streetcar Named Desire*, by Tennessee Williams
1948–49 *Death of a Salesman*, by Arthur Miller
1949–50 *South Pacific*, by Richard Rodgers, Oscar Hammerstein II, and Joshua Logan
1950–51 No award.
1951–52 *The Shrike*, by Joseph Kramm
1952–53 *Picnic*, by William Inge
1953–54 *The Teahouse of the August Moon*, by John Patrick
1954–55 *Cat on a Hot Tin Roof*, by Tennessee Williams
1955–56 *The Diary of Anne Frank*, by Albert Hackett and Frances Goodrich
1956–57 *Long Day's Journey into Night*, by Eugene O'Neill
1957–58 *Look Homeward, Angel*, by Ketti Frings
1958–59 *J. B.*, by Archibald MacLeish
1959–60 *Fiorello!*, by Jerome Weidman, George Abbott, Sheldon Harnick and Jerry Bock

CRITICS CIRCLE AWARDS

1935–36 *Winterset*, by Maxwell Anderson
1936–37 *High Tor*, by Maxwell Anderson
1937–38 *Of Mice and Men*, by John Steinbeck
1938–39 No award.
1939–40 *The Time of Your Life*, by William Saroyan
1940–41 *Watch on the Rhine*, by Lillian Hellman
1941–42 No award.
1942–43 *The Patriots*, by Sidney Kingsley
1943–44 No award.
1944–45 *The Glass Menagerie*, by Tennessee Williams
1945–46 No award.
1946–47 *All My Sons*, by Arthur Miller
1947–48 *A Streetcar Named Desire*, by Tennessee Williams

1948–49   *Death of a Salesman*, by Arthur Miller
1949–50   *The Member of the Wedding*, by Carson McCullers
1950–51   *Darkness at Noon*, by Sidney Kingsley
1951–52   *I Am a Camera*, by John van Druten
1952–53   *Picnic*, by William Inge
1953–54   *The Teahouse of the August Moon*, by John Patrick
1954–55   *Cat on a Hot Tin Roof*, by Tennessee Williams
1955–56   *The Diary of Anne Frank*, by Albert Hackett and Frances
          Goodrich
1956–57   *Long Day's Journey into Night*, by Eugene O'Neill
1957–58   *Look Homeward, Angel*, by Ketti Frings
1958–59   *A Raisin in the Sun*, by Lorraine Hansberry
1959–60   *Toys in the Attic*, by Lillian Hellman

OTHER AWARDS

The Critics Circle, which usually bestows two other blessings after its Best American Play citation, voted that *Fiorello!* was the best musical and *Five Finger Exercise* was the best foreign play. Both these attractions have been dealt with extensively in other pages of this book.

The American Theatre Wing's Antoinette Perry Awards, called Tonys, were given for outstanding work, but were, as has been the custom of the Wing, not labeled best. Winners included *The Miracle Worker* in the drama division; *Fiorello!* and *The Sound of Music* as musicals; Mary Martin, for her performance in *The Sound of Music*; Jackie Gleason, for his performance in *Take Me Along*; Anne Bancroft, for her performance in *The Miracle Worker*; Melvyn Douglas, for his acting in *The Best Man*; Anne Revere, for acting in *Toys in the Attic*, and Roddy McDowall for acting in *The Fighting Cock*; Tom Bosley, for his title performance in *Fiorello!* and Patricia Neway for hers in *The Sound of Music*; Arthur Penn for directing *The Miracle Worker* and George Abbott for staging *Fiorello!* Other Tonys went to Michael Kidd for staging the dances in *Destry Rides Again*, Oliver Smith for his *The Sound of Music* settings, Howard Bay for the sets in *Toys in the Attic* and Cecil Beaton for the costumes in *Saratoga*. Special awards were bestowed on Burgess Meredith and James Thurber for *A Thurber Carnival* and John D. Rockefeller III for his presidency of the now-building Lincoln Center for the Performing Arts.

The Clarence Derwent Awards, financed by the estate of the late Derwent, went, as is stipulated, to non-featured players. They were for Rochelle Oliver, the child bride of *Toys in the Attic*, and William Daniels, playing the publisher in the off-Broadway *The Zoo Story*.

For his direction and co-authorship of *Fiorello!*, George Abbott was given traditional prizes by the Barter Theatre of Abingdon, Virginia, —an acre of land, a ham and the opportunity to name two students for scholarships at the theater. The ladies of the Aegis Theatre Club honored José Ferrer for his direction of *The Andersonville Trial*, the entire cast of *Destry Rides Again*, the cast of *Silent Night, Lonely Night*, and Mary Martin for being Mary Martin.

Another important ladies' matinee group, the Drama League, gave its Delia Austrian medal to Jessica Tandy for her performance in *Five Finger Exercise*. The American National Theatre and Academy named Anne Bancroft and Tom Bosley as its prize-winners. Sol Hurok was given the medal of the Sam S. Shubert Foundation for his contributions to the art of the theater. And one Michael Tolan, actor in *A Majority of One*, was given the Bill Johnson Memorial Trophy as the most valuable player in the Broadway Show League's softball tournament, which is held Sundays in the springtime in Central Park.

THE LONGEST RUNS

Herewith are listed the New York plays and musicals which have had five hundred or more performances. Attractions marked with an asterisk were still running as of June 1, 1960.

Life with Father: 3224
Tobacco Road: 3182
Abie's Irish Rose: 2327
Oklahoma!: 2248
South Pacific: 1925
*My Fair Lady: 1757
Harvey: 1775
Born Yesterday: 1642
The Voice of the Turtle: 1557
Arsenic and Old Lace: 1444
Hellzapoppin: 1404
Angel Street: 1295
Lightnin': 1291
The King and I: 1246
Guys and Dolls: 1200
Mister Roberts: 1157
Annie Get Your Gun: 1147
The Seven Year Itch: 1141
Pins and Needles: 1108
Kiss Me, Kate: 1070
The Pajama Game: 1063
The Teahouse of the August
   Moon: 1027
*The Music Man: 1024
Damn Yankees: 1022
Anna Lucasta: 957
Kiss and Tell: 957
Bells Are Ringing: 933
The Moon Is Blue: 928
Can-Can: 894
Carousel: 890
Hats Off to Ice: 889
Fanny: 888
Follow the Girls: 882
The Bat: 867

My Sister Eileen: 865
White Cargo: 864
Song of Norway: 860
A Streetcar Named Desire: 855
Comedy in Music (Victor
   Borge): 849
You Can't Take It with
   You: 837
Three Men on a Horse: 835
Stars on Ice: 830
Inherit the Wind: 803
No Time for Sergeants: 798
Where's Charley?: 792
The Ladder: 789
State of the Union: 765
The First Year: 760
Gentlemen Prefer Blondes: 750
Two for the Seesaw: 750
Death of a Salesman: 742
Sons o' Fun: 742
The Man Who Came to
   Dinner: 739
West Side Story: 734
Call Me Mister: 734
High Button Shoes: 727
Finian's Rainbow: 725
Claudia: 722
The Gold Diggers: 720
The Diary of Anne Frank: 716
I Remember Mama: 714
Junior Miss: 710
Seventh Heaven: 704
Cat on a Hot Tin Roof: 694
Li'l Abner: 693
Peg o' My Heart: 692

The Children's Hour: 691
Tea and Sympathy: 691
Dead End: 687
The Lion and the Mouse: 686
Dear Ruth: 683
East Is West: 680
The Most Happy Fella: 678
The Doughgirls: 671
Irene: 670
Boy Meets Girl: 669
Blithe Spirit: 657
The Women: 657
A Trip to Chinatown: 657
Bloomer Girl: 654
The Fifth Season: 653
Rain: 648
Witness for the Prosecution: 645
Call Me Madam: 644
Janie: 642
The Green Pastures: 640
Auntie Mame: 639
The Fourposter: 632
Is Zat So?: 618
Anniversary Waltz: 615
The Happy Time: 614
Separate Rooms: 613
Affairs of State: 610
Star and Garter: 609
The Student Prince: 608
Broadway: 603
Adonis: 603
Street Scene: 601
Flower Drum Song: 601
Kiki: 600
Wish You Were Here: 598
A Society Circus: 596
Blossom Time: 592
The Two Mrs. Carrolls: 585
Detective Story: 581
Brigadoon: 581

Kismet: 580
Brother Rat: 577
Show Boat: 572
The Show-Off: 571
Sally: 570
One Touch of Venus: 567
Happy Birthday: 564
Look Homeward, Angel: 564
The Glass Menagerie: 561
Sunrise at Campobello: 558
Rose Marie: 557
Strictly Dishonorable: 557
Jamaica: 557
Wonderful Town: 556
Floradora: 553
Dial M for Murder: 552
Good News: 551
Let's Face It: 547
Pal Joey: 542
Within the Law: 541
The Music Master: 540
What a Life: 538
The Red Mill: 531
The Solid Gold Cadillac: 528
The Boomerang: 522
Rosalinda: 521
Chauve Souris: 520
Blackbirds: 518
Sunny: 517
Victoria Regina: 517
The Vagabond King: 511
The New Moon: 509
The World of Suzie Wong: 508
Shuffle Along: 504
Up in Central Park: 504
Carmen Jones: 503
The Member of the
    Wedding: 501
Personal Appearance: 501
Panama Hattie: 501

Bird in Hand: 500
Sailor, Beware!: 500
Room Service: 500
Tomorrow the World: 500

THE HOLDOVERS

These are the attractions continued from previous seasons which closed during the season of 1959–60, with the totals of their performances on Broadway.

Two for the Seesaw: 750
West Side Story: 734
Flower Drum Song: 601
The World of Suzie Wong: 508
The Pleasure of His Company: 474
Redhead: 453
The Marriage-Go-Round: 433
Sweet Bird of Youth: 383
J. B.: 364
A Touch of the Poet: 284
Once More With Feeling: 263
The Gazebo: 218
Rashomon: 159

THE SEASON IN FULL

Broadway productions from June 1, 1959, to May 31, 1960

MUCH ADO ABOUT NOTHING

Opened September 17, 1959; closed November 7, 1959;
60 performances.

Comedy by William Shakespeare. Settings and costumes after designs by Mariano Andreu, supervision and lighting by Paul Morrison, costumes executed by Ray Diffen, music by Leslie Bridgewater, dances by Pauline Grant, staged by John Gielgud, Myles Eason assistant. Produced by The Cambridge Drama Festival by arrangement with The Producers Theatre, Roger L. Stevens, Robert Whitehead, Robert Dowling and Louis Lotito at the Lunt-Fontanne Theatre.

The cast

Don Pedro, Prince of Arragon	Micheal MacLiammoir
Don John, his bastard brother	Hurd Hatfield
Claudio, a young lord of Florence	Barrie Ingham
Benedick, a young lord of Padua	John Gielgud
Leonato, governor of Messina	Malcolm Keen
Antonio, an old man, his brother	Herbert Ranson
Balthasar, attendant on Don Pedro	Jonathan Anderson
Borachio ⎫ Conrade ⎬ Followers of Don John	Paul Sparer, Mark Lenard
Friar Francis	David King-Wood
Dogberry, a constable	George Rose
Verges, a headborough	Donald Moffat
A Sexton	Barry Macollum
A boy	Willie Wade
1st Watch	Howard Fischer
2nd Watch	Graham Jarvis
A Messenger	Donald Moffat
Hero, daughter to Leonato	Jean Marsh
Beatrice, niece to Leonato	Margaret Leighton
Margaret ⎫ Waiting Gentlewomen	Betsy von Furstenberg
Ursula ⎬ Attending on Hero	Nancy Marchand
Watch	Theodore Tenley, Joe Ponazecki
Pages	Edward Moor, Ralph Williams, Louis Negin, John Valva, Arthur Teno Pollick, D. F. Gilliam
Ladies	Virginia Robinson, Juliete Hunt, Joan Hackett, Fay Tracey, Elizabeth Winship
Lords	Neil Vipond, Allessandro Giannini, David Thurman, Martin Herschberg
Captains	Donald Barton, Richard Buck, Joseph Hoover
An Acolyte	Peter deVise

THE PLAY:

More often than not, a new theatrical season begins with a dull thud. This time it opened most promisingly and splendidly, with John Gielgud and Margaret Leighton as Benedick and Beatrice. In my first-night notice I wrote, "I cannot recall as fine a production of a Shakespeare comedy . . . and the part of my heart which belongs to the theatre has been hopelessly lost to Miss Leighton.

"Gielgud, in addition to playing a most lucid and keenly humorous Benedick, has managed what amounts to an orchestration of the comedy, so that I half imagined that, beneath the lines, I was hearing some music by Mozart. Miss Leighton's Beatrice is a perfect high-comedy performance, quick of wit, feather-light and wonderfully cool in its assurance."

AN EVENING WITH YVES MONTAND

*Opened September 22, 1959; closed October 31, 1959;
43 performances.*

Songs in French. Staged and lighted by Yves Montand. Produced by Norman Granz in association with Jacques Canetti at Henry Miller's Theatre.

The cast

Yves Montand
Bob Castella, piano
Nick Perito, accordion
Al Hall, bass
Jim Hall, guitar
Charles Persip, drums
Jimmy Giuffre, clarinet
Billy Byers, trombone

Program

PREMIÈRE PARTIE

LES AMIS (The Friends)

Paroles—Francis Lemarque, Musique—Bob Castella

When a guy meets the girl he loves for good, it's time for him to say goodbye to his friends. They have been the most important thing in his life, he has shared everything with them. Now, for a little while, he wants to be alone with his girl. But they'll meet again, soon; he is sure they'll understand, and like her.

LA FETE A LOULOU (The Birthday of Loulou)

Paroles—Rene Rouzaud, Musique—Bob Castella

A man invites his friend to a party, his friend is blue. "Come on, have a bite with us, have a drink, you'll meet some nice people, ordinary people like us. Nenette will be there, you'll like Nenette. It's Loulou's birthday party, we'll have ourselves a ball!"

UNE DEMOISELLE SUR UNE BALANCOIRE (A Young Lady in a Swing)

Paroles—Jean Nohain, Musique—Mireille

There was this young lady at the fair, standing on a swing, swinging. Up and down she went swinging; nothing could stop her from swinging. She was apparently mad about swinging. Matter of fact, as I soon discovered, she preferred swinging to doing anything else. And I mean ANYTHING else. Moral: There is no arguing about this, but enough is enough.

MA MOME, MA P'TITE MOME

Paroles—Henri Contet, Musique—Marguerite Monnot

This is what the French man calls the woman he adores . . . "Je t'adore, ma mome, ma p'tite mome." The American man might say, "I love you, baby."

SIR GODFREY

Paroles—Jacques Mareuil, Musique—Georges Liferman

If you can imagine a very British gentleman, a veddy, veddy British gentleman, the kind who might feed oysters to his horse, who plays billiards, rides to hounds, plays golf, is received in the best of society, but . . . but what nobody knows is that late at night—and I am sorry to have to tell you the surprise in the song— he's a gangster, not an ordinary gangster, his father was a gangster. His grandfather was a gangster. It's a matter of tradition suh, tradition; Sir . . . Godfrey!

LE CARROSSE   (The Golden Chariot)

Paroles—Henri Contet, Musique—Mireille

He did not play "cowboys and Indians" with us at school. He was waiting for his golden chariot, building his castle in Spain, dreaming of a slow boat to China— whatever YOU call a dream. Later on, while he sold flint stones on the street, I met him; he was still waiting, and building and sailing . . . and dreaming.

LUNA-PARK

Paroles—Jean Guigo, Musique—Loulou Gaste

When a fellow has finished his week's work, he puts on his clean clothes and goes to LUNA-PARK. There he is greeted, like some others are at the "ROTARY CLUB." He knows everybody, everybody knows him . . . He is SOMEBODY!

LES FEUILLES MORTES

Paroles—Jacques Prevert, Musique—Joseph Cosma

LES GRANDS BOULEVARDS

Paroles—Jacques Plante, Musique—Norbert Glanzberg

This is the song of an auto-worker who walks. At night when he leaves the plant, he strolls along the grands boulevards of Paris; not the elegant Paris, the popular Paris. Here he finds his own crowd, his own fun, his own history, his own hopes, and in his little room, he still hears the music of the grands boulevards.

FLAMENCO DE PARIS

Paroles—Leo Ferre, Musique—Leo Ferre

You did not tell me, my Spanish friend, that a guitar in exile rings like a trumpet. When we met on a street in Paris, you told me nothing. But one word rang out in the winter air . . . Patience—Patiencia.

UN GARCON DANSAIT   (A Boy Was Dancing)

Paroles—Jacques Mareuil, Musique—Georges Liferman

This is about a boy who used to dance on the sidewalks of Paris, in the slums. He has a great ambition, a dream of becoming a big star, the equal of Fred Astaire. We see him go to an audition. And later we see him as a waiter. His is not a big star. But he still dreams of success.

DEUXIEME PARTIE

LES PETITS RIENS   (The Little Daily Nothings)

Paroles—Frances Lemarque, Musique—Frances Lemarque

This is a song about the little ordinary things of life—we say "Les petits riens quotidiens," the little daily nothings. It speaks of the work, the daily work of the farmer, the miner, the carpenter, the sailor. It speaks of the laugh of a child, the echo of a song, the sun, the sky, the birth of new love. You understand? All the things that are not really important.

SIMPLE COMME BONJOUR (Simple as Bonjour)

Paroles—Jacques Prevert, Musique—Henri Crolla

This song says: Love is clear as day, love is simple as bonjour . . . without it life is a slow waltz without music, a child who never laughs, or an unread novel.

MAIS QU'EST-CE QUE J'AI? (What's Wrong With Me?)

Paroles—Edith Piaf, Musique—Henri Betti

It's not a new idea that when you're in love your pals think you are coo-coo. This song says "What's wrong with me? When I start raving about my girl, my pals laugh at me. They're the ones who are coo-coo."

LA MARIE-VISON (Marie's Mink Coat)

Paroles—Roger Varnay, Musique—Marc Heyral

Back in Nineteen-Ten, men drank champagne from her slipper, she was the toast of Paris, drove in a carriage, made much love and gave none, ended on skid row. Wasted her life, and for what? A goddam mink coat. Gracious ladies: Let the sad story of Marie-Vison be a lesson to you: Vice doesn't pay, and there must be other ways for a girl to keep warm.

PLANTER CAFE

Paroles—Eddy Marnay, Musique—Emil Stern

Working on a coffee plantation, it's very hard work. Coffee may keep you awake if you drink it. But it's hard to stay awake if you have to work in the hot sun. Planter Cafe.

LE CHEF D'ORCHESTRE EST AMOUREUX (The Conductor Is in Love)

Paroles—Jacques Mareuil, Musique—Georges Liferman

What happens when a certain conductor—very high-brow and long-haired—falls in love with a young lady who can't stand music—except the Viennese Waltz.

A PARIS

Paroles—Frances Lemarque, Musique—Frances Lemarque

It says a lot of things about Paris, a lot of things which have already been said, and some which have never been said. Like for instance:

"Des ennuis,
Y en n'a pas qu'a Paris,
Y en a dans le monde entier,
Oui mais dans le monde entier,
Y a pas partout Paris . . . v'la l'ennui"

—which means: "There are troubles not only in Paris, they are all over the world; but all over the world, there is not everywhere a Paris! That's the trouble!"

IL FAIT DES . . . (LE FANATIQUE DE JAZZ)

Paroles—Edith Piaf, Musique—Edouard Chekle

This one's about the French equivalent of a hipster, a phony intellectual, a real cool cat who thinks he digs it all, but doesn't.

MON MANEGE A MOI

Paroles—Jean Constanin, Musique—Norbert Glanzberg

You have a phrase, and a song: "You Go To My Head." We have a phrase and a song: "You Turn My Head . . . You Are My Carousel."

THE ENTERTAINER:

Yves Montand, an Italian whose family took him to Marseille when he was two, is a charming and persuasive French singer, doing the narrative songs of which Frenchmen—and we—are so fond. Montand is married to Simone Signoret, and his theatrical skills go considerably beyond his ability to sing charming songs charmingly. For example, he played a year in Paris in the French adaptation of Arthur Miller's *The Crucible* with Mlle. Signoret, and then he and his wife duplicated these performances in Jean-Paul Sartre's screen version of the drama.

THE GANG'S ALL HERE

Opened October 1, 1959; closed January 23, 1960; 133 performances.

Play by Jerome Lawrence and Robert E. Lee. Settings and lighting by Jo Mielziner, costumes by Patricia Zipprodt, staged by George Roy Hill. Produced by Kermit Bloomgarden Productions, Inc., in association with Sylvia Drulie at the Ambassador Theatre.

The cast

Walter Rafferty	E. G. Marshall
Joshua Loomis	Bernard Lenrow
Charles Webster	Paul McGrath
Tad	Bill Zuckert
Higgy	Howard Smith
Judge Corriglione	Victor Kilian
Doc Kirkaby	Fred Stewart
Frances Greeley Hastings	Jean Dixon
Griffith P. Hastings	Melvyn Douglas
Cobb	Edwin Cooper
Maid	Anne Shropshire
Bruce Bellingham	Arthur Hill
Arthur Anderson	Bram Nossen
Axel Maley	Bert Wheeler
Laverne	Yvette Vickers
Renee	Alberta MacDonald
Piano Player	John Harkins
John Boyd	Clay Hall

THE PLAY:

Jerome Lawrence and Robert E. Lee wrote a fine play, *Inherit the Wind*, about the memorable clash between William Jennings Bryan and Clarence Darrow at the Scopes "monkey" trial in Dayton, Tennessee. They gave their characters fictitious names, but there was no doubt who was who. In *The Gang's All Here* the dramatists turned their attention to President Warren G. Harding and the Ohio Gang—and here, too, everybody was fictionalized. So were most of the events.

Melvyn Douglas had the first of the two political roles he has played this season—the other being the Presidential hopeful in *The Best Man*. He played an Ohioan who had never dreamed of the Presidency, yet suddenly found himself in the White House. A loyal and gregarious man, he put a number of cronies in key government posts. Varying types of political gangsters and sycophants were colorfully played by E. G. Marshall, Paul McGrath, Bert Wheeler, Victor Kilian, Howard Smith, and Fred Stewart.

The gangsterism became too evident, and a Senate investigation began closing in. The President, dismayed at his betrayal by his poker-playing pals, committed suicide with poison.

George Roy Hill directed the play in a sound melodramatic style, and Douglas' best scene was the one in which, as the small-town editor who never wanted to be President, he found himself entering the White House with his wife, played by Jean Dixon.

This was not the first play about the Harding administration. In 1927 there appeared a dramatization by Maureen Watkins of a novel by Samuel Hopkins Adams, *Revelry*. It was a failure, but even so I thought it was a better piece of theatre. In the Watkins-Adams piece of careful fiction, the President also committed suicide—but from a different motive; he was driven to it by threats of exposure by a woman.

Concerning *The Gang's All Here*, Richard Watts, Jr., wrote: "While the portrait of the good-hearted weakling of a President is touching, it is not a particularly moving play. The reaction to it is more likely to be one of recognition and, perhaps, of chastening meditation. And it falls off in interest in the final sections, although the last act contains one of its most appealing scenes, an incident where the doomed President, still an editor at heart, shows a frightened young reporter how to take notes on a statement he is dictating, denouncing his betrayers."

THE GREAT GOD BROWN

Opened October 6, 1959; closed October 31, 1959; 31 performances.

Play by Eugene O'Neill. Settings and costumes by Will Steven Armstrong, lighting by Tharon Musser, music by David Amram, staged by Stuart Vaughan. Produced by the Phoenix Theatre, a project of Theatre Incorporated, T. Edward Hambleton-Norris Houghton, founders, at the Coronet Theatre.

The cast

Mrs. Brown	Sasha von Scherler
William A. Brown	Robert Lansing
Mr. Brown	Patrick Hines
Mrs. Anthony	Patricia Ripley
Mr. Anthony	J. D. Cannon
Dion Anthony	Fritz Weaver
Margaret	Nan Martin
Cybel	Gerry Jedd
Eldest Son	John Hillerman
Second Son	Murray Levy
Youngest Son	Corydon Erickson
Older Draftsman	Elliott Sullivan
Younger Draftsman	John Heffernan
A Client	Eric Berry
Committeemen	Ray Reinhardt, Albert Quinton, Eric Berry
Police Captain	Albert Quinton
Policemen	Ray Reinhardt, Tom Bellin

THE PLAY:

In one of its few forays from off-Broadway to Broadway, the Phoenix Theatre essayed a revival of Eugene O'Neill's murky mask drama. To me, time had not dispelled the murkiness, and some of the stagecraft now looked a little silly. In his review, the *Post*'s Richard Watts, Jr., reminded one that *The Great God Brown* "is Eugene O'Neill's most tortured, enigmatic and tormenting drama." I felt that if the beatniks of Greenwich Village could see this play they would begin wearing masks instead of beards. It is much easier to cry woe from behind a mask than through whiskers, and somehow it sounds louder.

In this early O'Neill work, the principal characters show themselves as others see them when they wear disguises, and reveal their inner selves only when they take off the masks. Thus it happens that a wife cannot stand the sight of her husband when he shows himself a lost and yearning boy, but he suits her when he is posing as a harsh, alcoholic misfit. When this husband dies, his rival picks up his mask and wears it, and the wife cannot tell the difference.

A first-rate production was squandered on a second-rate drama.

HAPPY TOWN

Opened October 7, 1959; closed October 10, 1959; 5 performances.

Musical with book adapted by Max Hampton, lyrics by Harry M. Haldane and music by Gordon Duffy. Settings by Curt Nations, lighting by Paul Morrison, costumes by J. Michael Travis, choreography by Lee Scott, additional music and lyrics by Paul Nassau, orchestrations by Nicholas Carras, musical direction and vocal arrangements by Samuel Krachmalnick, staged by Allan A. Buckhantz. Produced by B & M Productions at the 54th Street Theatre.

The cast

Lint Richards	George Blackwell
Bub Richards	Bruce MacKay
Sib Richards	George Ives
Glenn Richards	Michael Kermoyan
Janice Dawson	Cindy Robbins
Craig Richards	Biff McGuire
Clint Yoder	Tom Williams
Bobbie Jo Hartman	Alice Clift
Molly Bixby	Lee Venora
Judge Ed Bixby	Dick Elliott
Jim Joe Jamieson	Frederic Tozere
A Reporter	Rico Froehlich
Pert Hawkins	Ralph Dunn
Claney	Charles May
Doc Spooner	Will Wright
Mrs. Hawkins	Liz Pritchett
Reverend Hornblow	Edwin Steffe
Mult	Roy Wilson
Luke Granger	Chester Watson

TOWNSWOMEN OF BACK-A-HEAP: Diana Baron, Lillian Bozinoff, Alice Clift, Colleen Corkrey, Dori Davis, Isabelle Farrell, Laurie Franks, Rita Golden, Connie Greco, Marian Haraldson, Marilyn Harris, Judy Keirn, Maxine Kent, Patricia Mount, Robbi Palmer

TOWNSMEN OF BACK-A-HEAP: John Buwen, Bob Daley, Rico Froehlich, James Gannon, George Jack, Danny Joel, Charles May, Jim McAnany, Nixon Miller, Howard Parker, Tom Pocoroba, Stewart Rose, Roy Wilson

UNDERSTUDIES: Stewart Rose, Laurie Franks, James Gannon, Alice Clift,

Diana Baron, Michael Kermoyan Bruce MacKay, Nixon Miller, George Blackwell, Rico Froehlich, Bob Daley, Rita Golden, Charles May, Colleen Corkrey, John Buwen

THE PLAY:

This musical about a Texas town which didn't have a millionaire was a monumental accident, a short-lived memorial to ineptness. There was one beguiling performance, by Tom Williams in the role of a lanky young ranch hand who has all the girls of the town trained to come to his whistle.

Synopsis of scenes

ACT I

Scene 1. A Private Office in the T.B.A. Exchange.
"It Isn't Easy" .... Janice, Glenn, Bub, Lint, Sib
Scene 2. Back-A-Heap Texas. The Main Street. A few hours later.
"Celebration!" .... Townspeople
"Something Special" .... Craig
Scene 3. Bixby's Super Market. A little later.
Scene 4. The Main Street. Immediately following.
"The Legend of Black-eyed Susan Grey" .... Susan Grey
and Townspeople
The role of Susan Grey is danced by Leigh Evans
"Opportunity!" .... Craig, Reverend Hornblow,
Mrs. Hawkins and Townspeople
"As Busy as Anyone Can Be" .... Clint and Girls
"Heaven Protect Me!" .... Janice and Girls
Scene 5. Bixby's Super Market. Immediately following.
Scene 6. The T.B.A. Office. A little later.
Scene 7. The Main Street. That evening.
"I Feel Like a Brother to You!" .... Craig and Molly
Scene 8. Back-A-Heap Town Hall. Immediately following.
"Hoedown!" .... Townspeople
Scene 9. The Main Street. Immediately following.
"I Am What I Am!" .... Craig and Molly
"The Beat of a Heart" .... Molly
"Mean" .... Janice
Scene 10. Fairgrounds. Next morning.
Scene 11. The T.B.A. Office
"It Isn't Easy Reprise" .... Glenn, Bub, Lint, Sib
Scene 12. The Prairie.
"When the Time Is Right" .... Reverend Hornblow

ACT II

Scene 1. The Main Street. Late the next day.
"Pick-Me-Up!" .... Townspeople
Scene 2. E Street. Immediately following.
"I'm Stuck With Love" .... Molly

Scene 3. The T.B.A. Office. At about the same time.
"It Isn't Easy Reprise" .... Glenn, Bub, Lint, Sib
Scene 4. Fairgrounds. Two weeks later.
"Nothing In Common" .... Janice and Molly
"Talkin' 'Bout You" .... Janice, Clint and Townspeople
"Something Special, Reprise" .... Craig and Molly
Scene 5. A street. Immediately following.
Scene 6. The Main Street.
Scene 7. T.B.A. Office.
Scene 8. Main Street. Later.
"Y' Can't Win" .... Janice
Scene 9. Bixby's Super Market.
Scene 10. A Street. Immediately following.
Scene 11. Town Hall. Later.
"Opportunity, Reprise" .... Entire Company

AT THE DROP OF A HAT

Opened October 8, 1959; closed May 14, 1960; 217 performances.

After-dinner farrago, with words by Michael Flanders and music by Donald Swann. Curtain by Al Hirschfeld, lighting by Ralph Alswang. Produced by Alexander H. Cohen in association with Joseph I. Levine at the John Golden Theatre.

The cast

>Michael Flanders
>Donald Swann

Program

>"A Transport of Delight"
>"Song of Reproduction"
>"The Hog Beneath the Skin"
>"The Youth of the Heart"
>(lyrics by Sydney Carter)
>"Greensleeves"
>"The Wompom"
>"Sea Fever"
>"A Gnu"
>"Judgement of Paris"
>"Songs for Our Time"
>"A Song of the Weather"
>"The Reluctant Cannibal"
>"In the Bath"
>"Design for Living"
>"Tried by the Centre Court"
>"Misalliance"
>"Kokoraki"
>"Madeira, M' Dear?"
>"The Hippopotamus"

THE ENTERTAINERS:

Fine, smooth, and witty were Michael Flanders, who wrote the words and did the talking, and Donald Swann, who wrote the music. In a captivatingly unpretentious way, they held their audiences and impelled them to laughter. Flanders is a hulking, bearded man who has long been confined to a wheelchair by polio. Swann looks like a scholar and is one. This Englishman and this Welshman first collaborated on a musical revue when they were students at Westminster School, near the Abbey. Among their classmates were Peter Ustinov, the actor and writer; Peter Brook, the noted director, and R. von Ribbentrop, son of a wine salesman who became Hitler's foreign minister. In 1941 Flanders joined the Royal Navy and Swann a Friends Ambulance Unit. Flanders was still in the Navy when he was invalided by polio in 1943.

After the war the two former schoolmates resumed collaborating on revue songs, and late in 1956 they launched *At the Drop of a Hat* in a small club on Notting Hill for $300. They planned on a two-week run. Londoners were so appreciative of their witty pleasantries that the pair moved to the West End, in the Fortune Theatre, on January 24, 1957, and remained there until May 3, 1959.

MOONBIRDS

Opened October 9, 1959; closed October 10, 1959; 3 performances.

Comedy by Marcel Aymé, adapted by John Pauker. Settings by Leo Kerz, costumes by Frank Thompson, staged by Leo Kerz. Produced by Leo Kerz, George Justin and Harry Belafonte at the Cort Theatre.

The cast

Alexander Chabert	Michael Hordern
Sylvie	Phyllis Newman
Elisa	Anne Meacham
Mrs. Martinon	Marjorie Nichols
Raoul Martinon	Mark Rydell
Duperrier	Carl Reindel
Valentine	Wally Cox
Mrs. Armandine Chabert	Helen Waren
Mrs. Bobignot	Dorothy Sands
Ariane	Dran Seitz
Arbelin	Dino Narizzano
Detective Inspector Petrov	Joseph Buloff
Detective Grindet	William H. Bassett
Mr. Perisson	Rex Everhart
Etienne Perisson	William Hickey
Martine	Peggy Pope
Inspector-General Davin	Arthur Malet
Seligmann	Peter Trytler
Escandier	Anthony Ray
Hermelin	Nick Hyams
Marchandeau	Bill Shawn

THE PLAY:

There was more than the usual number of two-performance and three-performance flops during the season, and *Moonbirds* was one. In times past, such a quick demise indicated that a play was so dreadful that the vigilantes should not even have allowed it to set foot in town. But in the hit-or-flop economy in which the theater now exists, a play of moderate merit and some charm gets as short a shrift as a deliberate dramatic crime. If all the next day's newspaper notices are without enthusiasm, there is nothing for a producer to do but close on the following Saturday; trying to keep a play running against disappointing reviews, in the hope that it will find and build a public, is throwing good money after bad.

Moonbirds certainly should not have been ridden out of town on a rail or hanged on the nearest traffic light. It had a certain charm, slight through it was, and there were three very pleasant performances by Wally Cox, in the role of a mild little chap who discovered that he could change people into birds merely by thinking about it; Michael Hordern as a distracted, fuzzy-minded professor, and Joseph Buloff in a delightful caricature of a French police inspector.

Marcel Aymé, the French author, and John Pauker, the adapter, got off to a fine start when they imagined that Mr. Cox could transmogrify unpleasant or unwanted people into birds. But, having had the idea, they didn't know where to go with it. All they could do was have Cox change more people into more birds—and blandly excuse his deeds by pointing out that people are happier as birds than they were as people. This fantasy could have been another *Harvey* or *Madwoman of Chaillot,* but it wasn't.

CHÉRI

Opened October 12, 1959; closed November 28, 1959;
56 performances.

Play adapted by Anita Loos from the novels *Chéri* and *The Last of Chéri* by Colette. Settings by Oliver Smith, lighting by Peggy Clark, costumes by Miles White, staged by Robert Lewis. Produced by the Playwrights' Company and Robert Lewis at the Morosco Theatre.

The cast

Charlotte Peloux	Edith King
Madame Valerie Aldonza	Frieda Altman
Baroness de Berche	Lucy Landau
Count Anthime Berthellmy	Jerome Collamore
Madame Lili	Jane Moultrie
Prince Guido Ceste	Angelo del Rossi
Butler	Byron Russell
Léa de Lonval	Kim Stanley
Patron	John Granger
Frédérick Peloux (Chéri)	Horst Buchholz
Rose	Margot Lassner
Edmée	Joan Gray
Coco	Lili Darvas
Fanchette	Ginger

THE PLAY:

If Anita Loos can have a resounding success by adapting for the theater a novel by Colette called *Gigi*, why can't she have twice the success by adapting *two* Colette novels and calling them *Chéri?* She could, one supposes, but she didn't.

And, if Helen Hayes can have her greatest dramatic triumph by growing old before one's eyes as Queen Victoria, why can't any other actress achieve similar renown with the same trick. Kim Stanley could have, one assumes, but she didn't.

The story of *Chéri* concerned a courtesan, or highly paid kept Frenchwoman, who indulged in a luxury of her own—the keeping of a handsome young man whom she affectionately called Dearie. He was played by an import from Germany, of whom I wrote, "He is pale, handsome, brooding and possessed of a rock-and-roll hairdo. After he kisses a woman he stands back and pants passionately. He can leap in a woman's lap or onto her bosom with nothing less than abandon. And when we catch him after a long night in a woman's boudoir he boldly displays a manly bare chest.

"The trouble with *Chéri* is that his seething affections, instead of being channeled in a proper direction, are bestowed upon a cocotte. A cocotte, says Miss Loos—or perhaps Colette said it first—is a lady who manages to receive more than she gives. Miss Stanley put a world of artifice into her portrayal of the cocotte, beginning in 1911 and lasting until 1929, but her talent was squandered on a sex drama that would have aroused pains of envy in David Belasco's cold heart."

GOLDEN FLEECING

Opened October 15, 1959; closed December 26, 1959; 84 performances.

Comedy by Lorenzo Semple, Jr. Designed and lighted by Frederick Fox, incidental music by Dana Suesse, staged by Abe Burrows. Produced by Courtney Burr and Gilbert Miller at Henry Miller's Theatre.

The cast

A Porter	Buck Kartalian
Ensign Beauregard Gilliam	Robert Carraway
Jackson Eldridge	Robert Elston
Lt. Ferguson Howard	Tom Poston
A Waiter	Alfred Hesse
Pete di Lucca	Ralph Stantley
Julie	Suzanne Pleshette
Ann Knutsen	Constance Ford
Benjamin Dane	John Myhers
Admiral Fitch	Richard Kendrick
Signalman Taylor	Mickey Deems
Shore Patrolman	Red Granger
Shore Patrolman	John Thomas

UNDERSTUDY: Pirie Macdonald

THE PLAY:

These are definitely not farcical times. In a more light-minded era, extending from *Nothing but the Truth*, *Up in Mabel's Room* and *Getting Gertie's Garter* to *Three Men on a Horse*, *Room Service* and *The Matchmaker*, this play would have run much longer than eighty-four performances. All it attempted to be was happy and light-minded —but some rapport between stage and audience always is necessary; the customers must be as light-minded as the actors if any real business is to be done.

Golden Fleecing was no great gem of farce, but it was enjoyable, and it was appealingly played by a company headed by Tom Poston. The story of the play had it that Poston was a lieutenant aboard a U.S. Navy ship loaded with top-secret electronic equipment. Since our Navy can drop anchor in many parts of the world without having to shoot its way in, Poston's vessel heaved to in the harbor of Venice and Poston and a couple of his shipmates found shore quarters in a palace on one of the famed canals.

A great gambling casino was operating at the Lido, and Poston was inspired to attempt to break the roulette bank there by using a modern method—an electronic computer aboard the vessel in the harbor. In his palatial shore suite he set up a blinker communication with the ship. If he broke the bank he would be wealthy enough to claim the admiral's daughter—and the admiral was a tough and suspicious officer and parent.

The trick with a farce is to get everybody as deeply in trouble as possible and then to get everybody out in the nick of time. This was done in *Golden Fleecing*. Poston, an ingratiating comedian with a gift for mugging and acrobatics, was pleasantly supported by Suzanne Pleshette as the daughter, Richard Kendrick as the admiral, Robert Elston as an electronics genius who couldn't think—and a bit-player, Mickey Deems, in the role of a Navy signalman who inadvertently got drunk in the performance of his duty.

In farce, the hero is in trouble right up to the last of the last act, and he has no faith in his fate. Poston, glumly facing the awful future, quoted something he called Murphy's Law: "If something can go wrong, it will." Too bad these are not farcical times.

HEARTBREAK HOUSE

Opened October 19, 1959, closed January 23, 1960; 112 performances.

Comedy by Bernard Shaw. Set and lighting by Ben Edwards, costumes by Freddy Wittop, staged by Harold Clurman. Produced by Maurice Evans and Robert L. Joseph at the Billy Rose Theatre.

The cast

Ellie	Diane Cilento
Nurse Guiness	Jane Rose
Captain Shotover	Maurice Evans
Lady Utterword	Pamela Brown
Mrs. Hushabye	Diana Wynyard
Mazzini Dunn	Alan Webb
Hector Hushabye	Dennis Price
Boss Mangan	Sam Levene
Randall	Patrick Horgan
Burglar	Sorrell Booke

THE PLAY:

This stylish, star-studded revival was appropriate for the opening of the new Billy Rose Theatre in West 41st St.—and it *was* a new theatre, completely rebuilt within the walls which had long contained the National. Oliver Messel, the artist and scene designer, did the décor, and it was splendid in its warm colors.

Six of the seven newspaper reviewers greeted *Heartbreak House* with extravagant enthusiasm; the seventh, Atkinson, reported "there is not much pith in this acting." My own reactions were delight and admiration. One does not often have the opportunity to see this comedy, in which Shaw wrote after World War I to warn Britain to give up its frivolous ways and careless attitude. When the play was first produced in 1920 by the Theatre Guild it had to be staged in full, of course, and it was extraordinarily long. In the production which Robert L. Joseph and Maurice Evans offered, a good forty minutes of conversation were excised, and I think this gave the play added sparkle.

Harold Clurman, the director, did a splendid job of giving the comedy style, pace, and unity, and this might not have been too easy —for he was dealing with a stageful of remarkable and individualistic actors. Captain Shotover, the retired seaman who "drinks rum in order to remain sober" in this out-of-joint world, was Shaw's chief spokesman, so it was fitting and amusing that Evans, as Shotover, should look just like Shaw, tweeds and all. (G.B.S. was no man to be content with having *one* spokesman per play, of course; he set all his men and women to talking for him.)

Yet, in spite of its brilliance and its critical reception, *Heartbreak House* was a failure. Theatergoers are fickle.

THE MIRACLE WORKER

Opened October 19, 1959; still running; 258 performances.. .

Play by William Gibson. Settings and lighting by George Jenkins, costumes by Ruth Morley, staged by Arthur Penn. Produced by Fred Coe at The Playhouse.

The cast

Doctor	Roger de Koven
Kate Keller	Patricia Neal
Captain Keller	Torin Thatcher
Martha	Miriam Butler
Percy	Caswell Fairweather
Viney	Beah Richards
Helen Keller	Patty Duke
James Keller	James Congdon
Aunt Ev	Kathleen Comegys
Anagnos	Michael Constantine
Annie Sullivan	Anne Bancroft

CHILDREN: Lori Heineman, Dale Ellen Bethea, Rita Levy, Lynn Schoenfeld, Eileen Musumeci, Donna Pastore

John	John Marriott
Mary	Juanita Bethea

One of Broadway's Best. See page 29.

THE WARM PENINSULA

Opened October 20, 1959; closed January 2, 1960; 88 performances.

Play by Joe Masteroff. Setting and lighting by Frederick Fox, costumes by Kenn Barr, staged by Warren Enters. Produced by Manning Gurian at the Helen Hayes Theatre.

The cast

Ruth Arnold	Julie Harris
Joanne de Lynn	June Havoc
Steve Crawford	Larry Hagman
Jack Williams	Farley Granger
Iris Floria	Ruth White
Howard Shore	Laurence Haddon
Tony Francis	Thomas Ruisinger

UNDERSTUDIES: Eileen Letchworth, Tom Carlin, George Petrarca

THE PLAY:

The simple trouble with this comedy was that I did not believe a word of what I was hearing—even with two such admirable ladies as Julie Harris and June Havoc acting it out. The story seemed to be a piece of slick-magazine fiction and therefore not convincing on a stage. The setting was a luxurious apartment in Miami Beach, occupied by a kept woman, Miss Havoc. She fell in love with a beach boy and garage monkey, played by Mary Martin's son, Larry Hagman. Sharing the apartment with Miss Havoc was Miss Harris, impersonating a mousy Milwaukee spinster—and she fell in love with a kept boy, played by Farley Granger.

Hagman couldn't marry Havoc because he was mourning the accidental drowning of his infant daughter. Granger wouldn't wed Miss Harris because he would rather be kept. Miss Harris did find a husband, though. She went home to Milwaukee and her job in a hardware store, and there became attached to a fellow worker with whom she had been taking coffee breaks for five years.

Love is wonderful. But not in *The Warm Peninsula*.

FLOWERING CHERRY

Opened October 21, 1959; closed October 24, 1959; 5 performances.

Play by Robert Bolt. Setting by Boris Aronson, lighting by Paul Morrison, costumes by Theoni V. Aldredge, staged by Frith Banbury. Produced by the Playwrights' Company and Don Herbert in association with Don Sharpe Enterprises, by arrangement with H. M. Tennent, Ltd. and Frith Banbury, Ltd. at the Lyceum Theatre.

The cast

Isobel Cherry	Wendy Hiller
Tom	Andrew Ray
Cherry	Eric Portman
Gilbert Grass	George Turner
Judy	Phyllis Love
David Bowman	Roy Poole
Carol	Susan Burnet

THE PLAY:

London playgoers are more relaxed and tolerant than their New York counterparts, and so it is that some times a West End success will be a sudden and sickening failure on Broadway. *Flowering Cherry* had no chance, even though its two principals, Wendy Hiller and Eric Portman, are favorites in this country; one wonders occasionally why American producers fail to take a hard American look at British play—or a French one—before risking its importation.

This drama was a quiet little affair of desperate yearning, a splinter, obviously, from one of Chekhov's cherry trees. Portman, as Mr. Cherry, played a middle-class suburbanite with an unimportant job with an insurance company. Cherry has a son and daughter, both strangers to him, and a gallant wife (played by Miss Hiller). Cherry dreams of something better than he has, and talks often of going back to the land and operating a little apple orchard. But he is a fake and a deceiver, and the one he deceives most is himself. He loses his job but pretends that he still has it until his money runs out and he is forced to pilfer from his wife's purse. When his wife comes forth with a sound scheme of selling their home and buying an orchard, he has to admit that he could never make a go of the project and never really wanted to try. A heart attack mercifully relieves him of the life he could never face squarely.

TAKE ME ALONG

Opened October 22, 1959; still running; 256 performances.

Musical, based on the play *Ah, Wilderness!* by Eugene O'Neill, with book by Joseph Stein and Robert Russell, music and lyrics by Bob Merrill. Production designed by Oliver Smith, lighting by Jean Rosenthal, costumes by Miles White, ballet and incidental music by Laurence Rosenthal, orchestrations by Philip J. Lang, musical direction and vocal arrangements by Lehman Engel, dances and musical numbers staged by Onna White, staged by Peter Glenville. Produced by David Merrick at the Sam S. Shubert Theatre.

The cast

Nat Miller	Walter Pidgeon
Mildred Miller	Zeme North
Art Miller	James Cresson
Tommy Miller	Luke Halpin
Essie Miller	Una Merkel
Lily	Eileen Herlie
Richard Miller	Robert Morse
Muriel Macomber	Susan Luckey
Dave Macomber	Fred Miller
Sid	Jackie Gleason
Wint	Peter Conlow
Lady Entertainers	Valerie Harper, Diana Hunter, Rae McLean
Bartender	Jack Collins
Belle	Arlene Golonka
The Drunk	Gene Varrone
Patrons of the bar	Elna Laun, Paula Lloyd, Janice Painchaud, Jack Konzal, Pat Tolson, Lee Howard
Salesman	Bill McDonald
The Beardsley Dwarf	Charles Bolender
Salome	Rae McLean

TOWNSWOMEN: Nicole Barth, Renee Byrns, Lyn Connorty, Barbara Doherty, Katia Geleznova, Valerie Harper, Diana Hunter, Elna Laun, Paula Lloyd, Nancy Lynch, Rae McLean, Janice Painchaud

TOWNSMEN: Alvin Beam, Frank Borgman, John Carter, Lee Howard, Jack Konzal, Bill McDonald, Henry Michel, Jack Murray, John Nola, Bill Richards, Harry Lee Rogers, Walter Strauss, Jimmy Tarbutton, Gene Varrone, Marc West, Pat Tolson, Rusty Parker, Chad Block, Bill Starr

UNDERSTUDIES: Ruth Warrick, Jack Collins, Henry Michel, Bill Starr, Zeme North, Gene Varrone, John Carter, Renee Byrns, Rusty Parker, Barbara Doherty, Bill McDonald, Frank Borgman

THE PLAY:

This is a heartwarming period piece based on the only heartwarming play—and the only comedy—Eugene O'Neill ever wrote. The story goes that O'Neill literally dreamed *Ah, Wilderness!* He was working on a drama when, one morning, he awoke with a play in mind about his youth. He wrote it very quickly, for him, and it was immediately produced by the Theatre Guild with George M. Cohan in the role played by Walter Pidgeon in the musical version.

The return of Jackie Gleason to the stage after his great success on television was an event to be applauded, but there were some doubters that the unpredictable Gleason might indulge in too many monkey-shines. The actor confounded the doubters by playing his role—that of Uncle Sid, a bibulous reporter—with straightforward simplicity and great personal charm. He was most ably abetted by his co-stars, Pidgeon and Eileen Herlie—and Robert Morse, playing the dreamy teen-ager whose knowledge of sex comes from poetry and drawings by Aubrey Beardsley, nearly stole *Take Me Along* from everybody.

The story is what happened on July 4, 1910, in the imaginary small town of Centerville, Connecticut. (There used to be a real Centerville, before it was absorbed into a bigger town, but O'Neill didn't know it.) Here, Pidgeon is the editor of the paper, and his life is generally pleasant, for he has a nice family—but he does have a few problems.

One of the problems is his brother-in-law (Gleason), who is a reporter in Waterbury, an interurban streetcar ride distant. He is not a sot, but he gets tiddly often enough to prevent Miss Herlie marrying him, even though anybody can see that these two were made for each other. Another problem is his younger son, a Galahad who reads Shaw, Wilde and the *Rubaiyat*. The most effective scene sequence is one in which the young man finds himself drunk for the first time in his life and in a brothel to boot. He offers a surprised harlot more money than she asks to let him alone. And then he has an alcoholic dream which becomes a splendid ballet staged by Onna White, in which all the characters he has read about, including Salome and Camille—and all costumed after Beardsley's grotesque black-and-whites—pursue him like fiends.

The time being 1910, when life was pleasant all over the world, everything comes out all right.

Synopsis of scenes

The action takes place in Centerville, Connecticut, 1910.

Musical numbers

ACT I

Scene 1. The Miller Home. Early morning of July 4th.
"The Parade" .... Nat and Townspeople
"Oh, Please" .... Nat, Essie, Lil and Family

Scene 2. The Macomber Home. The same morning.
"I Would Die" .... Muriel and Richard

Scene 3. The Car Barn. Later that morning.
"Sid, Ol' Kid" .... Sid and Townspeople

Scene 4. The Miller Home. A little later.
"Staying Young" .... Nat
"I Get Embarrassed" .... Sid and Lily
"We're Home" .... Lily

Scene 5. A Street.
"Take Me Along" .... Sid and Nat

Scene 6. The Picnic Grounds. That afternoon.
"For Sweet Charity" .... Sid, Nat, Lady Entertainers &
Townsmen

Scene 7. The Miller Home. That evening.
"Pleasant Beach House" .... Wint
"That's How It Starts" .... Richard

ACT II

Scene 1. Bar Room of the Pleasant Beach House. The same night.
"The Beardsley Ballet" .... Richard Muriel, The Dwarf,
Salome and Ensemble

Scene 2. The Miller Home. Later that night.
"Oh, Please" (Reprise) .... Nat and Essie
"Promise Me a Rose" .... Lily and Sid
"Staying Young" (Reprise) .... Nat

Scene 3. Richard's Bedroom. Afternoon of the following day.
"Little Green Snake" .... Sid

Scene 4. The Beach. That evening.
"Nine O'Clock" .... Richard

Scene 5. The Miller Home. A little later.
"But Yours" .... Sid and Lily

Scene 6. The Car Barn. Later that evening.
"Take Me Along" (Reprise) .... Lily, Sid and Townspeople

THE GIRLS AGAINST THE BOYS

Opened November 2, 1959; closed November 14, 1959;
16 performances.

Musical revue with sketches and lyrics by Arnold B. Horwitt and music by Richard Lewine and Albert Hague. Sets and lighting by Ralph Alswang, costumes by Sal Anthony, orchestrations by Sid Ramin and Robert Ginzler, dance music arranged by John Morris, musical direction by Irving Actman, dances and musical numbers staged by Boris Runanin, sketches directed by Aaron Ruben. Produced by Albert Selden at the Alvin Theatre.

The cast

Bert Lahr
Nancy Walker
Shelley Berman
Dick Van Dyke
Joy Nichols
Imelda De Martin
Richard France
June L. Walker
Maureen Bailey
Buzz Halliday
Mace Barrett

UNDERSTUDIES: Phil Leeds, Dorothy Greener, Martin Charnin

Program

ACT I

The Girls Against The Boys	Dick Van Dyke, Mace Barrett, Buzz Halliday and Ensemble
Rich Butterfly	
Husband	Shelley Berman
Wife	Nancy Walker
Can We Save Our Marriage?	
Counselor	Dick Van Dyke
Stella	June L. Walker
Harry	Bert Lahr
I Gotta Have You	Imelda De Martin, Richard France, Caroljane Abney, Sandra Devlin, Ray Pointer, Noel Schwartz

Home Late
        Husband .... Dick Van Dyke
        Wife .... Buzz Halliday
I Remember .... Bert Lahr
        Butler .... Mace Barrett
Assignation
        Jock .... Dick Van Dyke
        Cynthia .... Joy Nichols
        Essie .... Nancy Walker
        Waiter .... Martin Charnin
        Counterman .... Ray Pointer
        Man at Center Table .... Bob Roman
        Max .... Noel Schwartz
        Other Patrons .... Cy Young, Jo Ann Tenney, Roger
                     LePage, Mal Throne, Mona Pivar, Al Fiorella
Shelley Berman .... Written by Mr. Berman
Where Did We Go? Out .... Mace Barrett, Maureen Bailey
                     Richard France, Imelda De Martin
Too Young To Live .... Bert Lahr, Nancy Walker
Overspend .... Shelley Berman, Joy Nichols and Ensemble

ACT II

Girls and Boys
        Observer .... Mace Barrett
        Mother .... Joy Nichols
        Groom .... Dick Van Dyke
        Bride .... Imelda De Martin
        Best Man .... Richard France
        Father .... Bob Roman
        Maid of Honor .... Maureen Bailey
        Bridesmaids ....Mona Pivar, Margaret Gathright,
                     Sandra Devlin, Buzz Halliday
        Guests .... The Ensemble
Nightflight .... By Arnold Horwitt and Aaron Ruben
        Passenger .... Bert Lahr
        Girl .... Joy Nichols
        Man .... Mal Throne
        Hostess .... June L. Walker
        Mother .... Buzz Halliday
        Four People ....Mace Barrett, Cy Young, Bob Roman,
                     Nina Popova
Light Travelin' Man (Music by Albert Hague) ...... Shelley Berman,
                     Richard France
        Girls .... Sandra Devlin, Caroljane Abney,
                     Margaret Gathright
He and She
        Introduction .... Shelley Berman
        He .... Dick Van Dyke
        Goat .... Noel Schwartz
        Skunks .... Caroljane Abney, Roger LePage
        Rabbits .... Mitchell Nutick, Beatrice Salten
        Ducks .... Ray Pointer, Nona Pivar
        Wolf .... Al Fiorella

Lamb .... Jo Ann Tenney
She .... Nancy Walker
Snake .... Sandra Devlin
It .... Jim Sisco
Old-Fashioned Girl
    Doorman .... Mal Throne
    Monroe Fuller .... Bert Lahr
    Tawny .... June L. Walker
    Usher .... Beatrice Salten
    Treasurer .... Sandra Devlin
    Male Dancer .... Roger LePage
    Show Girls .... Buzz Halliday, Margaret Gathright,
       Caroljane Abney, Jo Ann Tenney, Ellen Graff, Mona Pivar
Shelley Berman .... Written by Mr. Berman
Hostility .... By Arnold Horwitt and Aaron Ruben
    Husband .... Bert Lahr
    Wife .... Nancy Walker
Nobody Else But You (Music by Albert Hague) .... Bert Lahr and
        Nancy Walker
Finale .... Entire Company

THE REVUE

Nancy Walker and Bert Lahr, two of the most gifted clowns still available to the American theatre, have been heard to moan, separately, "We always get good notices from the critics, but our shows don't." This again was the case with *The Girls Against the Boys*. It was a good title and a good premise for a revue, but the entertainment lacked the crispness, the pace, the variety, and the songs which a really good revue needs.

But it was not a total loss—not with Walker and Lahr working. They were amusing as a pair of extravagantly costumed teen-agers doing a rock-and-roll turn, and they were at the best of the evening in a long and hilarious pantomime of domestic life. A newcomer to the stage, Dick Van Dyke, from television, showed to advantage in a sketch concerning a husband who comes home very intoxicated but manages to act sober in the presence of his wife. Van Dyke had a second chance later in the season and this time he arrived in a leading role in a hit, the musical *Bye Bye Birdie*.

THE HIGHEST TREE

Opened November 4, 1959; closed November 21, 1959; 21 performances.

Play by Dore Schary. Setting and lighting by Donald Oenslager, costumes by Marvin Reiss, staged by Dore Schary. Produced by the Theatre Guild and Dore Schary, Walter Reilly associate, at the Longacre Theatre.

The cast

Aaron Cornish	Kenneth MacKenna
Isabel	Miriam Goldina
Dr. Robert Leigh	William Prince
Susan Ashe	Natalie Schafer
Frederick Ashe	Howard St. John
Frederick Ashe, Jr. (Buzz)	Robert Redford
Steven Cornish	Frank Milan
Caleb Cornish	Richard Anderson
Amy Cornish	Gloria Hoye
Mary Macready	Diana Douglas
Bronislau Partos	Joe De Santis
Jane Ashe	Elizabeth Cole
Arkady Clark	Robert Ritterbusch
John Devereaux	Larry Gates
Gloria Cornish	Shirley Smith

UNDERSTUDIES: Joe De Santis, Dee Victor, Shirley Smith, Nick Pryor, Gloria Hoye

THE PLAY:

Dore Schary, whose *Sunrise at Campobello* was so splendid and inspiring, bent his mind and writing talent to the cosmic menace of nuclear force in *The Highest Tree*. Its critical reception was mixed, with John McClain of the *Journal-American* calling it timely and absorbing, Robert Coleman of the *Mirror* labeling it dull. In the New York *Post* Richard Watts, Jr., summed it up, "Rarely has a play had its heart more firmly set in the right place. Its purposes are lofty and serious, its subject matter is of the utmost importance, its voice is clear and frank, and it is well acted. But unfortunately these are not enough, and Dore Schary's earnest new drama has its virtues more than counteracted by its curious failure to come to life in the stage as either a movingly emotional narrative or as a stimulating and provocative discussion."

The Highest Tree brought back to the stage in the leading role Kenneth MacKenna, who had abandoned Broadway twenty-two years previously to become story editor for Metro-Goldwyn-Mayer. He played a nuclear scientist who has been doomed by his own research; he has leukemia and no more than six months to live. So the scientist determines to spend this rest of the life trying to undo what he has done by seeking to put a stop to all bomb tests. But there was no firm conclusion in or to the drama; Schary said in a letter to this writer that he did not know what to do with or against nuclear tests, but he did know they presented a problem of the greatest import to all mankind, and he wrote his play to get people to think about the problem.

THE TENTH MAN

Opened November 5, 1959; still running; 238 performances.

Play by Paddy Chayefsky. Settings and lighting by David Hays, costumes by Frank Thompson, staged by Tyrone Guthrie. Produced by Saint Subber and Arthur Cantor, Caroline Swann associate, at the Booth Theatre.

The cast

Hirschman	Arnold Marlé
Sexton	David Vardi
Schlissel	Lou Jacobi
Zitorsky	Jack Gilford
Alper	George Voskovec
Forman	Jacob Ben-Ami
Evelyn Forman	Risa Schwartz
Arthur Brooks	Donald Harron
Harris	Martin Garner
Rabbi	Gene Saks
Kessler Boys	{ Alan Manson { Paul Marin
Policeman	Tim Callaghan

UNDERSTUDIES: Morris Strassberg, Sandra MacDonald, Carl Don

One of Broadway's Best. See page 51.

THE SOUND OF MUSIC

Opened November 16, 1959; still running; 226 performances.

Musical play with book by Howard Lindsay and Russel Crouse, music by Richard Rodgers and lyrics by Oscar Hammerstein II, suggested by Maria Augusta Trapp's *The Trapp Family Singers*. Settings by Oliver Smith, lighting by Jean Rosenthal, costumes by Lucinda Ballard and Mainbocher, choral arrangements by Trude Rittman, orchestrations by Robert Russell Bennett, musical numbers staged by Joe Layton, musical director Frederick Dvonch, staged by Vincent J. Donehue. Produced by Leland Hayward, Richard Halliday, Richard Rodgers and Oscar Hammerstein II at the Lunt-Fontanne Theatre.

The cast

Maria Rainer, A Postulant at Nonnberg Abbey	Mary Martin
Sister Berthe, Mistress of Novices	Elizabeth Howell
Sister Margaretta, Mistress of Postulants	Muriel O'Malley
The Mother Abbess	Patricia Neway
Sister Sophia	Karen Shepard
Captain Georg Von Trapp	Theodore Bikel
Franz, The Butler	John Randolph
Frau Schmidt, The Housekeeper	Nan McFarland
Liesl	Lauri Peters
Friedrich	William Snowden
Louisa	Kathy Dunn
Kurt — Children of Captain Von Trapp	Joseph Stewart
Brigitta	Marilyn Rogers
Marta	Mary Susan Locke
Gretl	Evanna Lien
Rolf Gruber	Brian Davies
Elsa Schraeder	Marion Marlowe
Ursula	Luce Ennis
Max Detweiler	Kurt Kasznar
Herr Zeller	Stefan Gierasch
Baron Elberfeld	Kirby Smith
A Postulant	Sue Yaeger
Admiral Von Schreiber	Michael Gorrin

Neighbors of Captain Von Trapp, nuns, novices, postulants, contestants in the Festival Concert: Joanne Birks, Patricia Brooks, June Card, Dorothy Dallas, Ceil Delly, Luce Ennis, Cleo Fry, Barbara George, Joey Heatherton, Lucas Hoving, Patricia Kelly, Maria Kova, Shirley Mendonca, Kathy

Miller, Lorna Nash, Keith Prentice, Nancy Reeves, Bernice Saunders, Connie Sharman, Gloria Stevens, Tatiana Troyanos, Mimi Vondra

UNDERSTUDIES: Renee Guerin, Kenneth Harvey, Sheppard Kerman, Elizabeth Howell, Karen Shepard, Joey Heatherton, David Gress, Frances Underhill, Mary Susan Locke, Dorothy Dallas, Nancy Reeves, Maria Kova, Keith Prentice, Lucas Hoving, Kirby Smith

Synopsis of scenes
The story is laid in Austrai early in 1938.

ACT I

Scene 1. Nonnberg Abbey.
Scene 2. Mountainside near the Abbey.
Scene 3. The Office of the Mother Abbess, the next morning.
Scene 4. A corridor in the Abbey.
Scene 5. The living room of the Trapp Villa, that afternoon.
Scene 6. Outside the Trapp Villa, that evening.
Scene 7. Maria's bedroom, later that evening.
Scene 8. The terrace of the Trapp Villa, six weeks later.
Scene 9. A hallway in the Trapp Villa, one week later.
Scene 10. The living room, the same evening.
Scene 11. A corridor in the Abbey.
Scene 12. The office of the Mother Abbess, three days later.

ACT II

Scene 1. The terrace, the same day.
Scene 2. A corridor in the Abbey, two weeks later.
Scene 3. The office of the Mother Abbess, immediately following.
Scene 4. A cloister overlooking the chapel.
Scene 5. The living room, one month later.
Scene 6. The concert hall, three days later.
Scene 7. The garden of Nonnberg Abbey, that night.

Musical numbers

ACT I

1. Preludium
2. "The Sound of Music" .... Maria
3. "Maria" ...... Mother Abbess, Sisters Margaretta, Berthe, Sophia
4. "My Favorite Things" .... Maria, Mother Abbess
5. "Do Re Mi" .... Maria, Children
6. "You Are Sixteen" .... Liesl, Rolf
7. "The Lonely Goatherd" .... Maria, Children
8. "How Can Love Survive?" .... Elsa, Max, Captain
9. "The Sound of Music" .... Maria, Captain, Children
10. "So Long, Farewell" .... Children
11. "Climb Every Mountain" .... Mother Abbess

ACT II

1. "No Way to Stop It" .... Captain, Max, Elsa

2. "Ordinary Couple" .... Maria, Captain
3. "Processional" .... Ensemble
4. "You Are Sixteen" .... Maria, Liesl
5. "Do Re Mi" .... Maria, Captain, Children
6. "Edelweiss" .... Captain, Maria, Children
7. "So Long, Farewell" .... Maria, Captain, Children
8. "Climb Every Mountain" .... Company

THE PLAY:

The popular success of *The Sound of Music* seemed foreordained. How could it miss, with a libretto by Lindsay and Crouse and songs by Rodgers and Hammerstein, with Mary Martin as the star? Everybody involved was so certain that no backers were invited in; all but $20,000 of the $400,000 production cost was paid for by Rodgers, Hammerstein, Leland Hayward, and Richard Halliday, who is Miss Martin's husband. More or less as a courteous gesture, the National Broadcasting Company was allowed to make a small investment—but half of the entire cost was assumed by Miss Martin's spouse. This was an interesting risk. Insiders guessed that, in lieu of taking a big salary and a big percentage, which would be taxed as personal income, Miss Martin took a nominal wage. Her money would come, not as a salaried performer, but as an investor—and this would be taxed at the lower capital gains rate.

More than three hundred theater parties were booked prior to the Broadway opening—something of a record for playing it safe. The newspaper reviews were not entirely ecstatic. I, for instance, felt that the story ended where it might have begun—with the arrival of the refugee Trapp family in America and their subsequent success here. Brooks Atkinson wrote, "The scenario has the hackneyed look of the musical theatre that Richard Rodgers and Oscar Hammerstein II replaced with *Oklahoma!*" But there was no doubt that Rodgers and Hammerstein had written a most enchanting set of songs.

Miss Martin plays the real-life Maria Augusta Trapp. A postulant in an Austrian abbey, she is engaged as a governess by Captain Georg Von Trapp, a seagoing martinet with seven children who orders everybody around with a bo'sun's whistle. The young woman teaches the children to sing. She takes over the captain's home and ultimately his heart. But Hitler is on the move in Austria and the captain will not accept *anschluss*. Rather than report for sea duty as ordered, he escapes with his family into Switzerland (although the real family escaped to Italy). There is hardly a hint that this little group of exiles found its way to the United States.

A superior cast supports Miss Martin—Theodore Bikel as Trapp, Kurt Kasznar as a small-time music impresario, and Patricia Neway, who has a grand opera voice, as the Mother Abbess of the abbey.

ONLY IN AMERICA

Opened November 19, 1959; closed December 12, 1959; 28 performances.

Play by Jerome Lawrence and Robert E. Lee, from the book by Harry Golden. Settings by Peter Larkin, lighting by Tharon Musser, costumes by Ruth Morley, staged by Herman Shumlin. Produced by Herman Shumlin at the Cort Theatre.

The cast

Helen Cheney	Lynn Hamilton
Herbert Loomis	Martin Huston
Mrs. Archer-Loomis	Enid Markey
Harry Golden	Nehemiah Persoff
Fred	Daniel Keyes
Wes	Howard Wierum
Ray	Wayne Tippit
Telephone Man	Alan Alda
I. Birnbaum	Ludwig Donath
Jed	Josh White, Jr.
Velma	Dinnie Smith
Lucius Whitmore	Shepperd Strudwick
Balthasar	Jerry Wimberly
Calvin	David Baker
Ruth-Ella	Charlotte Whaley
Kate Golden	Shannon Bolin
Hershey M. Stoddard	Edwin Whitner
Chairman	Vincent Gardenia
State Senator Claypool	Harry Holcombe
Dr. Leota Patterson	Flora Campbell
Legislator	Laurens Moore
Stenotypist	Edmund Williams
Bill Drake	Don Fellows
Young Man	Norris Borden

THE PLAY:

The saying goes that there is nothing as dead as yesterday's newspaper. But exceptions make the rule. Harry Golden, publisher and editor of the *Carolina Israelite* in Charlotte, North Carolina, was persuaded to put a batch of his homilies together and allow them to be brought forth as a book titled *Only in America*. It was a great success.

Golden himself is quite a story—a man who fitted himself easily and charmingly in an alien environment. A Jew from New York, and an ex-convict, he turned up in the Southland and began putting out a little paper. He made friends locally and when his book came out he made them nationally.

The play script by Lawrence and Lee, compounded of the career of Golden and some of his writings, was only intermittently lively as a piece of theater; Golden remained better silent. But the production was carefully staged by Herman Shumlin, and Nehemiah Persoff gave a most ingratiating performance as Golden, the small-paper editor who types out random thoughts, throws the little scripts into a barrel beside his desk and then fishes some out when it is time to put together another issue of the paper. The dramatic—and acting—highlight was when Persoff confessed that he once did a five-year stretch in prison.

FIORELLO!

Opened November 23, 1959; still running; 219 performances.

Musical with book by Jerome Weidman and George Abbott, lyrics by Sheldon Harnick and music by Jerry Bock. Scenery, lighting and costumes by William and Jean Eckart, choreography by Peter Gennaro, orchestrations by Irwin Kostal, dance music arranged by Jack Elliott, musical direction by Hal Hastings, staged by George Abbott. Produced by Robert E. Griffith and Harold S. Prince at the Broadhurst Theatre.

The cast

Announcer	Del Horstmann
Fiorello	Tom Bosley
Neil	Bob Holiday
Morris	Nathaniel Frey
Mrs. Pomerantz	Helen Verbit
Mr. Lopez	H. F. Green
Mr. Zappatella	David Collyer
Dora	Pat Stanley
Marie	Patricia Wilson
Ben	Howard Da Silva
Ed Peterson	Del Horstmann
2nd Player	Stanley Simmonds
3rd Player	Michael Quinn
4th Player	Ron Husmann
5th Player	David London
6th Player	Julian Patrick
Seedy Man	Joseph Toner
1st Heckler	Bob Bernard
2nd Heckler	Michael Scrittorale
3rd Heckler	Jim Maher
4th Heckler	Joseph Toner
Nina	Pat Turner
Floyd	Mark Dawson
Sophie	Lynn Ross
Thea	Ellen Hanley
Secretary	Mara Landi
Senator	Frederic Downs
Commissioner	Michael Quinn
Frankie Scarpini	Michael Scrittorale
Mitzi	Eileen Rodgers
Florence	Deedy Irwin

Reporter .... Julian Patrick
1st Man .... Scott Hunter
2nd Man .... Michael Scrittorale
Tough Man .... David London
Derby .... Bob Bernard
Frantic .... Stanley Simmonds
Judge Carter .... Joseph Toner
SINGERS: David Collyer, Barbara Gilbert, Del Horstmann, Deedy Irwin, Mara Landi, David London, Julian Patrick, Ginny Perlowin, Patsy Peterson, Silver Saundors, Ron Husmann
DANCERS: Charlene Carter, Bob Bernard, Elaine Cancilla, Ellen Harris, Patricia Harty, Scott Hunter, Bob La Crosse, Lynda Lynch, James Maher, Gregg Owen, Lowell Purvis, Dellas Rennie, Lynn Ross, Dan Siretta, Michael Scrittorale, Pat Turner
UNDERSTUDIES: Harvey Lembeck, Eileen Rodgers, Ginny Perlowin, Pat Harty, David Collyer, Patsy Peterson, Ron Husmann, Mara Landi

Synopsis of scenes

ACT I

New York City, shortly before World War One.

ACT II

Ten years later.

Musical numbers

ACT I

"On the Side of the Angels" .... Bob Holiday, Nathaniel Frey, Patricia Wilson
"Politics and Poker" .... Howard Da Silva and Politicians
"Unfair" .... Tom Bosley, Pat Stanley and Girls
"Marie's Law" .... Patricia Wilson and Nathaniel Frey
"The Name's LaGuardia" .... Tom Bosley and Company
"The Bum Won" .... Howard Da Silva and Politicians
"I Love A Cop" .... Pat Stanley
"I Love A Cop" Reprise ....Pat Stanley and Mark Dawson
"Till Tomorrow" .... Ellen Hanley and Company
"Home Again" .... Company

ACT II

"When Did I Fall in Love" .... Ellen Hanley
"Gentleman Jimmy" .... Eileen Rodgers and Dancing Girls
"Gentleman Jimmy" Reprise .... Company
"Little Tin Box" .... Howard Da Silva and Politicians
"The Very Next Man" .... Patricia Wilson
"The Very Next Man" Reprise .... Patricia Wilson
Finale

One of Broadway's Best. See page 41.

A LOSS OF ROSES

*Opened November 28, 1959; closed December 19, 1959;
25 performances.*

Play by William Inge. Setting by Boris Aronson, lighting by Abe
Feder, costumes by Lucinda Ballard, music edited by Robert Emmett
Dolan, staged by Daniel Mann. Produced by Saint Subber and Lester
Osterman at the Eugene O'Neill Theatre.

The cast

Mrs. Helen Baird	Betty Field
Kenny (Her Son)	Warren Beatty
Geoffrey Beamis (Jelly)	Michael J. Pollard
Lila Green	Carol Haney
Ronny Cavendish	James O'Rear
Mme. Olga St. Valentine	Margaret Braidwood
Ricky Powers	Robert Webber
Mrs. Mulvaney	Joan Morgan

UNDERSTUDIES: Anne Hegira, Joan Morgan, Dennis Cooney, Athan
Karras

One of Broadway's Best. See page 140.

THE PLAY:

William Inge, a dramatist who is accustomed to success, awoke on
the morning of November 30—he had to wait a day for the reviews
because the opening was on a Saturday—to find his newest drama
labeled "dull," "very bad," "unfortunate," and "a loss." I found it
"gentle, introspective and well played."

In *A Loss of Roses* Inge was more interested in character than event,
and he probed with sympathy into the characters of three people.
These three want something they haven't got, and it isn't material;
they have the simple yearning for understanding and love.

One, played by Betty Field, is a widow living in a modest bungalow
in Kansas City. Another is her twenty-one-year-old son, played by
Warren Beatty. It is depression time—1933—but they have jobs; she
as a hospital nurse and he as a gas-station attendant. The boy is
petulant and demanding, and his mother mournfully wishes he were
half the man his father was.

Into the home comes a stranded tank-town actress (Carol Haney), a friend from times past. She finds temporary sanctuary here—and, she thinks, true love at last from the boy. But, after an offstage affair, the young man sensibly curbs his passion, and the ending is a tragic one for the actress: she has to go back to the dreary life she has led for so long—entertaining at smokers and making dirty movies.

FIVE FINGER EXERCISE

Opened December 2, 1959; still running; 207 performances.

Play by Peter Shaffer. Setting by Oliver Smith, lighting by Tharon Musser, staged by John Gielgud. Produced by Frederick Brisson and the Playwrights' Company by arrangement with H. M. Tennent, Ltd. at the Music Box.

The cast

Louise Harrington	Jessica Tandy
Stanley Harrington	Roland Culver
Clive Harrington	Brian Bedford
Pamela Harrington	Juliet Mills
Walter Langer	Michael Bryant

One of Broadway's Best. See page 130.

SILENT NIGHT, LONELY NIGHT

Opened December 3, 1959; closed March 19, 1960; 125 performances.

Play by Robert Anderson. Setting by Jo Mielziner, costumes by Theoni V. Aldredge, staged by Peter Glenville. Produced by the Playwrights' Company at the Morosco Theatre.

The cast

Katherine	Barbara Bel Geddes
Mae	Eda Heinemann
John	Henry Fonda
Janet	Lois Nettleton
Philip	Bill Berger
Jerry	Peter De Visé

THE PLAY

My first-night report on this drama began thus:

"*Silent Night, Lonely Night,* which the Playwrights' Company presented at the Morosco Theatre, has been beautifully and tenderly written by Robert Anderson. In it, Barbara Bel Geddes and Henry Fonda give true and splendid performances. Even so, the play is a bore.

"This is another drama which is all art and no event. The setting is a New England inn and the time Christmas Eve. Fonda is here because his wife is in a looney-bin up the hill. Miss Bel Geddes is here because her son is in the school infirmary.

"Henry and Barbara have adjoining rooms. So what happens? They talk each other to sleep and they very nearly talked me to sleep too. He talks about what has happened between him and his wife in the past and she talks about a traveling husband.

"They talk good stories, but I'd rather see Fonda and his wife and Bel Geddes and her husband on the stage and find out for myself what has happened. Anderson's offstage drama might be more interesting than the one they are doing at the Morosco."

JOLLY'S PROGRESS

Opened December 5, 1959; closed December 12, 1959; 9 performances.

Play by Lonnie Colemen. Settings by George Jenkins, costumes by Gene Coffin, staged by Alex Segal. Produced by the Theatre Guild and Arthur Loew at the Longacre Theatre.

The cast

Robie Sellers	Charles McClelland
Warren Holly	James Knight
Buford Williams	Peter Gumeny
Charlie	Joseph Boland
Lon Keiler	Drummond Erskine
Mr. Scarborough	Laurie Main
Mr. Mendelsohn	Nat Burns
Reverend Furze	Ellis Rabb
Emma Ford	Anne Revere
David Adams	Wendell Corey
Jolly Rivers	Eartha Kitt
Portia Bates	Joanne Barry
Dora	Vinnette Carroll
Thompson Bates	Humphrey Davis
Thelma	Eulabelle Moore

UNDERSTUDIES: Cicely Tyson, Ellis Rabb, Eulabelle Moore, James Knight, Joseph Boland, Drummond Erskine, Peter Gumeny

THE PLAY:

There was this to say about *Jolly's Progress:* Among so many introspective and introverted plays, this one had some action, including Eartha Kitt, who played the title role, running up and down trees and in and out of woods.

This was a flashing, mercurial performance by Miss Kitt in the role of an underprivileged Negro girl in her early teens, and it was abetted by a speedy, assured one by Wendell Corey as the writing man who determined to play Pygmalion to her Galatea. He nurtured the native intelligence of this spooky little waif, defying the Ku Klux Klan in so befriending her, and saw her change from a hunted animal to a bright and intellectually eager chatterbox. What ruined the play was, I guess, that it was so obviously make-believe.

SARATOGA

Opened December 7, 1959; closed February 13, 1960; 80 performances.

Musical by Morton Da Costa, based on the novel *Saratoga Trunk* by Edna Ferber. Music by Harold Arlen, lyrics by Johnny Mercer, settings and costumes by Cecil Beaton, lighting by Jean Rosenthal, choreography by Ralph Beaumont, music for dances by Genevieve Pitot, orchestrations by Philip J. Lang, vocal arrangements by Herbert Greene, musical direction by Jerry Arlen, staged by Morton Da Costa. Produced by Robert Fryer at the Winter Garden.

The cast

Cupide	Tun Tun
Clio Dulaine	Carol Lawrence
Kakou	Carol Brice
Belle Piquery	Odette Myrtil
The Drapery Man	Mark Zeller
The Carpenter	Albert Popwell
Shorty	Augie Rios
Maudey	Brenda Long
The Charwoman	Virginia Capers
Mrs. LeClerc	Martha King
M. Augustin Haussy	Richard Graham
Clint Maroon	Howard Keel
M. Begué	Truman Gaige
Grandmother Dulaine	Natalie Core
Madame Dulaine	Beatrice Bushkin
Charlotte Thérèse	Jeannine Masterson
Léon, a Waiter	Mark Zeller
Editor	Truman Gaige
Haberdashery Clerk	Frank Green
Fabric Salesman	Barney Johnston
M. LaFosse	Lanier Davis
Mrs. Sophie Bellop	Edith King
Mrs. Porcelain	Natalie Core
Mr. Gould	Truman Gaige
Bart Van Steed	Warde Donovan
Mr. Bean	James Millhollin
Daisy Porcelain	Gerrianne Raphael
Clarissa Van Steed	Isabella Hoopes
Miss Diggs	Janyce Wagner

MARKET VENDORS, TOWNSPEOPLE, WAITERS, BUSBOYS, GAMBLERS,

CROUPIERS, HOTEL GUESTS ETC.: Betsy Bridge, Beatrice Bushkin, Virginia Capers, Martha King, Ina Kurland, Jeannine Masterson, Carol Taylor, Gerrianne Raphael, Lois Van Pelt, Janyce Wagner, Beverley Jane Welch, Socrates Birsky, John Blanchard, Joseph Crawford, Lanier Davis, Paul Dixon, Vito Durante, José Falcion, Julius Fields, John Ford, Jerry Fries, Gene Gavin, Frank Green, Nathaniel Horne, Barney Johnston, Louis Kosman, Jack Matthew, Oran Osburn, John Pero, Harold Pierson, Albert Popwell, Charles Queenan, Mark Zeller and Merritt Thompson

CHILDREN: Brenda Long, Linda Wright, Augie Rios, Wayne Robertson

THE PLAY:

On paper before it opened, this musical had everything: A libretto based on a best-seller by Edna Ferber, written by Morton Da Costa, who made his mark by staging *The Music Man*; songs by two old pros, Harold Arlen and Johnny Mercer, and sets and costumes by Cecil Beaton. But at the opening it turned out that *Saratoga* had too much; in trying to encompass a long novel which ranged from New Orleans to Saratoga, New York. It was difficult to understand what the two leading characters, played by Carol Lawrence and Howard Keel, were up to, and because of this difficulty audiences didn't seem to care much *what* the pair were up to—which, if it had been boiled down properly, was simply musical comedy love.

This was one of the two costliest theatrical productions of the season, and its losses ran close to $400,000—mostly National Broadcasting Company money. But it also was the most beautiful big production of the season both as to costumes and sets.

Synopsis of scenes and musical numbers

ACT I

Scene 1.   The Rampart Street House, New Orleans, 1880.
"I'll Be Respectable" .... Clio
"One Step—Two Step" ... Clio, Shorty, Maudey & Ensemble
"Gettin' a Man" .... Belle and Kakou
Scene 2.   Exterior of the Rampart Street House.
Scene 3.   The Waterfront Market.
"Petticoat High" ...... Charwoman, Clio, Belle, Cupide and
Ensemble
Scene 4.   The Museum.
Scene 5.   Begué's Restaurant.
"Why Fight This?" .... Clio & Clint
"Game of Poker" .... Clint & Clio
Scene 6.   The Garden of the Rampart Street House.
"Love Held Lightly" .... Belle
"Game of Poker" Reprise .... Clio, Clint & Belle

Scene 7. The Casino.
          "The Gamblers" .... Clio & the Gamblers & Croupiers
          "Saratoga" .... Clint & Clio
Scene 8. The United States Hotel, Saratoga.
          "Saratoga" Reprise .... Ensemble
          "The Gossip Song" .... Mrs. Bellop & Ensemble
Scene 9. Clint's and Clio's Rooms in the United States Hotel.
          "Countin' Our Chickens" .... Clio & Clint
          "You or No One" .... Clint

ACT II

Scene 1. The Springs, Saratoga.
          "The Cure" .... Ensemble
          "The Men Who Run the Country" .... The Robber Barons
Scene 2. Corridor of the United States Hotel.
Scene 3. Clint's and Clio's Rooms.
          "The Man in My Life" .... Clio & Clint
Scene 4. The Verandah.
          "The Polka" .... Clio, Bart & Ensemble
          "Love Held Lightly" Reprise .... Clio
Scene 5. The Corridor.
          "Goose Never Be a Peacock" .... Kakou
Scene 6. On a Flatcar and at the Railroad Station, Binghamton, N.Y.
          "Dog Eat Dog" .... Clint & His Men
          "The Railroad Fight" .... Clint, Cupide & the Men
Scene 7. The Corridor.
Scene 8. The Ballroom of the United States Hotel.
          "Petticoat High" Reprise .... Clio & Ensemble

THE FIGHTING COCK

Opened December 8, 1959; closed February 20, 1960;
87 performances.

Play by Jean Anouilh, adapted by Lucienne Hill. Settings and costumes by Rolf Gérard, lighting by Howard Bay, staged by Peter Brook. Produced by Kermit Bloomgarden Productions, Inc., at the ANTA Theatre.

The cast

The General	Rex Harrison
The Doctor	Geoffrey Lumb
Toto, the General's Son	Claude Gersene
Marie-Christine, the General's Daughter	Judy Sanford
The Milkman's Son	Rhoden Streeter
The Milkman	Roger De Koven
Father Gregory	Michael Gough
Sophie, the General's Daughter	Margo Anders
Tarquin Edward Mendigales	Roddy McDowall
Bise, the General's Sister	Jane Lillig
Aglae, the General's Wife	Natasha Parry
Lebelluc	Arthur Treacher
Michepain	Gerald Hiken
Baron Henri Belazor	Alan MacNaughtan

UNDERSTUDIES: Elizabeth Hubbard, Bill Howe, Avra Petrides, Roger De Koven, Don Doherty

THE PLAY:

The return of Rex Harrison, the original 'Enry 'Iggins of *My Fair Lady*, was an event, but his drama wasn't. Like another of Jean Anouilh's comedies, and a much better one, *Waltz of the Toreadors*, this one considered another retired French general who found that his present life was out of joint with the times.

The play was a literate and witty adaptation by Lucienne Hill, and many of its lines had spark and crackle. It had, indeed, almost everything it needed, including direction by Peter Brook and a supporting cast including Arthur Treacher and Roddy McDowall. But it did need a more interesting story; sophistication without interest is like caviar without chopped onions; a little of it is enough and more of it is too much.

In *The Fighting Cock* Harrison was a warrior who liked the past he had led, couldn't abide the present and was unable to contemplate the future. Walter Kerr wrote in the *Herald Tribune:* "The play, lacking a clear core around which its glistening flying saucers can soar, comes to seem fragile and thin before its philosophizing is done. . . . For all the lively nuance, a heartbeat is lacking."

GOODBYE CHARLIE

Opened December 16, 1959; closed March 19, 1960;
109 performances.

Comedy by George Axelrod. Setting by Oliver Smith, lighting by
Peggy Clark, staged by George Axelrod. Produced by Leland Hayward at the Lyceum Theatre.

The cast

Greg Morris	Frank Roberts
George Tracy	Sydney Chaplin
Franny Saltzman	Michelle Reiner
Irving	Clinton Anderson
Mr. Shriber	Dan Frazer
Rusty Mayerling	Sarah Marshall
Charlie	Lauren Bacall

THE PLAY:

Samuel Goldwyn is reported to have told a writer, a long time ago,
that he had the mucus of an idea. So did George Axelrod when he
penned or typed the fantasy, *Goodbye Charlie*. He gave himself a good
start but couldn't figure out how to keep going. There was, however,
an engaging first Broadway performance by Lauren Bacall, and
Sydney Chaplin revealed himself as a comedian of high polish.

It was Axelrod's notion that a man named Charlie, a charming
Hollywood libertine who would rather play at romance than write
screenplays, is shot dead by a properly outraged husband. As punish-
ment for all his earthly sins, Charlie is brought back to life—in the
person of a beautiful young woman. He doesn't realize at first that
he is different now, and he tries to resume the old life with his writing
partner—played by Chaplin. In due course, however, Charlie realizes
that he is a she and that love cannot be taken as casually as it once
was.

The play was part farce, part whimsey, but Axelrod's invention
failed him after he got his play going.

THE ANDERSONVILLE TRIAL

Opened December 29, 1959; closed June 1, 1960; 179 performances.

Play by Saul Levitt. Production designed and lighted by Will Steven Armstrong, staged by José Ferrer. Produced by William Darrid, Eleanore Saidenberg and Daniel Hollywood at Henry Miller's Theatre.

The cast

General Lew Wallace	Russell Hardie
President of the Court	
Lieutenant	Robert Burr
Clerk of the Court	
Lt. Col. N. P. Chipman	George C. Scott
The Judge Advocate	
Otis H. Baker	Albert Dekker
The Defense Counsel	
Captain Williams	Al Henderson
Henry Wirz	Herbert Berghof
The Defendant	
Louis Schade	James Arenton
Assistant Defense Counsel	
Lt. Col. Chandler	Robert Carroll
Dr. John C. Bates	Ian Keith
Ambrose Spencer	Moultrie Patten
Dr. C. M. Ford	Douglas Herrick
Prison Surgeon	
Major D. Hosmer	Howard Wierum
Assistant Judge Advocate	
James H. Davidson	James Greene
Jasper Culver	Robert Gerringer
George W. Gray	Frank Sutton
Union Soldiers	Robert Downey, Martin West, Lou Frizzell
Newspapermen	Robert Mayer, Richard Poston, William Scharf

General Mott		Clifford Carpenter
General Thomas		Taylor Graves
General Geary		John Leslie
General Fessenden	Assisting Judges	Owen Pavitt
General Ballier		William Hussung
Colonel Allcock		Archie Smith
Colonel Stibbs		Freeman Meskimen

UNDERSTUDIES: Robert Burr, William Hussung, Reuben Singer, Owen Pavitt, John Leslie, Richard Poston, Lou Frizzell, Freeman Meskimen, Clifford Carpenter, Archie Smith, Al Henderson.
One of Broadway's Best. See page 97.

A MIGHTY MAN IS HE

Opened January 6, 1960; closed January 9, 1960; 5 performances.

Comedy by Arthur Kober and George Oppenheimer. Setting and lighting by Frederick Fox, costumes by Virginia Volland, song by Sherman Edwards, staged by Reginald Denham. Produced by Edward Joy and Diana Green at the Cort Theatre.

The cast

Edwards	Claud Allister
Rachel Krupp	Nancy Cushman
Jason Smith	Doug Lambert
Frederick McMahon	Gene Blakely
Barbara Smith	Nancy Kelly
Elizabeth Talbot	Kimetha Laurie
Doctor Holden	John Cecil Holm
Phyllis Clyde	Polly Rowles
Jennifer Grant	Diana van der Vlis

UNDERSTUDIES: Richard O'Reilly, Judy Tucker

THE PLAY:

Two first-rate humorists, Arthur Kober and George Oppenheimer, pooled their talents with meagre results in writing *A Mighty Man Is He*. This comedy of sex lacked the depth for an entire evening in the theatre, and an attractive cast, including Nancy Kelly, Polly Rowles, and Diana van der Vlis were as helpful as could be—but not helpful enough.

As I saw it, the chief shortcoming of the comedy was that the mighty man of the title never appeared onstage; he was heard on a house intercom once, and that was not enough. Offstage events and offstage characters are never as interesting as they should be—including the murders which Lady Macbeth finished.

The Kober-Oppenheimer work told of a philandering theatrical producer and clashes over his unseen body by three women—his wife (Miss Kelly), his sophisticated mistress (Miss Rowles) and a young blonde he has recently acquired (Miss van der Vlis). Each thought him fascinating, but I could never learn why because I didn't see him. In the interest of morality, the authors arranged for the wife to defeat both rivals.

A DISTANT BELL

Opened January 13, 1960; closed January 16, 1960; 5 performances.

Play by Katherine Morrill. Setting by Mordecai Gorelik, lighting by Peggy Clark, costumes by Theoni V. Aldredge, staged by Norman Twain. Produced by Norman Twain at the Eugene O'Neill Theatre.

The cast

Keene Stanfield	Frieda Altman
Dora Greer	Nydia Westman
Burton Greer	Richard Nicholls
Mrs. Brighton	Mabel Cochran
Lucy Greer	Martha Scott
Barrett Greer	Patricia Roe
Waverly Greer	Phyllis Love
Flagg Greer	Evans Evans
Mr. Wilbur	Louis Girard
John Creighton	Andrew Prine
Clara Hurd	Lynda Carr
Jackson Dunne	Mark Fleischman
Arthur Wilson	Dale Helward
Newsboy	Michael Gleason

One of Broadway's Best. See page 107.

CUT OF THE AXE

Opened February 1, 1960; closed February 2, 1960; 2 performances.

Play by Sheppard Kerman, based on the novel by Delmar Jackson. Setting and lighting by Howard Bay, costumes by André, staged by John O'Shaughnessy. Produced by Rita Allen and Milton Cassel at the Ambassador Theatre.

The cast

Roy Slater	Charles Carlson
John Brown	Paul Sparer
Morales	Cal Bellini
Homer Fry	James Westerfield
Paul Carr	Robert Lansing
Harry Nichols	Milo Boulton
Rollie Evans	Thomas Mitchell
Martha Evans	Susan Brown
Doc	John Gibson
Charlie	Raymond Van Sickle
Johnson	William Severs
John Nichols	John Stark
Pete	John Thomas

TOWNSPEOPLE: Ernesto Gonzales, Joe Hardy, James Carville, Michael Egan, Herbert Voss

UNDERSTUDIES: Robert Crawley, Judith Hunter, John Thomas, Ernesto Gonzales, Raymond Van Sickle, William Severs

THE PLAY:

The author tried for a good melodrama but it wasn't exciting enough, even with two of the best left-handed character actors in the business, Thomas Mitchell and James Westerfield, in the leading roles.

Mitchell was the political power in a small town and Westerfield the honest town marshal. (He was, at base, honest, even though he had a case of contraband liquor in his truck, and his heart was as big as his paunch.)

The story concerned the stabbing to death of a young wife, the arrest of two vagrants suspected of the killing and the defense of the prisoners by the marshal against a lynch mob. It turned out that

Mitchell, though innocent of the crime, knew more about it than he let on. In the *Times*, Brooks Atkinson wrote: "It is a melodrama of many words, many characters and offstage noises. The bad guys yell not only at the good guys, but at the bad guys too. On stage things are tough enough. Off stage they are very threatening."

THE DEADLY GAME

Opened February 2, 1960; closed March 5, 1960; 39 performances.

Play by James Yaffee, based on a novel by Friedrich Duerrenmatt. Setting and lighting by Wolfgang Roth, staged by William Gaskill. Produced by Alton Wilkes and Joe Manchester in association with Emil Coleman, Morton Segal and Barbara Griner at the Longacre Theatre.

The cast

Emile Carpeau	Ludwig Donath
Bernard Laroque	Claude Dauphin
Joseph Pillet	Pat Malone
Pierre	Frank Campanella
Howard Trapp	Pat Hingle
Gustave Kummer	Max Adrian
A Visitor	Frances Helm

UNDERSTUDIES: Curt Conway, Richard Everhart

One of Broadway's Best. See page 90.

ROMAN CANDLE

Opened February 3, 1960; closed February 6, 1960; 5 performances.

Comedy by Sidney Sheldon. Settings and lighting by David Hays, costumes by Ruth Morley, staged by David Pressman. Produced by Ethel Linder Reiner at the Cort Theatre.

The cast

Sgt. Eddie Remick	Eddie Firestone
Eleanor Winston	Julia Meade
Mrs. Otis	Mildred Chandler
Sgt. Smitty	Stan Watt
Mark Baxter	Robert Sterling
Senator John Winston	Lauren Gilbert
Lieut. General Dayton	Walter Greaza
Admiral Trenton	Stephen Elliott
Colonel Grey	Lon Clark
Elizabeth Brown	Inger Stevens
Fire Control Officer	John Lasell
Range Officer	Chester Doherty
Secretary of Defense	Stan Watt
Sgt. Seidel	Tony Kraber
Dr. Alden	Lloyd Gough

UNDERSTUDIES: John Lasell, Elizabeth Ashley, Lon Clark, Stephen Elliott, Stan Watt, Tony Kraber.

THE PLAY:

Roman Candle may not have lit up the Broadway sky too brightly, but in my mind it should have more than the five performances it got. It was a simple, unpretending farce, and quite a bit of it was funny—and there were pleasant performances by Inger Stevens, Robert Sterling, and Eddie Firestone—Firestone having a character part of a sergeant who dreams of a fortune by using extrasensory perception on horse races.

The plot dealt principally with Sterling, a scientist who has devised the latest thing in space rockets, and Miss Stevens, a cool college woman who has gone far with ESP. Quite often she can figure out what is going to happen. Among other things, she figures out that she is going to get Sterling for her own.

The subsidiary characters are strictly clay pigeons—or brass pigeons, being self-important Army, Navy and senatorial figures. There were many well-delivered farce lines like, "The Army likes to restrict democracy to civilians" and "No expense is too unnecessary for the Army."

A LOVELY LIGHT

Opened February 8, 1960; closed February 20, 1960; 16 performances.

A dramatization of the poems and letters of Edna St. Vincent Millay by Dorothy Stickney through arrangement with Norma Millay. Setting and lighting by Lee Watson, gown by Helène Pons, staged by Howard Lindsay. Produced by S. Hurok at the Hudson Theatre.

The cast

    Dorothy Stickney
The program

ACT I

"The world stands out on either side
No wider than the heart is wide."

ACT II

"I know not how such things can be!
I breathed my soul back into me."

ACT III

"The soul can split the sky in two
And let the face of God shine through."

One of the sweetest, most charming theatrical events of the season was Dorothy Stickney's limited engagement in a solo performance about the poet, Edna St. Vincent Millay. Miss Stickney made no attempt to impersonate "Vincent," but she magically evoked her presence by "reading" from Millay's verses and letters. And she had made her selections so artfully that the performance was an absorbing narrative of Miss Millay's life, from girlhood to death.

BEG, BORROW OR STEAL

Opened February 10, 1960; closed February 13, 1960; 5 performances.

Musical, based on a story by Marvin Seiger and Bud Freeman, with book and lyrics by Bud Freeman and music by Leon Pober. Scenery, lighting and costumes by Carter Morningstar, dances and musical numbers by Peter Hamilton. Directed by David Doyle, orchestrations by Peter Matz and Hal Hidey, musical direction by Hal Hidey, staged by Billy Matthews. Produced by Eddie Bracken with Carroll and Harris Masterson at the Martin Beck Theatre.

The cast

Mrs. Plonsky	Jean Bruno
Junior	Biff McGuire
Ollie	Estelle Parsons
Phil	Betty Rhodes
Judy	Karen Sargent
Clara	Betty Garrett
Pistol	Eddie Bracken
Rafe	Larry Parks
Jason	Roy Stuart
Ethel	Bernice Massi
Lovers	Mary Sullivan and Del Hanley
Modern Dance Leader	Sally Lee
Dance Class	Carmen Morales, Garold Gardner, Ellen Halpin and Willard Nagel
Rug Hooker	Michael Davis
Pottery Girl	Colleen Corkrey
Bar Girl	Esther Horrocks
Knitters	Fran Leone and Keith Willis
Painter	Tom Hester
Chess Players	Michael Stuart and Arthur Whitfield
Flamenco Dancers	Adriana Keathley and Harold Da Silva
Guitarist	Fred Kimbrough
Kibitzer	Mara Wirt
Poet	John Tormey
Poetry Lovers	Shelia Dee, Georgia Kennedy and Virginia Barnes
Sculptor	Chuck Arnett
Model	Beti Seay
Mobile Artist	Lucinda Stevens
Frieda	Claiborne Cary
Patriot	Jack Drummond

Sam Lee Howard .... Richard Armbruster
Muscle .... Bill Linton
Koppisch .... Richard Woods
Blanding .... David Doyle
UNDERSTUDIES: Cris Kane, Richard Armbruster, Jack Drummond, Colleen Corkrey, Del Hanley, Lucinda Stevens, Sally Lee, Bruce Blaine

THE PLAY:

Elsewhere in these pages I have expounded the theory that one may find it difficult to satirize such things as advertising and television because they are satires in themselves. The same goes for beatniks. Two attempts have been made to spoof these creatures and both have failed. In *Beg, Borrow or Steal* Biff McGuire, a typical American Boy Salesman, was revealed as the idol of the beatnik set because of the poetry he wrote under a pseudonym. He wrote his poetry by taking six assorted books and a pair of dice and shooting craps for various lines from each book. The librettist of the musical may have used the same formula.

Synopsis of scenes

The action takes place in a run-down section of a monster American city in the 1950s.

ACT II

Scene 1. The Street.
Scene 2. The Store.
Scene 3. The Street.
Scene 4. The Pit.
Scene 5. The Park.
Scene 6. The Street.
Scene 7. The Pit.
Scene 8. Rafe's Attic.
Scene 9. The Store.
Scene 10. The Street.
Scene 11. The Pad.
Scene 12. The Pit.

ACT II

Six Months Later.

Scene 1. The Office.
Scene 2. The Street.
Scene 3. Chez Pit.
Scene 4. The Office.
Scene 5. The Street.

Scene 6. The Pad.
Scene 7. Chez Pit.
Scene 8. The Street.
Scene 9. The Store.

Musical numbers

ACT I

"Some Little People" .... The Ensemble
"Rootless" .... Biff McGuire
"What Are We Gonna Do Tonight?" .... Estelle Parsons,
                              Betty Rhodes and Karen Sargent
"Poetry and All That Jazz" .... Claiborne Cary and the Ensemble
"Don't Stand Too Close To The Picture" ... Larry Parks, Betty Garrett
                             and Ensemble
"Beg, Borrow or Steal," Recitative .... Larry Parks
"Beg, Borrow or Steal" .... Larry Parks
"No One Knows Me," .... Betty Garrett
"Zen Is When" .... Eddie Bracken, Biff McGuire, Bernice Massi and
                              Roy Stuart
Ballet danced by the Ensemble
Soloist: Colleen Corkrey
The Lovers: Carmen Morales and Arthur Whitfield
"Clara" .... Biff McGuire
"You've Got Something To Say" .... Larry Parks and Betty Garrett
Reprise: "You Got Something To Say" ...... Larry Parks, Betty Garrett,
               Eddie Bracken, Biff McGuire and the Company

ACT II

"Presenting Clara Spencer" ...... Betty Garrett. Assisted by Keith Willis,
          Michael Stuart, Chuck Arnett, Harold Da Silva, Willard Nagel,
                    Garold Gardner and Arthur Whitfield
"I Can't Stop Talking" .... Betty Garrett and Biff McGuire
"It's All in Your Mind" .... Larry Parks and Betty Garrett
"In Time" .... Biff McGuire
"Think" .... Betty Garrett
"Little People" .... Eddie Bracken and the Company
Danced by Keith Willis, Sally Lee and Michael Stuart
"Rafesville, U.S.A." .... Bernice Massi and Roy Stuart
Reprise: "Beg, Borrow or Steal" .... Larry Parks and the Ensemble
"Let's Be Strangers Again" .... Betty Garrett and Biff McGuire
Reprise: "Little People" .... The Entire Company

CALIGULA

Opened February 16, 1960; closed March 19, 1960; 38 performances.

Play by Albert Camus, adapted by Justin O'Brien. Settings and costumes by Will Steven Armstrong, lighting by Jean Rosenthal, music by David Amram, staged by Sidney Lumet. Produced by Chandler Cowles, Charles Bowden, and Ridgely Bullock at the 54th Street Theatre.

The cast

Octavius	Frederic Tozere
Darling	Sorrell Booke
Lucius	Edgar Daniels
Cassius	James O'Rear
Helicon	Edward Binns
Cherea	Philip Bourneuf
Scipio	Clifford David
Guard	Gene Pellegrini
Caligula	Kenneth Haigh
Caesonia	Colleen Dewhurst
Major Domo	Frederic Warriner
Mucius	Victor Thorley
Mereia	Harrison Dowd
Mucius' Wife	Sandra Kazan
Metullus	John Ramondetta
1st Poet	Paul Cambeilh
2nd Poet	Ralph Lee
3rd Poet	Roger C. Carmel
4th Poet	John Wynne-Evans
5th Poet	Dal Jenkins
6th Poet	Gene Gregory

WIVES: Marion Barker, Francesca Fontaine, Barbara Hall

SLAVES: Henri Leon Baker, Michael Baseleon, Ralph Newman, Barth Pillsbury

SOLDIERS: Matt Bennett, Gordon Blackmon, Cliff Carnell, Bill Fletcher, Frank Koomen, Grant Michaels, T. J. Murphy, John Tyrános

THE PLAY:

Albert Camus, Frenchman born in Algeria, was a novelist and essayist as well as a dramatist. He won the Nobel prize for literature in 1957. He was killed in an automobile accident six weeks before the first of his works to reach the New York stage was presented. The adapter, Justin O'Brien, is a professor of French at Columbia University, and is known for his translations of André Gide.

In the Broadway production, Kenneth Haigh, English actor who first scored here in *Look Back in Anger*, played the Roman emperor Caligula "between youthful petulance and demoniac fury," as Brooks Atkinson reported it.

Caligula failed New Yorkers as a piece of theater, although it was staged and costumed to be a work of great dramatic and philosophical import. It concerned an emperor who could have anything he wanted except the moon, but enjoyed nothing. In his search for satisfaction he tried everything—murder and assassination in many forms, sexual adventure and degradation and all the powers of a despot. But he found pleasure in nothing except his ultimate adventure, death. He courted assassination and literally flung himself into the midst of a throng of knife-wielders, and, dying of many wounds, he found that at last he was having fun. The irreparable weakness of the drama was, to me, that I did not care if Caligula died or lived. He was a philosophical abstraction.

THE LONG DREAM

Opened February 17, 1960; closed February 20, 1960; 5 performances.

Play by Kette Frings, based on the novel by Richard Wright. Settings by Zvi Geyra, lighting by Tharon Musser, costumes by Ruth Morley, music by Pembroke Davenport, staged by Lloyd Richards. Produced by Cheryl Crawford and Joel Schenker in association with October Productions, Inc., at the Ambassador Theatre.

The cast

Rex (Fishbelly) Tucker	Al Freeman, Jr.
Tyree Tucker	Lawrence Winters
Emma Tucker	Gertrude Jeannette
Tony	Josh White, Jr.
Chris	Clarence Williams, III
Zeke	Edward Phifer
Chief of Police Gerald Canley	R. G. Armstrong
Clem	Clifton James
Phil	Jim Jeter
Doc Bruce	Stanley Greene
Lt. Harvey	Charles A. McDaniel
Gladys	Isabelle Cooley
Maude Carter	Helen Martin
Vera Mason	Joya Sherrill
Jim Bowers	Walter Mason
Mr. McWilliams	Arthur Storch
Rev. Ragland	John Garth, III
White Girl	Barbara Loden
Other Citizens of Clintonville	Jeannette DuBois, Marshall Hill, Peggy Pope, Leonard Parker, Mary Louise, Sylvia Ray

UNDERSTUDIES: Peggy Pope, Jeannette DuBois, Marshall Hill, James E. Wall, Walter Matthews, Leonard Parker, Sylvia Ray

THE PLAY:

It has been many years since I have walked out on a play on its first night, but I did depart after the first act of this one and reported in my newspaper that this act of *The Long Dream* was shoddy and lascivious—a degradation of my seat companion and of several admirable Negro actors. This act included teen-age boys discussing the theories and practice of birth control, a policeman threatening to geld a frightened Negro boy with his knife, a tough madam urging her girls to keep busy and the assumption by white policemen that all Negroes must be guilty of something. It seemed impossible that this play could have been adapted by the lady who did such a beautiful job of adapting Thomas Wolfe's *Look Homeward, Angel.*

THE COOL WORLD

Opened February 22, 1960; closed February 23, 1960; 2 performances.

Play by Warren Miller and Robert Rossen, based on the novel by Warren Miller. Settings and lighting by Howard Bay, costumes by Ann Roth, staged by Robert Rossen. Produced by Lester Osterman at the Eugene O'Neill Theatre.

The cast

Duke Custis	Billy Dee Williams
Hurst	P. Jay Sidney
Priest	Raymond Saint-Jacques
Gramma Custis	Eulabelle Moore
Mrs. Custis	Lynn Hamilton
Mrs. Thurston	Alice Childress
Foxy	Clebert Ford
Mau Mau	Philip Hepburn
Cowboy	George Gatlin
Rod	Martin Golar
Cherokee	Cheyenne Sorocki
Saint	Herb Coleman
Savage	Donald Blakely
Little Man	Lamont Washington
Blood	Calvin Lockhart
Lu Ann	Alease Whittington
Royal Baron	Roscoe Lee Browne
Miss Dewpont	Hilda Simms
Father Christmas	Wardell Saunders
Hermit	Melvin Stewart
Girl	Cicely Tyson
Boy	David Downing
Pusher	Maxwell Glanville
Harrison Thurston	James Earl Jones
Chester	Harold Scott
Bebop	Marvin Camillo
Lucky	Art Aveilhe
Old Man	Jim Oyster
Woman at the Beach	Ethel Ayler
First Policeman	Jim Oyster
Second Policeman	Duke Williams

UNDERSTUDIES: Martin Golar, Cicely Tyson, Ethel Ayler, Maxwell Glanville, Calvin Lockhart, Duke Williams, Lurlean Smaulding, James Earl Jones

THE PLAY:

The *Herald Tribune*'s Walter Kerr led off his review of *The Cool World* thus: "The constant whine of knives being sharpened is the predominant sound. Indeed, by the end of the ninth scene what seems like the entire juvenile-delinquent population of Harlem is hard at work honing machetes, switchblades and stolen kitchen utensils. Unfortunately, as the boys' knives get sharper, their tongues get duller."

My estimate of the play was that, as a story of teen-age life in Harlem, it was now and again vivid, sordid, exciting, pitiful and shameful, but that the authors had not been able to reach a dramatic conclusion. The big gang rumble which was being led up to most of the evening occurred offstage, and everything afterward was anticlimax.

The basis of the story was the preparation by a gang of Negroes to wreak vengeance upon a gang of Puerto Ricans for the wounding of one of their friends. This beginning was not unlike *West Side Story*, but here the resemblance ended. *The Cool World* had no comparable emotional depth, being a documentary and not a romance. But some of the scenes were written and played vividly, and Howard Bay's unit setting of a crumbling Harlem brownstone was the most imaginative and poetic investiture of the season—but, with only two performances, scarcely anybody had opportunity to see it.

Synopsis of scenes

ACT I

Prologue: The Street
Scene 1. The Street. Morning.
Scene 2. The Custis Apartment. Immediately following.
Scene 3. The Clubhouse of the Royal Crocodiles. That evening.
Scene 4. Royal Baron's Apartment. Thirty minutes later.
Scene 5. Lu Ann's bedroom. Late that night.
Scene 6. Hermit's Luncheonette. Several days later.

ACT II

Scene 1. The Clubhouse. Later.
Scene 2. Chester's Apartment. That evening.
Scene 3. The Clubhouse. Evening of the next day.
Scene 4. Coney Island. The next day.
Scene 5. The Street. Later the same night.
Scene 6. Hurst's Apartment. An hour later.

THE SERVANT OF TWO MASTERS

Opened February 23, 1960; closed March 5, 1960; 16 performances.

Play by Carlo Goldoni performed in Italian by the Piccolo Teatro di Milano, Paolo Grassi and Giorgio Strehler directors. Décor and costumes by Ezio Frigerio, masks by Amleto Sartori, music by Fiorenzo Carpi, staged by Giorgio Strehler. Produced by Jerry Hoffman in association with the New York City Center at the New York City Center.

The cast

Pantalone de'Bisognosi	Gianrico Tedeschi
Clarice, his daughter	Giulia Lazzarini
Doctor Lombardi	Bruno Lanzarini
Silvio, his son	Giancarlo Dettori
Beatrice, from Turin; she is in man's clothes impersonating Federigo Rasponi	Relda Ridoni
Florindo Aretusi, from Turin, her lover	Warner Bentivegna
Brighella, Innkeeper	Gianfranco Mauri
Smeraldina, Clarice's maid	Narcisa Bonati
Arlecchino, servant to Beatrice and then to Florindo	Marcello Moretti
A Servant of the Inn, who speaks	Vincenzo De Toma
A Porter, who speaks	Angelo Corti
A Servant	Ferruccio Soleri
Other Servants	Augusto Salvi, Giuliano Mariani, Fernando Mazzola

THE PLAY:

Carlo Goldoni's *Arlecchino, Servitore di due Padroni,* two centuries old, is a pioneer work in farce, and the Italian visitors played it for slapstick with such amusing effect that the language barrier was minimal. The comedians from Milan were unpretentious and charming, and they performed with zest a charade about mistaken identities and girls dressed as boys. All the way from Shakespeare to Mozart and Richard Strauss it has been a hilarious fancy to have a girl masquerade as a boy or to have a boy impersonate a girl. The most popular of all such masquerades, by far, has been *Charley's Aunt*.

Marcello Moretti, the leader of the Piccolo Teatro, was so exceptionally gifted a pantomimist that I longed to see him in a silent movie directed by Mack Sennett.

THE TUMBLER

Open February 24, 1960; closed February 27, 1960; 5 performances.

Play by Benn W. Levy, setting by Roger Furse, lighting by Tharon Musser, staged by Laurence Olivier. Produced by Alfred de Liagre, Jr., and Roger L. Stevens in association with Laurence Olivier, Don Herbert associate producer, at the Helen Hayes Theatre.

The cast

Lennie	Rosemary Harris
Kell	Charlton Heston
Nina	Martha Scott
The Doctor	William Mervyn
George	Donald Moffat

THE PLAY:

This was a dismaying mixture of overheated writing and bad acting. The narrative, if it could be discovered in a clutter of words, seemed to concern a girl who had a roll in the hay in a barn with her mother's second husband. She loved this manly fellow on sight, but she hated him, too, because she suspected him of having killed her beloved father in order to become intimate with her mother.

The auspices of this offering seemed all to the good. The author is a respected writer of jolly British comedies. The director, Laurence Olivier, is titled. The principals were Rosemary Harris, a young and attractive Old Vic graduate, and Charlton Heston, the hero of the Oscar-winning movie, *Ben-Hur*. But Levy chose to couch his rather commonplace narrative in poetic cadences, and the director, Olivier, felt impelled to make everybody yell on the stage.

How can so many people be wrong all at the same time?

TOYS IN THE ATTIC

Opened February 25, 1960; still running; 111 performances.

Play by Lillian Hellman. Setting and lighting by Howard Bay, costumes by Ruth Morley, staged by Arthur Penn. Produced by Kermit Bloomgarden at the Hudson Theatre.

The cast

Carrie Berniers	Maureen Stapleton
Anna Berniers	Anne Revere
Gus	Charles McRae
Albertine Prine	Irene Worth
Henry Simpson	Percy Rodriguez
Julian Berniers	Jason Robards, Jr.
Lily Berniers	Rochelle Oliver
Taxi Driver	William Hawley
3 Moving Men	Clifford Cothren, Tom Manley, Maurice Ellis

One of Broadway's Best. See page 62.

A THURBER CARNIVAL

Opened February 26, 1960; still running; 110 performances.

Revue by James Thurber. Scenery by Marvin Reiss, lighting by Paul Morrison, men's costumes by Ramsé Stevens, music composed and performed by Don Elliott, entire production conceived and staged by Burgess Meredith, "Word Dance" and "Fables" staged by James Starbuck, Don Elliott associate director. Produced by Michael Davis, Helen Bonfils and Haila Stoddard at the ANTA Theatre.

The cast

> Tom Ewell
> Peggy Cass
> Paul Ford
> John McGiver
> Alice Ghostley
> Peter Turgeon
> Wynne Miller
> Margo Lungreen
> Charles Braswell
> Don Elliott Quartet
> > Jack Six, Jim Raney, Ronnie Bedford, Don Elliott

Program

ACT I

WORD DANCE (PART I)

Peggy Cass	Peter Turgeon
Paul Ford	Wynne Miller
John McGiver	Margo Lungreen
Alice Ghostley	Charles Braswell

THE NIGHT THE BED FELL
Tom Ewell
FABLES (PART I)
The Wolf at the Door

Narrator .... Alice Ghostley
Daughter .... Wynne Miller
Mother .... Peggy Cass
Father .... Paul Ford
Wolf .... Charles Braswell

The Unicorn in the Garden

Narrator .... Peter Turgeon
Man .... Paul Ford
She .... Alice Ghostley
Psychiatrist .... John McGiver
Policeman .... Charles Braswell

The Little Girl and the Wolf

Narrator .... Peggy Cass
Wolf .... Paul Ford
Little Girl .... Wynne Miller

IF GRANT HAD BEEN DRINKING AT APPOMATTOX

Narrator .... Peter Turgeon
Shultz .... Charles Braswell
Grant .... Tom Ewell
Lee .... Paul Ford
Lee's Staff Man .... John McGiver
Officer .... Peter Turgeon

CASUALS OF THE KEYS

Visitor .... John McGiver
Darrel Darke .... Paul Ford

THE MACBETH MURDER MYSTERY

He .... Tom Ewell
She .... Peggy Cass

GENTLEMEN SHOPPERS

Salesgirl .... Alice Ghostley
Westwater .... John McGiver
Bargirl .... Wynne Miller
Anderson .... Tom Ewell
Bailey .... Paul Ford

THE LAST FLOWER
Tom Ewell

ACT II

PET DEPARTMENT

The Pet Counsellor .... Tom Ewell
Miss Whittaker .... Alice Ghostley
A Girl .... Wynne Miller

MR. PREBLE GETS RID OF HIS WIFE

Preble .... Paul Ford
Miss Daley .... Wynne Miller
Mrs. Preble .... Peggy Cass

FILE AND FORGET

James Thurber .... Tom Ewell
Miss Bagley .... Margo Lungreen
Miss Alma Winege .... Peggy Cass

Miss Wynne .... Wynne Miller
Jeannette Gaines .... Alice Ghostley
Clint Jordan .... Paul Ford
H. F. Cluffman .... John McGiver
TAKE HER UP TENDERLY
John .... Paul Ford
Nellie .... Alice Ghostley
Lou .... Peggy Cass
FABLES (PART II)
The Owl Who Was God
Narrator .... Alice Ghostley
Owl .... John McGiver
Moles .... Peter Turgeon, Charles Braswell
Secretary Bird .... Paul Ford
Red Fox .... Margo Lungreen
The Clothes Moth and the Luna Moth
Narrator .... Tom Ewell
Luna Moth .... Wynne Miller
Clothes Moth .... Charles Braswell
THE SECRET LIFE OF WALTER MITTY
Narrator .... Peter Turgeon
Walter Mitty .... Tom Ewell
Mrs. Mitty .... Peggy Cass
First Voice .... Charles Braswell
Lt. Berg .... Peter Turgeon
Nurse .... Wynne Miller
Dr. Renshaw .... John McGiver
Dr. Benbow .... Charles Braswell
Dr. Remington .... Peter Turgeon
Mr. Pritchard-Mitford .... Paul Ford
The Leader .... Paul Ford
WORD DANCE (PART II)

Tom Ewell	John McGiver	Wynne Miller
Peggy Cass	Alice Ghostley	Margo Lungreen
Paul Ford	Peter Turgeon	Charles Braswell
	Don Elliott Quartet	

THE IDEA

James Thurber is noted as a wit, a cartoonist, a philosopher, an auto-
biographer with total recall and a fictioneer. With Elliott Nugent he
once wrote a first-rate comedy, *The Male Animal*. But who would
ever think of putting a mélange of Thurber fragments on a stage and
calling it a show?

Burgess Meredith thought of it, and the result was the lighthearted
masterpiece of the season. *A Thurber Carnival* has some interesting
jazz music by the Don Elliott Quartet, but the music is mainly used

to fill in stage-waits quite pleasantly. The entertainment, ranging from shocking sanity to captivating lunacy, is pure Thurber. And it is presented by a perfectly chosen little group of comedians and comediennes.

THERE WAS A LITTLE GIRL

Opened February 29, 1960; closed March 12, 1960; 16 performances.

Play by Daniel Taradash, from a novel by Christopher Davis. Settings and lighting by Jo Mielziner, costumes by Patton Campbell, original music by Lehman Engel, staged by Joshua Logan, production manager Robert Linden. Produced by Robert Fryer and Lawrence Carr at the Cort Theatre.

The cast

Toni Newton	Jane Fonda
Stan Walters	Dean Jones
Waiter	Val Ruffino
Nicky Walters	Peter Helm
Harry Adams	Michael Vandever
Mr. Newton	Whitfield Connor
Mrs. Newton	Ruth Matteson
Lucille Newton	Joey Heatherton
Neill Johns	Sean Garrison
Ralph	Gary Lockwood
Lt. Goldman	William Adler
Policeman	Mark Slade
Bartender	Phillip Pruneau
Tom Fraser	Tom Gilleran

DANCERS: Val Ruffino, Sharon Forsmoe, Mark Slade, Barbara Davis

THE PLAY:

This could have been a provocative drama, but it wasn't. It concerned a college freshman who had a tendency toward sexual adventure in a nice schoolgirl fashion, but whose only real adventure was to be abducted, beaten and assaulted by two roadhouse thugs.

This girl should have been an object of sympathy and pity, but she became a celebrity and a freak. The suspicion got around that she wasn't exactly abducted and that the crime against her person was not uninvited. As a result, being an intelligent and sensitive lass, she almost lost her mind. In the nick of curtain time she decided to forget the past and resume her studies in college—not a very stirring finish for a play. There was an admirable début performance of the leading role by Henry Fonda's young and talented daughter, Jane.

There must and perhaps there will be a profound drama about what happens afterward to a well-born girl who has been ravished. What will be society's attitude toward her, and her attitude toward society? These questions deserve an answer in theatrical terms—a better one than this play offered.

THE GOOD SOUP

Opened March 2, 1960; closed March 19, 1960; 21 performances.

Play by Félicien Marçeau, adapted by Garson Kanin from the original Paris production by André Barsacq. Sets and costumes by Jacques Noel, supervised by William Pitkin, lighting by Albert Alloy, staged by Garson Kanin, production stage manager Neil Hartley. Produced by David Merrick at the Plymouth Theatre.

The cast

The Croupier	Jules Munshin
The Barman	Pat Harrington
Marie-Paule I	Ruth Gordon
Monsieur Gaston	Ernest Truex
Marie-Paule II	Diane Cilento
Marie-Paule's Mother	Mildred Natwick
Roger	Morgan Sterne
The Customer	Bill Becker
Madame Roger	Dorothy Whitney
The Doorman	George S. Irving
The Shady One	Lou Antonio
The Skater	Barbara Lou Mattes
Odilon	Sam Levene
The First Patron	John Myhers
Irma	Sasha von Scherler
The Second Patron	Morgan Sterne
Mauricette	Hilda Brawner
The Third Patron	Lou Antonio
Monsieur Alphonse	George S. Irving
The Chambermaid	Barbara Lou Mattes
The Fourth Patron	Bill Becker
Lecasse	Lou Antonio
Joseph	Ernest Truex
Angele	Mildred Natwick
Raymond	George S. Irving
The House Painter	Bill Becker
Jacquot	Charles Robinson
Minouche	Hilda Brawner
The Tough	George S. Irving
The Second Tough	Pat Harrington
Armand	John Myhers
The Other Man	George S. Irving
Armand's Mother	Mildred Natwick
Ernest	Bill Becker

Berthe .... Hilda Brawner
Madame Desvaux .... Sasha von Scherler
Madame Thonnard .... Dorothy Whitney
Jeannine .... Nicola Lubitsch
Mollard .... Morgan Sterne

UNDERSTUDIES: Karen Morley, Collin Wilcox, Rex Williams, Barbara Lou Mattes, Allan Stevenson, Bill Becker

THE PLAY:

The advance buildup of *The Good Soup* may have been the most stupendous of the season. It had been adapted from a great Paris hit by Garson Kanin, and was to be directed by him. The star would be Ruth Gordon, one of the most gifted of American comédiennes. The supporting cast would include such important players as Diane Cilento, Ernest Truex, and Mildred Natwick. The play would be very French and therefore very naughty.

It struck me as being no more French than a dirty postcard, and even with Miss Gordon doubling all the extravagant stage tricks she used in Thornton Wilder's delightful *The Matchmaker*, it was dull and tasteless. It told the life story, in flashback form, of a cocotte who goes from man to man until she reaches middle age and finds herself with nothing better to do than tell this life story to a stranger —a croupier at the Monte Carlo Casino.

There was originality in the scheme of the play, with Miss Cilento acting out the sleazy life Miss Gordon led while Miss Gordon told it to the impressionable croupier, amusingly played by Jules Munshin. Munshin was, indeed, far more interested than I was in this overblown and remarkably tasteless farce.

GREENWILLOW

Opened March 8, 1960; closed May 28, 1960; 96 performances.

Musical, based on the novel by B. J. Chute, with book by Lesser Samuels and Frank Loesser, music and lyrics by Frank Loesser. Settings by Peter Larkin, lighting by Feder, costumes by Alvin Colt, choreography by Joe Layton, orchestrations by Don Walker, musical direction by Abba Bogin, staged by George Roy Hill. Produced by Robert A. Willey in association with Frank Productions, Inc., at the Alvin Theatre.

The cast

Jabez Briggs	John Megna
Clara Clegg	Dortha Duckworth
Mrs. Hasty	Maggie Task
Mr. Preebs	Jordon Howard
Mrs. Lunny	Marie Foster
Reverend Lapp	William Chapman
Gramma Briggs	Pert Kelton
Maidy	Elaine Swann
Emma	Saralou Cooper
Gideon Briggs	Anthony Perkins
Dorrie Whitbred	Ellen McCown
Amos Briggs	Bruce MacKay
Micah Briggs	Ian Tucker
Martha Briggs	Lynn Brinker
Sheby Briggs	Brenda Harris
Thomas Clegg	Lee Cass
Reverend Birdsong	Cecil Kellaway
Young Churchgoer	Thomas Norden
Will	David Gold
Nell	Margery Gray
Andrew	Grover Dale

SINGERS: Kenny Adams, Betsy Bridge, Marie Foster, Rico Froehlich, Russell Goodwin, Jordon Howard, Marion Mercer, Carl Nicholas, Virginia Oswald, Bob Roman, Shelia Swenson, Maggie Task, Karen Thorsell

DANCERS: Jere Admire, Don Atkinson, Estelle Aza, Joan Coddington, Ethelyne Dunfee, Richard Englund, David Gold, Margery Gray, Mickey Gunnerson, Patsi King, Jack Leigh, Nancy Van Rhein, Jimmy White

UNDERSTUDIES: Grover Dale, Clarence Nordstrom, Rico Froehlich, Karen Thorsell, Marie Foster, Jordon Howard, Russell Goodwin, Marion Mercer,

Maggie Task, Thomas Norden, Ave Marie Megna, Edmund Gaines, Virginia Oswald, Bob Roman, Ralph Linn, Patsi King, Jack Leigh

THE PLAY:

The story was not as satisfactory on the stage as it might have been —perhaps because it clung too faithfully to Miss Chute's fanciful novel. But it was admirably cast and set, and Frank Loesser provided some admirable songs.

The fantasy concerns a young man who, though cursed with the wanderlust as his father was before him, returns to his home town of Greenwillow on the Meander River, and here he falls in love with a girl. In the end, the wandering curse is put down.

Synopsis of scenes

The action takes place in four seasons in and about Greenwillow.

ACT I

Scene 1. The Square.
Scene 2. Briggs Farm.
Scene 3. The Mill.
Scene 4. The Willow.
Scene 5. The Square.
Scene 6. Cleggs Farm.
Scene 7. The Mill.
Scene 8. Briggs Farm.
Scene 9. The Church.
Scene 10. The Square.

ACT II

Scene 1. The Square.
Scene 2. Briggs Farm.
Scene 3. Cleggs House.
Scene 4. The Square.
Scene 5. Briggs Farm.

Musical numbers

ACT I

1. "A Day Borrowed from Heaven" .... The Villagers
2. "A Day Borrowed from Heaven" .... Gideon
3. "Dorrie's Wish" .... Dorrie
4. "The Music of Home" .... Amos, Gideon and the Villagers
5. "Gideon Briggs, I Love You" .... Gideon and Dorrie
6. "The Autumn Courting" .... All the Villagers

7. "The Call to Wander" .... Amos
8. "Summertime Love" .... Gideon and the Villagers
9. "Walking Away Whistling" .... Dorrie
10. "The Sermon" .... Reverend Lapp and Reverend Birdsong
11. "Could've Been a Ring" .... Clegg and Gramma
12. "Gideon Briggs, I Love You" .... Dorrie
13. "Halloweve" .... The Young Villagers
14. "Never Will I Marry" .... Gideon
15. "Greenwillow Christmas" (Carol) ...... Martha and the Villagers

ACT II

1. "The Music of Home" .... The Villagers
2. "Faraway Boy" .... Dorrie
3. "Clang Dang the Bell" .... Gideon, Gramma, Martha, Micah,
                                      Sheby and Jabez
4. "What a Blessing" .... Reverend Birdsong
5. "He Died Good" .... The Villagers
6. "The Spring Courting" .... Andrew, Dorrie and the Young Villagers
7. "Summertime Love" .... Gideon
8. "What a Blessing" .... Reverend Birdsong
9. "The Call" .... Gideon
10. "The Music of Home" .... All of Greenwillow

THE VISIT

Opened March 8, 1960; closed March 20, 1960; 16 performances.

Revival of play by Friedrich Duerrenmatt, adapted by Maurice Valency. Sets by Teo Otto, supervision and lighting by Paul Morrison, Miss Fontanne's clothes by Castillo, staged by Peter Brook. The Producers Theatre production presented by the City Center of Music and Drama by arrangement with The American Theatre Society under the auspices of The Council of Living Theatre at the New York City Center.

The cast

Hofbauer	William Callan
Helmsberger	David Clarke
Wechsler	Geoffrey Bryant
Vogel	Lance Cunard
The Painter	Burford Hampden
Station Master	Joseph Leberman
Burgomaster	Thomas Gomez
Professor Muller	Glenn Anders
Pastor	William Hansen
Anton Schill	Alfred Lunt
Claire Zachanassian	Lynn Fontanne
Conductor	Frank Hamilton
Pedro Cabral	Myles Eason
Bobby	John Wyse
Police Chief Schultz	Michael Lewis
1st Grandchild	Donna Francis
2nd Grandchild	Katharine Dunfee
Mike	Lucky Kargo
Max	James MacAaron
1st Blind Man	James Dukas
2nd Blind Man	Roy Johnson
Frau Burgomaster	Nora Dunfee
Frau Block	Edna Preston
Frau Schill	Edith Gresham
Ottilie Schill	Aina Niemela
Karl Schill	John Vickers
Doctor Nusslin	Ronald Bishop
Athlete	Larry Casey
Truck Driver	John Kane
Reporter	Jack DeMave

GENERAL UNDERSTUDY: Edward Moor

THE PLAY:

This great acting team brought profit to the City Center in this return of Duerrenmatt's thriller about the implacable vengeance of a cigar-smoking woman.

SEMI-DETACHED

Opened March 10, 1960; closed March 12, 1960; 4 performances.

Play by Patricia Joudry. Production designed by Boris Aronson, lighting by Klaus Holm, costumes by Helène Pons, staged by Charles S. Dubin. Produced by Philip Rose at the Martin Beck Theatre.

The cast

Joy Friar	Rosalyn Newport
Papa	Edgar Stehli
Paper Boy	Paul Mace
Emile Duschene	Frank Silvera
Frank Friar	Ed Begley
Winnie Friar	Jean Muir
Chris Friar	Ronnie Tourso
Marie Duschene	Vivian Nathan
Jean-Michel Duschene	Brad Herrman
Milkman	Frank Chase
Pierre Boudreau	James Dimitri
Simone	Doris Belack
Father Gagnon	Dana Elcar
Workman	Robert Alvin

UNDERSTUDIES: Dana Elcar, Vera Stough, Manny Sloane, Robert Alvin, Doris Belack, Frank Chase, James Dimitri, Paul Mace, Margaret Thomson

THE PLAY:

This play, by a Canadian actress, Patricia Joudry, was a case of great good will but very little play. It told of the jealousies, prejudices, and differences between a family of French stock and a family of French stock who lived in a semi-detached house, and how all the big and little quarrels were finally resolved. *Abie's Irish Rose*, heaven rest its tattered soul, told a more interesting tale.

DEAR LIAR

Opened March 17, 1960; closed April 30, 1960; 52 performances.

A comedy of letters adapted for the stage from the correspondence of Mrs. Patrick Campbell and Bernard Shaw by Jerome Kilty. Décor by Donald Oenslager, lighting by Jean Rosenthal, costumes by Cecil Beaton, incidental music by Sol Kaplan, staged by Jerome Kilty. Produced by Guthrie McClintic in association with S. Hurok at the Billy Rose Theatre.

The cast

Mrs. Patrick Campbell	Katharine Cornell
Bernard Shaw	Brian Aherne

THE PLAY:

There was not, perhaps, the dramatic bite in *Dear Liar* that one might expect, since it was based on the letters between two tempestuous characters, Mrs. Patrick Campbell and George Bernard Shaw. But it did have charm and it was presented with good taste.

Miss Cornell and Mr. Aherne had toured through sixty-six cities before coming to the Billy Rose Theatre with their high-style recital. From this graceful summary of published correspondence, I gained the impression that G.B.S. never wrote to Mrs. Pat and she never wrote to him; they only wrote *back at* each other, and this made their correspondence through forty years lively enough to be of interest even now.

Neither player attempted an impersonation—a wise conceit, for Mr. Aherne was not as peppery as Shaw and Miss Cornell was too gentle a lady to be the sharp-tongued and volatile Mrs. Pat.

In the pre-opening publicity buildup of *Dear Liar* speculation was offered that these letters were love letters, and that the attachment of the playwright and the actress was not entirely cerebral. I came away from the first performance with the impression that this love-letter theory was true. Shaw was in love with Shaw and Mrs. Campbell was mad about Mrs. Pat.

ONE MORE RIVER

Opened March 18, 1960; closed March 19, 1960; 3 performances.

Play by Beverly Cross. Setting and lighting by George Jenkins, costumes by Anna Hill Johnstone, staged by Windsor Lewis. Produced by Mary K. Frank by arrangement with Laurence Olivier at the Ambassador Theatre.

The cast

Louis, cook	Louis Guss
Ross, a cadet	Thomas Hawley
Danny, deck boy	David Winters
Jacko, ordinary seaman	Robert Drivas
Johnny Condell, bo's'n	Lloyd Nolan
Smitty, able seaman	Don Gantry
Colombus, able seaman	Al Lewis
Pompey, able seaman, ex-Navy	Harry Guardino
Kelly, "Chips," carpenter	John McLiam
Trim, wiper	Lance Taylor
Mick, wiper	Buck Kartalian
Sewell, mate	Alfred Ryder

UNDERSTUDIES: Walter Kinsella, John Matthews, Charles Taylor, Ralph Williams, Louis Guss, Paul Leaf

THE PLAY:

It was the spring which made theater observers say that this was the worst season in memory. Plays opened and closed like camera shutters, including *One More River*, which trickled through three performances. The interesting thing about most of the failures, including this one, had high purpose and were not too bad; they were driven out of town by economics, not the populace.

With Lloyd Nolan, the memorable Queeg of *The Caine Mutiny Court Martial*, cast as a seasoned bo'sun aboard a tramp freighter anchored in a West African river, the drama gave promise in the first act that it would be tough, picturesque, and exciting. The author, Beverly Cross, had a good knack for theatrical talk, and he obviously knew life aboard a freighter.

There was something like a mutiny aboard, and only the intervention of Nolan prevented the lynching of Alfred Ryder, who played a first mate who hid a weak will under a hard shell. But the cause for the rebellion struck me as unsound, being a small incident in which a happy-go-lucky cabin boy was blinded by a pot of boiling water—which the first mate may have thrown at him but, on the other hand, which the lad might accidentally have spilled on himself.

There was a picturesque drinking scene followed by a menacing attempt at hanging. But the two most important events, plotwise, the death of the boy from the shock of his burns and the death by accident of the first mate, occurred offstage—and I have always held that the only place to make things happen is onstage.

THE BEST MAN

Opened March 31, 1960; still running; 40 performances.

Play by Gore Vidal. Settings and lighting by Jo Mielziner, costumes by Theoni V. Aldredge, staged by Joseph Anthony. Produced by The Playwrights' Company, Lyn Austin associate producer, at the Morosco Theatre.

The cast

Dick Jensen	Karl Weber
First Reporter	Howard Fischer
William Russell	Melvyn Douglas
Mike	Martin Fried
Second Reporter	Tony Bickley
Third Reporter	Barbara Berjer
Fourth Reporter	Tom McDermott
Alice Russell	Leora Dana
Ass't to Dick Jensen	Ruth Maynard
Mrs. Gamadge	Ruth McDevitt
Arthur Hockstader	Lee Tracy
Mabel Cantwell	Kathleen Maguire
Bill Blades	Joseph Sullivan
Joseph Cantwell	Frank Lovejoy
Senator Carlin	Gordon B. Clarke
Dr. Artinian	Hugh Franklin
Sheldon Marcus	Graham Jarvis
Reporters, Delegates, Etc.	John Dorrin, Mitchell Erickson, Ruth Tobin

UNDERSTUDIES: Hugh Franklin, Tony Bickley, Barbara Berjer, Ruth Maynard, Howard Fischer, Tom McDermott

One of Broadway's Best. See page 119.

VIVA MADISON AVENUE!

Opened April 6, 1960; closed April 7, 1960; 2 performances.

Comedy by George Panetta. Scenery and lighting by William and Jean Eckart, costumes by Frank Thompson, staged by Aaron Frankel. Produced by Selma Tamber and Martin H. Poll, Alex Singer associate producer, at the Longacre Theatre.

The cast

Joe Caputo	Buddy Hackett
Copy Chief	Carl Low
George Caruso	Lee Krieger
Jim Leary	William Windom
Sandy Neal	Robert Dowdell
Dee Jones	Frances Sternhagen
The Stag	Jed Allan
Toro	Paul E. Richards
Peggy	Jan Miner
Head of Research	Burt Berger
Research Assistant	Richard Poston
Frank O'Boyle	Earl Rowe
Ed Noone	Fred Clark
Jane, Receptionist	Mary Alice Bayh
Girl in the hotel	Peggy Pope
Engineer	Edward Earle

UNDERSTUDIES: Carl Low, Burt Berger, Mary Alice Bayh, Richard Poston, Richard Merrell.

THE PLAY:

This one didn't rate many more than two performances, even though it did have a fine comic performance by Buddy Hackett as an imaginative advertising agency underling.

One would think that such enterprises as Hollywood, advertising, radio, and television were prime subjects for satire—but they aren't. Why? Because they are satires to begin with and one must not paint the lily. The only memorable Hollywood spoof was *Once in a Lifetime*, and I cannot recall a good one about radio or TV. Long years ago Willie Collier appeared in *It Pays to Advertise*, and this farce was funny. *Viva Madison Avenue!* was not.

A SECOND STRING

Opened April 13, 1960; closed May 7, 1960; 29 performances.

Play dramatized by Lucienne Hill from a novel by Colette. Settings and lighting by Ben Edwards, costumes by Robert Mackintosh, staged by Raymond Gerome. Produced by Leonard Sillman and Carroll and Harris Masterson, Dan Fisher associate producer and Jacqueline Adams production associate, at the Eugene O'Neill Theatre.

The cast

Paul	Ben Piazza
Jane	Nina Foch
Fanny	Shirley Booth
Clara	Cathleen Nesbitt
Inez	Carrie Nye
Farou	Jean Pierre Aumont

UNDERSTUDIES: Ward Costello, Ann Driscoll, Ursula Stevens, Franklin Kaiser

THE PLAY:

Lucienne Hill, French-English writer, translated Anouilh's *The Waltz of the Toreadors*, which was a success, and *The Fighting Cock*, which wasn't. *A Second String* was her dramatization of a novel by Colette, *La Seconde*.

The French estimate of sex, everybody has been telling me since I was swept by nature into puberty, is supposed to be the most—urbane, witty, delightfully naughty but ever so sensible. This play had all these qualities plus another one which proved fatal: it was a bore. In it, Jean Pierre Aumont impersonated a playwright with a roving disposition, and Shirley Booth played his case-hardened wife. To complete the triangle, Nina Foch was his so-called secretary. (Why, in the theatre, do mistresses always have to be passed off as secretaries? Couldn't they, for a change, be the cleaning woman?)

At the end of three occasionally interesting acts, the two women decided that they might as well be civilized and share the playwright —but to me this character was not interesting enough to be shared by one, let alone two. In this comedy, the French attitude toward sex seemed quaint—almost Victorian.

BYE BYE BIRDIE

Opened April 14, 1960; still running; 54 performances.

Musical with book by Michael Stewart, music by Charles Strouse and lyrics by Lee Adams. Scenery by Robert Randolph, lighting by Peggy Clark, costumes by Miles White, orchestrations by Robert Ginzler, dance arrangements by John Morris, musical direction by Elliot Lawrence, choreography and staging by Gower Champion. Produced by Edward Padula, in association with L. Slade Brown, at the Martin Beck Theatre.

The cast

Albert Peterson	Dick Van Dyke
Rose Grant	Chita Rivera
Teen-Agers:	
Helen	Karin Wolfe
Nancy	Marissa Mason
Alice	Sharon Lerit
Margie Ann	Louise Quick
Penelope Ann	Lada Edmund
Deborah Sue	Jessica Albright
Suzie	Lynn Bowin
Linda	Judy Keirn
Carol	Penny Ann Green
Martha Louise	Vicki Belmonte
Harold	Michael Vita
Karl	Jerry Dodge
Harvey	Dean Stolber
Henry	Ed Kresley
Arthur	Bob Spencer
Freddie	Tracy Everitt
Peyton	Gary Howe
Ursula Merkle	Barbara Doherty
Kim MacAfee	Susan Watson
Mrs. MacAfee	Marijane Maricle
Mr. MacAfee	Paul Lynde
Teen Trio	Louise Quick, Jessica Albright, Vicki Belmonte
Sad Girl	Sharon Lerit
Another Sad Girl	Karin Wolfe
Mae Peterson	Kay Medford
Reporters	Lee Howard, Jim Sisco, Don Farnworth, John Coyle
Conrad Birdie	Dick Gautier
Guitar Man	Kenny Burrell

```
Conductor ....................................... Kasimir Kokich
Cheerleaders ............................... Judy Keirn, Lynn Bowin
Mayor ............................................. Allen Knowles
Mayor's Wife ....................................... Amelia Haas
Hugo Peabody ................................... Michael J. Pollard
Randolph MacAfee ................................. Johnny Borden
Mrs. Merkle ........................................ Pat McEnnis
Old Woman ........................................... Dori Davis
Neighbors .............. Amelia Haas, Jeannine Masterson, Ed Becker,
                        Oran Osburn, George Blackwell, Lee Howard
Mr. Henkel .................................. Charles Nelson Reilly
Gloria Rasputin ................................. Norma Richardson
Ed. Sullivan's Voice .................................. Will Jordan
TV Stage Manager ................................. Tony Mordente
Charles F. Maude ................................ George Blackwell
SHRINERS ................... Allen Knowles, John Coyle, Dick Crowley,
                Don Farnworth, Bud Fleming, Kasimir Kokich, Jim Sisco
```

UNDERSTUDIES: Patti Karr, Charles N. Reilly, Tony Mordente, Pat McEnnis, Lee Howard, Dean Stobler, Vicki Belmonte, Don Farnworth, Bob Spencer, Ed Becker, Jessica Albright, Jeannine Masterson, Amelia Haas, Lee Howard, Ed Kresley, Bud Fleming, Lynn Bowin, Penny Ann Green.

Musical synopsis of scenes

ACT I

Prologue
Scene 1. Office of Almaelou Music, New York.
    "An English Teacher" .... Rose with Albert
Scene 2. Sweet Apple, Ohio.
    "The Telephone Hour" .... Sweet Apple Kids
Scene 3. MacAfee Home, Sweet Apple.
    "How Lovely To Be A Woman" .... Kim
Scene 4. Pennsylvania Station, New York.
    "We Love You, Conrad!" .... Teen Trio
    "Put On A Happy Face" .... Albert and Two Sad Girls
    "Normal American Boy" .... Rose, Albert and Chorus
Scene 5. Railroad Station, Sweet Apple.
    "One Boy" .... Kim, Deborah Sue and Alice
    Reprise: "One Boy" .... Rose
Scene 6. Courthouse Steps, Sweet Apple.
    "Honestly Sincere" .... Conrad and Townspeople
Scene 7. MacAfee Home, Sweet Apple.
    "Hymn For A Sunday Evening" ...... Mr. MacAfee, Mrs.
                        MacAfee, Kim, Randolph and Neighbors
Scene 8. Stage, Central Movie Theatre, Sweet Apple.
Scene 9. Backstage Office, Central Movie Theatre, Sweet Apple.
    Ballet: "How To Kill A Man" .. Rose, Albert and Company
Scene 10. Stage, Central Movie Theatre, Sweet Apple.
    "One Last Kiss" .... Conrad and Company

ACT II

Prologue The World At Large
Scene 1. MacAfee Home, Sweet Apple.
"What Did I Ever See In Him?" .... Rose with Kim
Scene 2. Street Outside MacAfee Home.
"A Lot of Livin' To Do" ...... Conrad, Kim and Teen-agers
Scene 3. MacAfee's Back Door.
"Kids" .... Mr. MacAfee and Mrs. MacAfee
Scene 4. Maude's Roadside Retreat.
"Baby, Talk To Me" .... Albert and Quartet
Scene 5. Private Dining Room, Maude's Roadside Retreat.
"Shriners' Ballet" .... Rose and Shriners
Scene 6. Back Door, Maude's Roadside Retreat.
Reprise: "Kids" .. Mr. MacAfee, Mrs. MacAfee, Randolph
and Townspeople
Scene 7. The Ice House
"Spanish Rose" .... Rose
Scene 8. Railroad Station, Sweet Apple.
"Rosie" .... Albert and Rose

One of Broadway's Best. See page 73.

DUEL OF ANGELS

Opened April 19, 1960; closed June 1, 1960; 51 performances.

Play by Jean Giraudoux, translated and adapted by Christopher Fry. Settings by Roger Furse, lighting by Paul Morrison, women's costumes by Christian Dior, staged by Robert Helpmann. Produced by Roger L. Stevens and S. Hurok at the Helen Hayes Theatre.

The cast

Joseph	James Valentine
Count Marcellus	Peter Wyngarde
Gilly	Aina Niemela
Paola	Vivien Leigh
Armand	John Merivale
Lucile	Mary Ure
Eugénie	Ludi Claire
Mace-Bearer	Felix Deebank
Barbette	Margaret Braidwood
Servant	Ken Edward Ruta
Mr. Justice Blanchard	Alan MacNaughtan
Clerk of the Court	Donald Moffat
Servant	Theodore Tenley
Customers at the Café	Key Meersman, Byron Mitchell, Donald Moffat, Virginia Robinson, Ken Edward Ruta, Alicia Townsend

One of Broadway's Best. See page 82.

FROM A TO Z

Opened April 20, 1960; closed May 7, 1960; 21 performances.

Revue. Sets, lighting and costumes by Fred Voelpel, choreography by Ray Harrison, orchestrations by Jay Brower and Jonathan Tunick, vocal arrangements by Milton Greene, dance arrangements by Jack Holmes, musical direction by Milton Greene, staged by Christopher Hewett. Produced by Carroll and Harris Masterson at The Plymouth Theatre.

The cast

Hermione Gingold
Elliott Reid
Alvni Epstein
Louise Hoff
Nora Kovach
Kelly Brown
Paula Stewart
Stuart Damon
Bob Dishy
Isabelle Farrell
Michael Fesco
Larry Hovis
Doug Spingler
Beryl Towbin
Virginia Vestoff

Program

ACT I

Best Gold .... Hermione Gingold,
Nora Kovach, Kelly Brown, Michael Fesco, Doug Spingler,
Beryl Towbin, Virginia Vestoff, Stuart Damon, Paula Stewart
Music and Words by Jerry Herman

Bardolatry .... Louise Hoff, Elliott Reid
Pill Parade
   Narrator .... Alvin Epstein
   Average Man .... Kelly Brown
Vitamins .... Michael Fresco, Doug Spingler
   Benzabang .... Beryl Towbin
   Pilltown .... Virginia Vestoff
   Sexaphine .... Nora Kovach

One More Pill .... Isabelle Farrell
Music and Words by Jay Thompson
Togetherness
Grandmother .... Hermione Gingold
Father .... Elliott Reid
Mother .... Louise Hoff
Daughter .... Paula Stewart
Son .... Stuart Damon
Music and Words by Dickson Hughes and Everett Sloane
Psychological Warfare
Sergeant .... Alvin Epstein
Privates .... Larry Hovis, Doug Spingler
Enemy .... Bob Dishy
Medics .... Stuart Damon, Michael Fesco
By Woody Allen
Balloons
Nora Kovach, Kelly Brown, Michael Fesco, Doug Spingler, Beryl
Towbin, Virginia Vestoff
Music and Words by Jack Holmes
Music Talk .... Hermione Gingold
Hire A Guy
The Star .... Louise Hoff
The Director .... Elliot Reid
The Writer .... Stuart Damon
Patsy .... Bob Dishy
Music by Mary Rodgers, Words by Marshall Barer
Interlude
Ladies .... Beryl Towbin, Virginia Vestoff, Isabelle Farrell
Gentlemen .... Kelly Brown, Michael Fesco, Doug Spingler
A Stranger .... Nora Kovach
A Man .... Stuart Damon
Music by Jack Holmes
Hit Parade
Girl .... Hermione Gingold
Boy .... Alvin Epstein
By Woody Allen
Conventional Behavior .... Elliott Reid
I Said To Love .... Louise Hoff
Music by Paul Klein, Words by Fred Ebb
Winter in Palm Springs
Colonel Spicer .... Alvin Epstein
Mrs. Twiceover .... Hermione Gingold
Alice .... Beryl Towbin
By Herbert Farjeon
Charlie .... Paula Stewart
Words and Music by Fred Ebb and Norman Martin
The Sound of Schmaltz

The cast

Head Nanny .... Louise Hoff
Nannies .... Nora Kovach, Beryl Towbin, Virginia Vestoff,
Isabelle Farrell
Alicia Cadwallader-Smith .... Hermione Gingold
Baron von Klaptrap .... Elliot Reid

Children .... Kelly Brown, Alvin Epstein, Michael Fesco,
Doug Spingler, Stuart Damon, Bob Dishy, Paula Stewart

Synopsis of scenes

    1. The Offices of "International Nannies, Ltd."
       (with an interlude in Central park)
    2. The von Klaptrap Nursery
    3. Baron von Klaptrap's Apartment
    4. The von Klaptrap Living Room
      Words by Don Parks, Music by William Dyer

Intermission

ACT II

Grand Jury Jump
    Nora Kovach, Paula Stewart, Beryl Towbin, Virginia Vestoff, Isabelle
    Farrell, Kelly Brown, Stuart Damon, Michael Fesco, Doug Spingler,
    Larry Hovis
        Music by Paul Klein, Words by Fred Ebb
South American Way .... Alvin Epstein, Bob Dishy
    Music by Norman Martin, Words by Norman Martin and Fred Ebb
Snapshots
    She .... Hermione Gingold
    He .... Elliott Reid
              By Herbert Farjeon
Time Step .... Kelly Brown
        Music by Paul Klein, Words by Fred Ebb
Bobo .... Elliott Reid
Queen of Song .... Hermione Gingold
Surprise Party
    Fred .... Bob Dishy
    Harry .... Kelly Brown
    Myrna .... Louise Hoff
    Linda .... Beryl Towbin
    Ruthie .... Nora Kovach
    Rita .... Isabelle Farrell
    Virginia .... Virginia Vestoff
    Blonde .... Paula Stewart
             By Woody Allen
On the Beach .... Alvin Epstein
    Devised by Mark Epstein and Christopher Hewett
Park Meeting
    Governess .... Hermione Gingold
    Woman .... Louise Hoff
           By Nina Warner Hook
Red Shoes
    Introduced by .... Bob Dishy
    Danced by .... Kelly Brown, Isabelle Farrell, Michael Fesco, Larry
          Hovis, Doug Spingler, Beryl Towbin, Virginia Vestoff
            Music by Jack Holmes
Four for the Road .... Hermione Gingold
    Music by Paul Klein, Lyrics by Lee Goldsmith and Fred Ebb
What Next? .... The Company
    Music by Charles Zwar, Words by Alan Melville

THE ENTERTAINMENT

It was a good idea to make a revue with a song or sketch for every letter of the alphabet, but *From A to Z* barely got from A to B as entertainment. Hermione Gingold's grotesqueries were not varied enough for a whole evening, and all the authors turned up mediocre stuff. There was an excellent pantomime sketch by Alvin Epstein in which, in violation of ordinances on public beaches, he undressed on a beach under cover of a raincoat.

WEST SIDE STORY

Opened April 27, 1960; still running; 39 performances.

Revival of musical, based on a conception of Jerome Robbins, with book by Arthur Laurents, lyrics by Stephen Sondheim and music by Leonard Bernstein. Settings by Oliver Smith, lighting by Jean Rosenthal, costumes by Irene Sharaff, choreography by Jerome Robbins and Peter Gennaro, Howard Jeffrey assistant dance director, orchestrations by Leonard Bernstein with Sid Ramin and Irwin Kostal, musical direction by Joseph Lewis, staged by Jerome Robbins. Produced by Robert E. Griffith and Harold S. Prince, by arrangement with Roger L. Stevens, Sylvia Drulie associate at the Winter Garden.

The cast

THE JETS

Riff, The Leader	Thomas Hasson
Tony, His Friend	Larry Kert
Action	George Liker
A-Rab	Alan Johnson
Baby John	Barry Burns
Big Deal	Martin Charnin
Diesel	Donald Corby
Snowboy	Eddie Gasper
Mouth Piece	Eddie Miller
Tiger	Richard Corrigan
Gee-Tar	Glenn Gibson
Their Girls	
Graziella	Sandy Leeds
Velma	Audrey Hays
Clarice	Lee Lewis
Pauline	Judy Aldene
Anybodys	Pat Birch
Minnie	Barbara Monte

THE SHARKS

Bernardo, The Leader	George Marcy
Maria, His Sister	Carol Lawrence
Anita, His Girl	Allyn Ann McLerie
Chino, His Friend	Miguel De Vega
Pepe	Ben Vargas
Indio	Robert Avian
Luis	Sterling Clark

Estella .... Danii Prior
Burro .... Vince Baggetta
Nibbles .... Ed Dutton
Toro .... Kent Thomas
Moose .... Marc Scott
Their Girls
   Rosalia .... Gloria Lambert
   Teresita .... Hope Clarke
   Francisca .... Anna Marie Moylan
   Marguerita .... Poligena Rogers
   Consuelo .... Genii Prior

THE ADULTS

Doc .... Albert M. Ottenheimer
Schrank .... Ted Gunther
Krupke .... Roger Franklin
Gladhand .... Ross Hertz

UNDERSTUDIES: Robert Kole, Jan Canada, Genii Prior, Glenn Gibson, Barry Burns, Sterling Clark, Vince Baggetta, Sandy Leeds, Ben Vargas, Marc Scott, Ross Hertz, Larry Pool, Eddie Miller, Judy Aldene

THE PLAY:

In its return engagement, *West Side Story* seemed more vibrant than ever, and Leonard Bernstein's score seemed to have taken on added depth, vigor, and individuality.

Synopsis of scenes

The action takes place on the West Side of New York City during the last days of summer.

ACT I

Prolouge: The Months Before

5:00 P.M. .... The Street
5:30 P.M. .... A Back Yard
6:00 P.M. .... The Bridal Shop
10:00 P.M. .... The Gym
11:00 P.M. .... A Back Alley
Midnight .... The Drugstore

The Next Day

5:30 P.M. .... The Bridal Shop
6:00 to 9:00 P.M. .... The Neighborhood
9:00 P.M. .... Under The Highway

ACT II

9:15 P.M. .... The Bedroom
10:00 P.M. .... Another Alley

11:30 P.M. .... The Bedroom
11:40 P.M. .... The Drugstore
11:50 P.M. .... The Cellar
Midnight .... The Street

Musical numbers

ACT I

Prologue .... Danced by Jets and Sharks
Jet Song .... Riff, Baby John, Snowboy and Jets
"Something's Coming" .... Tony
The Dance At The Gym .... Jets and Sharks
"Maria" .... Tony
"Tonight" .... Tony and Maria
"America" .... Anita, Rosalia, and Shark Girls
"Cool" .... Riff and the Jets
"One Hand, One Heart" .... Tony and Maria
"Tonight" (Quintet and Chorus) .... Company
The Rumble .... Danced by Riff, Bernardo, Jets and Sharks

ACT II

"I Feel Pretty" .... Maria, Rosalia, Estella, Marguerita
"Somewhere" .... Danced by Company; Sung by Jan Canada
"Gee, Officer Krupke" .... Big Deal, Gee-Tar and Jets
"A Boy Like That" .... Anita and Maria
"I Have A Love" .... Anita and Maria
Taunting .... Anita and the Jets
Finale .... Company

FINIAN'S RAINBOW

Opened April 27, 1960; closed May 8, 1960; 16 performances.

Revival of musical with book by E. Y. Harburg and Fred Saidy, lyrics by E. Y. Harburg and music by Burton Lane. Scenery and lighting by Tom McElhany, costumes by Stanley Simmons, choreography by Herbert Ross and Peter Conlow, orchestrations by Robert Russell Bennett and Don Walker, musical direction by Max Meth, staged by Herbert Ross. Produced by the New York City Center Light Opera Company at the New York City Center.

The cast

Buzz Collins	Eddie Bruce
Sheriff	Tom McElhany
1st Sharecropper	John McCurry
2nd Sharecropper	Knute Sullivan
Susan Mahoney	Anita Alvarez
Henry	Michael Darden
Maude	Carol Brice
Finian McLonergan	Bobby Howes
Sharon McLonergan	Jeannie Carson
Sam	Arthur Garrison
Woody Mahoney	Biff McGuire

Synopsis of scenes

ACT I

Scene 1. The Meetin' Place, Rainbow Valley, Missitucky.
Scene 2. The same. That Night.
Scene 3. The Colonial Estate of Senator Billboard Rawkins.
                    The Next Morning.
Scene 4. The Meetin' Place. Following Day.
Scene 5. A Path in the Woods.
Scene 6. The Meetin' Place. Next morning.

ACT II

Scene 1. Rainbow Valley. A Few Weeks Later.
Scene 2. A Wooded Section of the Hills.
Scene 3. The Meetin' Place.
Scene 4. Just Before Dawn.

Musical numbers

ACT I

1. "This Time of the Year" .... Singing Ensemble
   Dance .... Anita Alvarez and Dance Ensemble
2. "How Are Things in Glocca Morra?" .... Jeannie Carson
3. "Look to the Rainbow" .... Jeannie Carson, Biff McGuire and
   Singing Ensemble
4. "Old Devil Moon" .... Biff McGuire and Jeannie Carson
5. Reprise: "How Are Things in Glocca Morra" .... Jeannie Carson
6. "Something Sort of Grandish" .. Howard Morris and Jeannie Carson
7. "If This Isn't Love" .... Biff McGuire, Jeannie Carson, Bobby
   Howes, Singing and Dancing Ensemble
   Dance .... Anita Alvarez
   Three Couples .... Ellen Halpin, Jaime Juan Rogers,
   Nat Horne, Myrna White, Wakefield Poole, Sandra Roveta
   The Adolescents .... Diane McDaniel, Ron Schwinn
   The Timids .... Mavis Ray, Loren Hightower
   The Inquisitives .... Marilynn Allwyn, Gene Gavin
   The Intense Pair .... Sally Lee, Paul Olson
   Triangle ...... Carmen Morales, Julius C. Fields, Jacqueline Walcott
   Others .... Ronald Lee, Jerry Fries
8. Reprise: "Something Sort of Grandish" .... Howard Morris
9. "Necessity" .... Carol Brice, Singing Ensemble
10. "Great Come-and-Get-It Day" ...... Biff McGuire, Jeannie Carson,
    Dancing, Singing Ensemble

ACT II

1. "When the Idle Poor Become the Idle Rich"
   A. Dance .... Anita Alvarez and Dance Ensemble
   B. Song .... Jeannie Carson and Singing Ensemble
2. Reprise: "Old Devil Moon" .... Jeannie Carson and Biff McGuire
3. Dance of the Golden Crock .... Anita Alvarez
   (Original Choreography by Michael Kidd)
4. "The Begat" .... Sorrell Booke, Jerry Laws, Tiger Haynes,
   Bill Glover
5. Reprise: "Look to the Rainbow" .... Jeannie Carson, Biff McGuire,
   Singing Ensemble
6. "When I'm not Near the Girl I Love" .... Howard Morris,
   Anita Alvarez
7. Reprise: "If This Isn't Love" .... Entire Ensemble
8. Finale. Reprise: "How Are Things in Glocca Morra?" .... Jeannie
   Carson and Entire Company

Og (A Leprechaun) .... Howard Morris
Senator Billboard Rawkins .... Sorrell Booke
1st Geologist .... Barney Johnston
2nd Geologist .... Robert Guillaume
Howard .... Jim McMillan
Diane .... Patty Austin
Mr. Robust .... Edgar Daniels
Mr. Shears .... Joe Ross
1st Passion Pilgrim Gospeleer .... Jerry Laws

2nd Passion Pilgrim Gospeleer .... Bill Glover
3rd Passion Pilgrim Gospeleer .... Tiger Haynes
1st Deputy .... Don Gray
2nd Deputy .... Larry Mitchell

SINGERS

GIRLS: Issa Arnal, Nan Courtney, Marnell Higley, Mary Louise, Lispet Nelson, Stephanie Reynolds, Alice Elizabeth Webb, Beverly Jane Welch

BOYS: John Boni, Hugh Dilworth, Bill Glover, Don Gray, Robert Guillaume, Tiger Haynes, Barney Johnston, Jerry Laws, John McCurry, Larry Mitchell, Knute Sullivan

DANCERS

GIRLS: Marilynn Allwyn, Ellen Halpin, Sally Lee, Diane McDaniel, Carmen Morales, Mavis Ray, Sandra Roveta, Jacqueline Walcott, Myrna White

BOYS: Julius C. Fields, Jerry Fries, Gene Gavin, Loren Hightower, Nat Horne, Ronald Lee, Paul Olsen, Wakefield Poole, Jaime Juan Rogers, Ron Schwinn

UNDERSTUDIES: Mavis Ray, Knute Sullivan, Robert Guillaume, John McCurry, Nan Courtney, Larry Mitchell

THE PLAY:

Things whimsical being longer-lived than things topical, this revival stood up most charmingly—so well, indeed, that the production was moved to a Broadway theatre (Forty-sixth Street Theatre) for a regular run that lasted till the actors' strike. There were such melodic and lyric highlights as Jeannie Carson singing "How Are Things in Glocca Morra?"; Biff McGuire and Miss Carson singing "Old Devil Moon" and Howard Morris singing "Something Sort of Grandish" and "When I'm not Near the Girl I Love." The latter songs were the ones which made a star of David Wayne.

CHRISTINE

Opened April 28, 1960; closed May 7, 1960; 12 performances.

Musical with book by Pearl S. Buck and Charles K. Peck, Jr., adapted from *My Indian Family* by Hilda Wernher, lyrics by Paul Francis Webster and music by Sammy Fain. Settings and lighting by Jo Mielziner, costumes by Alvin Colt, choreography and musical numbers by Hanya Holm, vocal and dance arrangements by Trude Rittman, orchestrations by Phil Lang, musical direction by Jay Blackton, associate conductor Sam Farber, staged by Jerome Chodorov and Cy Feuer. Produced by Oscar S. Lerman and Martin B. Cohen in association with Walter Cohen, Ben Frye associate producer, at the Forty-sixth Street Theatre.

The cast

Beggar	Joseph Crawford
Servants to Dr. Singh	Arthur Tookoyan / Tony Gardell / John Anania
Auntie	Nancy Andrews
Uncle	Phil Leeds
Rainath	Bhaskar
Jaya	Leslye Hunter
Rajendra	Augie Rios
Krishna	Steve Curry
Mohan Roy	Jonathan Morris
Servant to Mohan Roy	Nicholas Bianchi
Station Master	Louis Polacek
Sita Roy	Janet Pavek
Lady Christine FitzSimons	Maureen O'Hara
Dr. Rashil Singh	Morley Meredith
Dr. MacGowan	Daniel Keyes
The Matchmaker	Barbara Webb
The Prospective Brides: Tara	Mai-Lan
Lakshmi	Jinja
Amora	Laurie Archer
The Twins	Anjali Devi, Sasha
Children of the Town	Donna Lyn / Jan Rhodes / Luis Hernandez

The Priest .... John Anania
Townspeople, Hindus, Muslims, Vendors, Beggars

DANCERS: Laurie Archer, Sandra Bowman, Anjali Devi, Jinja, Mai-Lan, Jonalee Sanford, Sasha, Vito Durante, Dino Laudicino, Joseph Nelson, Alan Peterson, Joe Rocco, Gil Schwartz

SINGERS: Bea Barrett, Diana Corto, Marceline Decker, Josephine Lang, Jen Nelson, Barbara Webb, John Anania, Nicholas Bianchi, Joseph Crawford, Tony Gardell, Louis Polacek, Arthur Tookoyan

UNDERSTUDIES: Jen Nelson, Arthur Tookoyan, Bea Barrett, John Anania, Nicholas Bianchi, Diana Corto, Joe Rocco, Luis Hernandez, Donna Lyn

THE PLAY:

Set in India, this was one of the most beautiful productions of the season. But its story, of an Irish woman who falls in love with an Indian doctor, in spite of differences of creed, custom and color, was not a holding romance. The film actress, Maureen O'Hara, did have the opportunity to show that she is really splendid as a "live" music-show star; she had beauty, charm, and a good voice.

Synopsis of scenes

The story is laid in the little town of Akbarabad, India, at the present time.

ACT I

Scene 1. The railroad station in Akbarabad.
Scene 2. The Study in Dr. Rashil Singh's home.
Scene 3. Outside the Clinic.
Scene 4. The Living Room, six days later.
Scene 5. The Veranda, two months later.
Scene 6. The Living Room.
Scene 7. The Veranda.
Scene 8. The Drawing Room.
Scene 9. The Clinic.
Scene 10. The City Square.

ACT II

Scene 1. The Veranda at Rashil's house.
Scene 2. An open plain.
Scene 3. A Shrine.
Scene 4. The Living Room.
Scene 5. The Veranda.
Scene 6. The Drawing Room.
Scene 7. The Veranda.
Scene 8. Mohan Roy's Home.

Musical numbers

ACT I

1. "Welcome Song" ...... Auntie, Uncle, Rainath, Children, Chorus
2. "My Indian Family" .... Christine
3. "A Doctor's Soliloquy" .... Rashil
4. "UNICEF" Song .... The Children
5. "My Little Lost Girl" .... Christine and Rashil
6. "I'm Just a Little Sparrow" .... Jaya, Auntie, Rainath, Servants and Children
7. "We're Just a Pair of Sparrows" .... Christine and Jaya
8. Cobra Ritual Dance .... Rainath and Dancers
9. "How to Pick a Man a Wife" .... Auntie, Uncle
10. "The Lovely Girls of Akbarabad" .... The Matchmaker and Chorus
11. "Room in My Heart" .... Christine
12. "The Divali Festival" .... Rainath, Dancers and Singers
13. "I Never Meant to Fall in Love" .... Rashil and Christine

ACT II

1. "Freedom Can Be a Most Uncomfortable Thing" ...... Auntie and Friends
2. "Ireland Was Never Like This" .... Christine and Dancers
3. "He Loves Her" .... Sita
4. "Christine" .... Rashil
5. "Room in My Heart" .... Christine
6. "Freedom Can Be a Most Uncomfortable Thing" .... Auntie and Uncle
7. a. Kathak (Plate Dance) .... Rainath and Girls
   b. Kathakali .... Dancing Boys
   c. Bharatha Natyan .... Rainath, Dancing Girls and Dancing Boys
8. "The Woman I Was Before" .... Christine
9. "A Doctor's Soliloquy" .... Christine and Rashil
10. "I Never Meant to Fall in Love" .... Christine and Rashil

BOOKS ABOUT THE THEATRE
PUBLISHED DURING THE SEASON

A COMPANION TO SHAKESPEARE STUDIES, edited by H. Granville-Barker and G. B. Harrison. Reissue of fifteen essays. Doubleday Anchor Book, $1.45.

A LIFE IN THE THEATRE, by Tyrone Guthrie. Professional autobiography of the stage director. McGraw-Hill Book Company, 357 pages, $5.95.

A LOSS OF ROSES, by William Inge. Text of the Broadway production. Random House, $2.95.

A MAJORITY OF ONE, by Leonard Spigelgass. Text of the Broadway production. Illustrated. Random House, 142 pages, $2.95.

A PHOENIX TOO FREQUENT, by Christopher Fry. New edition of the comedy in verse. Illustrated by Ronald Searle. Oxford University Press, $3.50.

A QUITE REMARKABLE FATHER, by Leslie Ruth Howard. Biography of Leslie Howard by his daughter. Harcourt, Brace and Company, 307 pages, $4.75.

A RAISIN IN THE SUN, by Lorraine Hansberry. Text of the Broadway production. Illustrated. Random House, 142 pages, $2.95.

A TASTE OF HONEY, by Shelagh Delaney. Text of the London production. Grove Press, 87 pages, $3.50.

A THEATRE IN YOUR HEAD, by Kenneth Thorpe Rowe. Analyzing a play and visualizing its production. Funk & Wagnalls, 434 pages, $6.95.

ACT ONE, by Moss Hart. Autobiography. Random House, 444 pages, $5.

ALL THE KING'S MEN, by Robert Penn Warren. Text of the play. Random House, $2.95.

ARTISTS' THEATRE, edited by Herbert Machiz. Four plays: TRY! TRY! by Frank O'Hara, THE HEROES by John Ashbery, THE BAIT by James Merrill, ABSALOM by Lionel Abel. Grove Press, $1.95.

BLUE DENIM, by James Leo Herlihy and William Noble. Text of the Broadway production. Bantam Books, 35 cents.

BRECHT: THE MAN AND HIS WORK, by Martin Esslin. Biographical study of the playwright. Doubleday, $4.50.

BROADWAY'S BEST 1959, edited by John Chapman. Critical and statistical survey of the 1958–59 theatrical season in New York with extended examination of twelve productions. Doubleday, 332 pages, $4.50.

BUT HE DOESN'T KNOW THE TERRITORY, by Meredith Willson. His experiences in writing *The Music Man*. G. P. Putnam's Sons, 190 pages, $3.50.

CHEKHOV PLAYS, translated by Elisaveta Fen. IVANOV, THE CHERRY ORCHARD, THE SEAGULL, UNCLE VANYA, THE THREE SISTERS, THE BEAR, THE PROPOSAL and A JUBILEE. Penguin Books, 453 pages, $1.25.

COMMUNITY THEATRE: IDEA AND ACHIEVEMENT, by Robert E. Gard and Gertrude S. Burley. Duell, Sloan & Pearce, 182 pages, $3.75.

COSTUMING FOR THE THEATRE, by Joseph D. Paterek. Details in costuming a stage production. Crown, $3.50.

DANIEL BLUM'S THEATRE WORLD: SEASON 1958–1959. Pictorial and statistical record. Chilton Company, 256 pages, $6.

DEAR AUDIENCE, by Blanche Yurka. A guide to the enjoyment of the theater. Illustrated by Rafaello Busoni. Prentice-Hall, $3.

DRAMA FOR WOMEN, by Alison Graham-Campbell and Frank Lambe with a foreword by Flora Robson. A discussion of problems of women engaged in producing amateur theatricals. G. Bell & Sons, Ltd., distributed by Sportshelf, 160 pages, $3.75.

DUEL OF ANGELS, by Jean Giraudoux, translated by Christopher Fry. English translation of Giraudoux's last play POUR LUCRECE. Oxford University Press, 66 pages, $3.

ED WYNN'S SON, by Keenan Wynn as told to James Brough. Illustrated. Doubleday, 236 pages, $3.95.

EDWIN FORREST: FIRST STAR OF THE AMERICAN STAGE, by Richard Moody. Illustrated. Alfred A. Knopf, 416 pages, $6.95.

ENGLISH DRAMA FROM EARLY TIMES TO THE ELIZABETHANS: ITS BACKGROUND, ORIGINS AND DEVELOPMENTS, by A. P. Rossiter. Barnes & Noble, 176 pages, $4.50.

EVERYMAN AND MEDIEVAL MIRACLE PLAYS, edited by A. C. Cawley. Fifteen plays. Dutton, 266 pages, $1.35.

EXPERIMENT THEATRE, edited by Carol Ely Harper. One-minute plays for intimate production. Allan Swallow, $2.50.

FAMOUS AMERICAN PLAYS OF THE NINETEEN FORTIES, selected and introduced by Henry Hewes. Dell-Laurel, 75 cents.

FAMOUS AMERICAN PLAYS OF THE 1930s, selected and introduced by Harold Clurman. Dell, 75 cents.

FAMOUS AMERICAN PLAYS OF THE 1920S, selected and introduced by Kenneth Macgowan. THE MOON OF THE CARIBBEES by Eugene O'Neill, WHAT PRICE GLORY? by Maxwell Anderson and Laurence Stallings, THEY KNEW WHAT THEY WANTED by Sidney Howard, PORGY by DuBose and Dorothy Heyward, STREET SCENE by Elmer Rice and HOLIDAY by Philip Barry. Dell-Laurel, 75 cents.

FARQUHAR, edited with an introduction by William Archer. The plays are: THE RECRUITING OFFICER, THE BEAUX' STRATAGEM, THE CONSTANT COUPLE and THE TWIN-RIVALS. Hill and Wang, 455 pages, $1.75.

FIORELLO!, book by Jerome Weidman and George Abbott, lyrics by Sheldon Harnick, music by Jerry Bock. Text of the Pulitzer Prize winning Broadway musical. Illustrated. Random House, 147 pages, $2.95.

FIVE FINGER EXERCISE, by Peter Shaffer. Text of the Broadway production. Harcourt, Brace and Co., 110 pages, $3.

FLOWER DRUM SONG, by Richard Rodgers, Oscar Hammerstein 2nd and Joseph Fields. Text of the Broadway musical based on a novel by C. Y. Lee. Farrar, Straus & Cudahy, 141 pages, $3.50.

FROM SHAKESPEARE TO EXISTENTIALISM: STUDIES IN POETRY, RELIGION AND PHILOSOPHY, by Walter Kaufmann. Beacon Press, 404 pages, $5.95.

GOETHE: FAUST PART II, newly translated with an introduction by Philip Wayne. Penguin Books, 95 cents.

GOETHE'S MAJOR PLAYS, by Ronald Peacock. An essay. Hill and Wang, 236 pages, $3.95.

GOLDEN ACES OF THE THEATER, by Kenneth Macgowan and William Melnitz. Spectrum Book, Prentice-Hall, $1.95.

GOODNESS HAD NOTHING TO DO WITH IT, by Mae West. Autobiography. Illustrated. Prentice-Hall, 271 pages, $3.95.

GREAT LADY OF THE THEATRE: SARAH BERNHARDT, by Iris Noble. Biography written for young people. Julian Messner, 192 pages, $2.95.

GROUCHO AND ME, by Groucho Marx. Memoir. Bernard Geis Associates, distributed by Random House, 344 pages, $3.95.

GYPSY, a musical, book by Arthur Laurents, music by Jule Styne and lyrics by Stephen Sondheim. Text of the Broadway production. Random House, 144 pages, $2.95.

HELOISE, by James Forsyth. Text of the drama. Theatre Arts Books, $1.50.

HERE LIES THE HEART, by Mercedes de Acosta. Autobiography of the poet and playwright. Reynal, $5.75.

HOW NOT TO WRITE A PLAY, by Walter Kerr. New edition of a discussion of contemporary playwriting. Simon and Schuster, 244 pages, $1.45.

HOW TO ACT, by Robert Graham Paris. Harper & Bros., 178 pages, $3.50.

IBSEN AND THE TEMPER OF NORWEGIAN LITERATURE, by James Walter McFarlane. Oxford University Press, 208 pages, $3.40.

INGRID BERGMAN: AN INTIMATE PORTRAIT, by Joseph Henry Steele. David McKay Company, 365 pages, $3.95.

INTERNATIONAL THEATRE ANNUAL, NO. 4, edited by Harold Hobson. Illustrated survey. Grove Press, 288 pages, $5 cloth, $2.45 paper.

JEAN GIRAUDOUX: HIS LIFE AND WORKS, by Laurent LeSage. Pennsylvania State University Press, 238 pages, $5.

JEAN RACINE: FIVE PLAYS, translated into English verse, with an introduction by Kenneth Muir. Mermaid Dramabook, Hill and Wang, $1.95.

KRAPP'S LAST TAPE, by Samuel Beckett. Also ALL THAT FALL, EMBERS, ACT WITHOUT WORDS I and ACT WITHOUT WORDS II by the same author. Grove Press, 141 pages, $1.95.

LETTERS OF STRINDBERG TO HARRIET BOSSE, edited and translated by Arvid Paulson. Strindberg's letters to his third and last wife. Illustrated. Thomas Nelson & Sons, 194 pages, $5.

LOOK BACK IN ANGER, by John Osborne. Text of the London and Broadway productions. Bantam Books, 35 cents.

LUIGI PIRANDELLO: THE RULES OF THE GAME, THE LIFE I GAVE YOU, LAZARUS, edited and introduced by E. Martin Browne. Penguin Books, 95 cents.

LYRICS ON SEVERAL OCCASIONS, by Ira Gershwin. Lyrics for stage and screen with the author's notes. Alfred A. Knopf, 362 pages, $5.

MAN AND SUPERMAN, by Bernard Shaw. Introduction by Brooks Atkinson. Bantam Books, 50 cents.

MARK TWAIN TONIGHT!, by Hal Holbrook. Prologue and selections from Mark Twain adapted and arranged for the Broadway re-creation of Mark Twain on the lecture platform. Illustrated. Ives Washburn, 272 pages, $4.50.

MEMOIRS OF A PROFESSIONAL CAD, by George Sanders. Autobiography. Illustrated. G. P. Putnam's Sons, 192 pages, $3.50.

MIRACLE PLAYS: SEVEN MEDIEVAL PLAYS FOR MODERN PLAYERS, adapted by Anne Malcolmson. For ages 10 to 14. Illustrated by Pauline Baynes. Houghton Mifflin Co., 142 pages, $3.

MIXED COMPANY, by Clay Franklin. Twenty-five monologues for men and women. Samuel French, 98 pages, $1.50.

MODERN GERMAN DRAMA, by H. F. Garten. A study. Essential Books, $6.

MOLIÈRE: THE COMIC MASK, by D. B. Wyndham Lewis. A biography. Coward-McCann, $4.

MOLIÈRE: THE MAN SEEN THROUGH HIS PLAYS, by Ramon Fernandez, translated from the French by Wilson Follett. Hill and Wang, 205 pages, $1.25.

MOOT PLAYS OF CORNEILLE, translated by Lacy Lockert. The Vanderbilt University Press, 486 pages, $6.50.

MY WICKED, WICKED WAYS, by Errol Flynn. G. P. Putnam's Sons, 438 pages, $4.95.

MY WONDERFUL WORD OF SLAPSTICK, by Buster Keaton with Charles Samuels. Autobiography. Illustrated. Doubleday, 282 pages, $4.50.

NAPOLEON AND MADEMOISELLE GEORGE, by Edith Saunders. Story of Napoleon's love affair with the Comedie Française actress. Illustrated. E. P. Dutton & Co., 248 pages, $4.50.

NEO-CLASSIC DRAMA IN SPAIN: THEORY AND PRACTICE, by John A. Cook. Southern Methodist University Press, 576 pages, $8.50.

NEW ENGLISH DRAMATISTS, edited by E. Martin Browne. EACH HIS OWN WILDERNESS by Doris Lessing, THE HAMLET OF STEPNEY GREEN by Bernard Kops and CHICKEN SOUP WITH BARLEY by Arnold Wesker. Penguin Books, 238 pages, 95 cents.

NINE PLAYS OF CHEKHOV. Four major plays: THE SEA GULL, THE CHERRY ORCHARD, THREE SISTERS, UNCLE VANYA, and five one-act plays. Universal-Grosset & Dunlap, 95 cents.

OBERAMMERGAU AND ITS PASSION PLAY, by Elisabethe H. C. Corathiel. Newman Press, $3.

OSCAR WILDE, by Frank Harris, including MY MEMORIES OF OSCAR WILDE, by George Bernard Shaw and an introduction by Lyle Blair. Reissue of a biography first published in 1916. Michigan State University, $7.

OVER THE HILLS: FOUR PLAYS FOR YOUTH, by James S. Wallerstein. Illustrated by Nitsa Savramis. Bellamy Press, $4.

PAUL VALERY: PLAYS, translated by David Paul and Robert Fitzgerald, introduction by Francis Fergusson and a memoir by Igor Stravinsky. Volume three in the Collected Works of Paul Valery. Bollingen, Pantheon Books, $4.50.

PIRANDELLO AND THE FRENCH THEATRE, by Thomas Bishop with a

foreword by Germaine Bree. Analysis of Pirandello and the French theatre of the twenties, thirties and postwar period. New York University Press, 170 pages, $4.50.

PLAYS OF THE YEAR, VOL. 19, 1958–1959, edited by J. C. Trewin. Four plays. Frederick Ungar, $3.50.

PLAYWRIGHTS ON PLAYWRITING, edited by Toby Cole, introduction by John Gassner. The meaning and making of modern drama from Ibsen to Ionesco. Hill and Wang, $3.95.

POINTERS ON PRODUCING THE SCHOOL PLAY, by Helen Louise Miller. Plays, Inc., 112 pages, $2.95.

PRODIGAL PURITAN, by Vivian C. Hopkins. A life of Delia Bacon who was obsessed with the idea that Shakespeare did not write his plays. The Belknap Press of Harvard University Press, 362 pages, $6.75.

RACINE: FIVE PLAYS, translated and introduced by David Magarshack. Mermaid Dramabook, Hill and Wang, $1.95.

RASHOMON, by Fay and Michael Kanin. Text of the Broadway production. Illustrated. Random House, 76 pages, $2.95.

RELIGIOUS DRAMA 3: AN ANTHOLOGY OF MODERN MORALITY PLAYS, selected and introduced by Marvin Halverson. Meridian Books, $1.45.

REMINISCENCES OF TOLSTOY, CHEKHOV AND ANDREYEV, by Maxim Gorky. From diaries, notes and letters. Viking-Compass $1.25.

SHAKESPEARE, by Jean Paris Schubert. Evergreen Profile Book, Grove Press, $1.35.

SHAKESPEARE: A PLAYER'S HANDBOOK OF SHORT SCENES, selected and arranged with acting directions by Samuel Selden. Holiday House, $2.75.

SHAKESPEARE AND HIS PLAYS, by H. M. Burton. For ages 10 to 14. Review of Elizabethan society and its theater, biography of Shakespeare and synopses of his plays. Illustrated. Roy Publishers, 68 pages, $2.95.

SHAKESPEARE AND THE CRAFT OF TRAGEDY, by William Rosen. Criticism. Harvard University Press, $4.75.

SHAKESPEARE MEMORIAL THEATRE, 1957–59, by Ivor Brown. Pictorial record of all the Stratford-on-Avon productions with photographs by Angus McBean and critical comment by Ivor Brown. Theatre Arts Books, 333 pages, $5.

SHAKESPEARE STUDIES: HISTORICAL AND COMPARATIVE IN METHOD, by Elmer Edgar Stoll. Corrected edition of a work published in 1942. Frederick Ungar, $6.50.

SHAKESPEARE SURVEY, edited by Allardyce Nicoll. An annual survey of Shakespearean study and production. Illustrated. Cambridge University Press, 163 pages, $4.75.

SHAKESPEAREAN SYNOPSES: OUTLINES OF ALL THE PLAYS OF SHAKESPEARE, by J. Walker McSpadden. Revised edition of a book first published in 1951. Crowell, $2.95.

SHAKESPEARE'S NAMES, by Helge Kökeritz. Pronouncing dictionary of all the proper names in Shakespeare. Yale University Press, 100 pages, $2.

SHAKESPEARE'S PROBLEM COMEDIES, by William Witherle Lawrence. Reissue of a study published in 1931. Frederick Ungar, $5.

SHAKESPEARE'S SONGS AND POEMS, edited by Edward Hubler. An anthology with explanatory notes. Illustrated. McGraw-Hill Book Company, 534 pages, $7.50.

SHAKESPEARE'S STAGE, by A. M. Nagler. Speculation about the Globe Theatre stage, based on historical research. Yale University Press, 111 pages, $2.

SHAKESPEARE'S WOODEN O, by Leslie Hotson. The form and method of the stage in Shakespeare's time. Illustrated. Macmillan, 335 pages, $6.50.

SHAW ON THEATRE, edited by E. J. West. Hill and Wang Dramabook, $1.35

SONS OF MEN, by Herschel S. Steinhardt. Text of the play. Bookman Associates, $3.

STAGE SCENERY: ITS CONSTRUCTION AND RIGGING, by A. S. Gillette. Illustrated. Harper & Bros., 315 pages, $8.

STEPS IN TIME, by Fred Astaire. Autobiography. Illustrated. Harper & Bros., 338 pages, $4.95.

SWEET BIRD OF YOUTH, by Tennessee Williams. Text of the Broadway production. New Directions, $3.25.

TALL STORY, by Howard Lindsay and Russel Crouse. Text of the Broadway production. Illustrated. Random House, 143 pages, $2.95.

THE AMERICAN SHAKESPEARE FESTIVAL: THE BIRTH OF A THEATRE, by John Houseman and Jack Landau. Illustrated. Simon and Schuster, 95 pages, $3.95.

THE ARDENT YEARS, by Janet Stevenson. Novel about the marriage of the English actress Fanny Kemble. Viking, $4.95.

THE ART OF DRAMATIC WRITING, by Lajos Egri. New edition. Simon and Schuster, 320 pages, $1.75.

THE ART OF RUTH DRAPER: HER DRAMAS AND CHARACTERS, with a memoir by Morton Dauwen Zabel. Illustrated. Doubleday, 373 pages, $4.95.

THE AUTOBIOGRAPHY OF CECIL B. DE MILLE, edited by Donald Hayne. Illustrated. Prentice-Hall, 465 pages, $5.95.

THE BEST OF MCDERMOTT, with a foreword by John Mason Brown. Selected writings by the late drama critic. World Publishing Co., 281 pages, $4.50.

THE BEST PLAYS OF 1958–1959, edited by Louis Kronenberger. The Burns Mantle Yearbook. Illustrated. Dodd, Mead & Co., 405 pages, $6.

THE BEST SHORT PLAYS OF 1958–1959, edited by Maragret Mayorga. Beacon Press, $3.95.

THE BLACKS: A CLOWN SHOW, by Jean Genet. English version of the Paris production. Grove Press, 128 pages, $3.50, Evergreen paperback $1.75.

THE BOOK OF JOB AS A GREEK TRAGEDY, by Horace M. Kallen. New edition of the text of the drama. Hill and Wang, 163 pages, $1.25.

THE CLASSIC THEATRE, VOLUME III, by Eric Bentley. Six Spanish plays. Doubleday Anchor Book, $1.45.

THE COLE PORTER SONG BOOK. Forty of his best-known songs, with a foreword by Moss Hart. Simon and Schuster, 222 pages, $12.50.

THE COMEDIES OF OSCAR WILDE: THE IMPORTANCE OF BEING EARNEST, LADY WINDERMERE'S FAN, A WOMAN OF NO IMPORTANCE AND AN IDEAL HUSBAND. Universal-Grosset & Dunlap, 95 cents.

THE COMPLETE GREEK TRAGEDIES, edited by David Grene and Richmond Lattimore. Thirty-three plays by Aeschylus, Sophocles and Euripides. University of Chicago Press, 4 volumes, boxed, $16.95.

THE CONNECTION, by Jack Gelber. Text of the play with introduction by Kenneth Tynan and photographs by John E. Wulp. Grove Press Evergreen Book, $1.75.

THE CULT OF SHAKESPEARE, by F. E. Halliday, Shakespeare's plays from his death to the present. Yoseloff, $5.

THE DEVIL AND THE GOOD LORD and TWO OTHER PLAYS, by Jean-Paul Sartre. Translated from the French. Alfred A. Knopf, 438 pages, $5.

THE FABULOUS SHOWMAN: THE LIFE AND TIMES OF P. T. BARNUM, by Irving Wallace. Illustrated. Alfred A. Knopf, 317 pages, $5.

THE FIGHTING COCK, by Jean Anouilh, adapted by Lucienne Hill. Text of the Broadway production. Coward-McCann, $3 cloth, $1.50 paper.

THE FIRST NIGHT GILBERT AND SULLIVAN, edited with a prologue and descriptive particulars by Reginald Allen, foreword by Bridget D'Oyly Carte. Complete librettos and facsimilies of first-night programs. Illustrated with contemporary drawings. Heritage Press Book. Dial Press, $6.95.

THE HERITAGE SHAKESPEARE: THE COMEDIES with an introduction by Tyrone Guthrie and illustrations by Edward Ardizzone, THE HISTORIES with introduction by James G. McManaway and wood engravings by John Farleigh, THE TRAGEDIES with introduction by George Rylands and wood engravings by Agnes Miller Parker. Heritage Press Book. Dial, $8.50 each, $25 3-volume set.

THE HEART OF HAMLET: THE PLAY SHAKESPEARE WROTE, by Bernard Grebanier. Thomas Y. Crowell Company, 311 pages, $4.95.

THE HIGHEST TREE, by Dore Schary. Text of the Broadway production. Random House, 130 pages, $2.95.

THE HOSTAGE, by Brendan Behan. Text of the drama. Grove Press, 92 pages, $3.50.

THE KILLER AND OTHER PLAYS, by Eugene Ionesco, translated by Donald Watson. Grove Press, $3.95. Evergreen Edition, $1.95.

THE LAUREL SHAKESPEARE: HENRY IV, PART I, with a modern commentary by Sir Ralph Richardson. THE WINTER'S TALE, with a modern commentary by D. A. Traversi. Dell, 35 cents each.

THE LAUREL SHAKESPEARE: OTHELLO, commentary by John Houseman. AS YOU LIKE IT, commentary by Esme Church. Dell, 35 cents each.

THE LIFE AND TIMES OF FREDERICK LEMAITRE, by Robert Baldick. Essential Books, 283 pages, $5.

THE LIVING THEATRE, by Elmer Rice. A collection of essays based on The Contemporary Theatre course which the playwright gave at New York University. Harper & Bros., 306 pages, $5.50.

THE LOWER DEPTHS AND OTHER PLAYS, by Maxim Gorky. Text of THE LOWER DEPTHS, ENEMIES and THE ZYKOVS, translated by Alexander Bakshy and Paul S. Nathan. Yale University Press, $1.25.

THE MERMAID MYTH: SHAKESPEARE NOT AMONG THOSE PRESENT, by Walter Hart Blumenthal. Westholm Publication, 32 pages, $5.

THE MODERN THEATRE, VOL. 6, edited by Eric Bentley. Five plays: LORENZACCIO, SPRING'S AWAKENING, THE UNDERPANTS, A SOCIAL

SUCCESS, and THE MEASURES TAKEN. Doubleday Anchor Book, 95 cents.

THE OFF-BROADWAY THEATRE: SEVEN PLAYS, edited by Richard A. Cordell and Lowell Matson. Random House, 481 pages, $5.

THE OPEN STAGE, by Richard Southern. Discussion about the usefulness of the platform stage of Elizabethan and other eras. Theatre Arts Books, 121 pages, $3.

THE PELICAN SHAKESPEARE: A MIDSUMMER NIGHT'S DREAM, edited by Madeleine Doran. Penguin Books, 50 cents. THE TRAGEDY OF RICHARD III, edited by G. Blakemore Evans. Penguin Books, 65 cents.

THE PLAY OF DANIEL: A THIRTEENTH-CENTURY MUSICAL DRAMA, edited for modern performance by Noah Greenberg, narration by W. H. Auden. Oxford University Press, $5.

THE PLEASURE OF HIS COMPANY, by Samuel Taylor with Cornelia Otis Skinner. Text of the Broadway comedy. Illustrated. Random House, 145 pages, $2.95.

THE POSSESSED, by Albert Camus. Text of a play in three parts. Alfred A. Knopf, 182 pages, $3.50.

THE RIGHT PLAY FOR YOU, by Bernice Wells Carlson. Twenty plays and skits designed for children of about 9 to 12 with suggestions for changes and production. Illustrated by Georgette Boris. Abingdon Press, 160 pages, $2.50 cloth, $1.60 paper.

THE ROAD TO DAMASCUS, by August Strindberg, translated by Graham Rawson, introduction by Gunnar Ollen. Grove Press, 286 pages, $1.95.

THE SHAKESPEARIAN ETHIC, by John Vyvyan. Barnes & Noble, 207 pages, $3.75.

THE SIGN OF JONAH, by Guenter Rutenborn, translated by George White. Text of a drama. Thomas Nelson & Sons, 91 pages, $2.50.

THE SIR THOMAS MORE CIRCLE: A PROGRAM OF IDEAS AND THEIR IMPACT ON SECULAR DRAMA, by Pearl Hogrefe. University of Illinois Press, 360 pages, $5.75.

THE STORM and Other Russian Plays, translated by David Magarshack. Gogol's THE INSPECTOR GENERAL, Ostrovsky's THE STORM, Tolstoy's THE POWER OF DARKNESS, Chekhov's UNCLE VANYA and Gorky's THE LOWER DEPTHS. Hill and Wang, 362 pages, $1.95.

THE TENTH MAN, by Paddy Chayefsky. Text of the Broadway production. Illustrated. Random House, 154 pages, $2.95.

THE THEATRE OF BERTOLT BRECHT, by John Willett. A study from eight aspects. Illustrated. New Directions, 272 pages, $8.

THE TRAGIC ACTOR, by Bertram Joseph. Survey of tragic acting in England from Richard Burbage to Sir Johnston Forbes-Robertson. Illustrated. Theatre Arts Books, 415 pages, $9.75.

THE WAY I SEE IT, by Eddie Cantor. A philosophy of life. Prentice-Hall, $2.95.

THE WORLD OF JEROME KERN, by David Ewen. A biography. Illustrated. Henry Holt & Co., 178 pages, $3.95.

THEATRE WORLD ANNUAL, NO. 10, edited by Frances Stephens. Pictorial review of the London 1958–59 theatrical season with statistics. Macmillan, 176 pages, $5.

THREE COMEDIES, by Ludvig Holber. THE TRANSFORMED PEASANT, THE THE ARABIAN POWDER, and THE HEALING SPRING. Theatre Arts Books, 91 pages, $1.50.

THREE FAMOUS PLAYS BY IVAN TURGENEV, translated by Constance Garnett. A MONTH IN THE COUNTRY, A PROVINCIAL LADY, and A POOR GENTLEMAN. Hill and Wang, 235 pages, $1.25.

THREE IRISH PLAYS: THE MOON IN THE YELLOW RIVER by Denis Johnston, THE IRON HARP by Joseph O'Conor, STEP-IN-THE-HOLLOW by Donagh MacDonagh, edited and introduced by E. Martin Browne. Penguin Books, 95 cents.

THREE JAPANESE PLAYS, edited with an introduction by Earle Ernst. Plays from the traditional theatre and essays on the No Theatre, the Doll Theatre and the Kabuki. Illustrated. Oxford University Press, 200 pages, $6.

THREE PLAYS, by Eugene O'Neill. Texts of DESIRE UNDER THE ELMS, STRANGE INTERLUDE, and MOURNING BECOMES ELECTRA. Random House Modern Library, $1.45.

TOYNBEE IN ELYSIUM, by Myra Buttle. Satirical fantasy in one act. Sagamore Press, $2.95.

TWO PLAYS AND A PREFACE: *Cards of Identity* and *The Making of Moo*, by Nigel Dennis. The Vanguard Press, 224 pages, $3.95.

UNDER MILK WOOD, by Dylan Thomas. Acting version of his poem about a Welsh community. New Directions, 96 pages, $1.85.

UNDERSTANDING TODAY'S THEATRE, by Edward A. Wright. Spectrum Book, Prentice-Hall, $1.95.

VOLTAIRE AND CANDIDE: A STUDY IN THE FUSION OF HISTORY, ART AND PHILOSOPHY, by Ira O. Wade. Princeton University Press, 369 pages, $8.50.

WILLIAM SHAKESPEARE: THE COMPLETE WORKS, edited by Charles
Jasper Sisson. Harper & Bros., 1376 pages, $7.50.

WITH POWDER ON MY NOSE, by Billie Burke with Cameron Shipp. Illustrated. Coward-McCann, 249 pages, $3.95.

OBITUARIES

ADAMS, FRANKLIN P., author, d. New York, March 23, 1960, age 78. A columnist whose work appeared in various New York newspapers, he was author of several books and the co-author of the musical comedies, *Lo* and *The 49ers*.

ADRIAN, GILBERT, d. Los Angeles, Sept. 13, 1959, age 56. Costume designer for many years at Metro-Goldwyn-Mayer, he was also responsible for costumes for the Broadway production *Music Box Revue*.

BARR, JOSEPH, actor, d. New York, June 12, 1959, age 38. He appeared in several outdoor productions of Shakespearean plays in New York City and off Broadway in *The Iceman Cometh* and *Children of Darkness*.

BARRYMORE, DIANA, actress, d. New York, Jan. 25, 1960, age 38. Daughter of actor John Barrymore, she appeared on Broadway in *The Happy Days*, *Rebecca*, and *Hidden Horizon*, and with the touring companies of *Streetcar Named Desire* and *Cat on a Hot Tin Roof*.

BARRYMORE, ETHEL, actress, d. Hollywood, June 18, 1959, age 79. With her brothers Lionel and John, she was one of the stage's "Royal Family" and began her career at the age of 14 in *The Rivals* with her grandmother, Mrs. John Drew, Sr. Her first starring role was in 1901 in *Captain Jinks of the Horse Marines*, later appearing in *The Corn Is Green*, *The Constant Wife*, *School for Scandal* and *The Kingdom of God* among others. She appeared in many motion pictures, including *None But the Lonely Heart*, and *Rasputin and the Empress* with her brothers.

BAZZI, MARIA, actress, d. Locarno, Switzerland, Aug. 24, 1959, age 61. She presented a number of American plays in Italian in Rome and other European cities.

BELLINGER, MARTHA, author, d. New York, Jan. 6, 1960, age 89. An editor and novelist, she was the author of a *Short History of the Drama*, published in 1927.

BISHOP, ANDREW, actor, d. Cleveland, Ohio, Sept. 9, 1959, age 66. He was a member of a Negro dramatic company that appeared at the Lincoln and the Lafayette theatres in New York City.

BISHOP, WILLIAM, actor, d. Los Angeles, Oct. 3, 1959, age 41. Actor in numerous motion pictures, he appeared on Broadway in *Victoria Regina*, *Tobacco Road* and other plays, and in many television shows.

BOSAN, ALONZO, actor, d. New York, June 24, 1959, age 73. He appeared in *Seventeen*, *Green Pastures*, and *The Wisteria Trees*.

BOYNE, EVA LEONARD, actress, d. New York, April 12, 1960, age 74. A star of the English stage, she first appeared on Broadway in *Fanny's First Play*, then in *Victoria Regina*, *The Corn Is Green*, *O Mistress Mine*, and *The Chalk Garden*.

BRODERICK, HELEN, actress, d. Los Angeles, Sept. 25, 1959, age 68. She appeared in *The Ziegfeld Follies*, *Oh Please*, *Fifty Million Frenchmen*, *The Band Wagon*, *As Thousands Cheer*, and in many motion pictures.

BROWN, GILMOR, d. Hollywood, Jan. 10, 1960, age 73. Head of the Pasadena Playhouse, he began his career as an actor and pageant director in the Midwest, went to Pasadena in 1917 as head of a small stock company.

CAHANE, HARRY, d. New York Jan. 22, 1960, age 65. He produced the plays, *The Rubicon* and *The Tyranny of Love*.

CAMUS, ALBERT, author, d. Villeneuve-la-Guyard, France, Jan. 4, 1960, age 46. Recipient of the Nobel prize for literature in 1957, he was the author of books, essays, criticisms, and dramas. His *Caligula* was presented in New York in 1960.

CHAUVEL, CHARLES, producer, d. Sydney, Australia, Nov. 11, 1959, age 62. He produced the motion pictures, *Forty Thousand Horsemen*, *Rats of Tobruk*, *Sons of Matthew*, and *Jedda*.

CHEVALIER, ALBERT, actor, d. London Nov. 11, 1959, age 60. A British character actor, he appeared on Broadway in *The Entertainer*.

CLARIOND, AIME, actor, d. Paris, Jan. 1, 1960, age 65. Dean of actors of the Comedie Française, he appeared in numerous French films including *Lucrezia Borgia*, *The Blue Veil*, *The Eternal Husband* and *My First Love*.

CLARK, BOBBY, d. New York, Feb. 12, 1960, age 71. A noted comedian, he appeared with his partner, Paul McCullough, in minstrel shows, circuses, vaudeville, burlesque, and musical comedy. Alone, he appeared in *The Ziegfeld Follies*, *Star and Garter*, *Streets of Paris*, *The Would-be Gentleman*, and *As The Girls Go*.

CLAXTON, OLIVER, author, d. South Londondery, Vt., Oct. 8, 1959, age 59. A former drama editor of *Cue* magazine, at the time of his retirement in 1950 he was literary editor and drama columnist for *Charm* magazine.

COLL, OWEN GRIFFITH, actor, d. New York, Feb. 7, 1960, age 81. He appeared in numerous plays, including *The Philadelphia Story, Call Me Madam, Another Part of the Forest* and *The Winning of Barbara Worth.*

COOKE, JAMES, d. Bala-Cynwyd, Pa., March 3, 1960, age 84. Author of several plays, he was a music publisher and editor of *Etude,* the music magazine, until his retirement in 1956.

CORBIN, JOHN, critic, d. Briarcliff Manor, N.Y., Aug. 30, 1959, age 89. Author of several books, he had been drama critic for *Harper's Weekly,* the New York *Times* and the New York *Sun.*

CURRIE, MAUDE, actress, d. London, July 28, 1959, age 79. Born in America, she was the wife of actor Finlay Currie.

DAVIES, JACK, agent, d. New York, Feb. 15, 1960, age 61. A theatrical agent for over thirty years, he represented such performers as Frank Fay, Bert Wheeler, Eddie Foy Jr., Gwen Verdon, and Romo Vincent.

DERWENT, CLARENCE, actor, d. New York Aug. 6, 1959, age 75. President of the American National Theatre and Academy, he was former president of Actors' Equity and appeared on Broadway in over 500 plays including *Queen Victoria, Electra, Serena Blandish, Kind Lady, The Eagle Has Two Heads, Madwoman of Chaillot,* and several motion pictures.

DORSAY, EDMUND, actor, d. New York, June 12, 1959, age 62. A comedian and character actor, he appeared in *Stage Door, Separate Rooms* and *Ah, Wilderness!*

DOUGLAS, PAUL, actor, d. Hollywood, Sept. 11, 1959, age 52. He appeared on Broadway in *Born Yesterday, A Hole in the Head,* a road company of *The Caine Mutiny Court Martial,* and in numerous motion pictures.

DOYLE, LEN, d. Port Jervis, N.Y., Dec. 6, 1959, age 66. An actor, director and producer, he appeared in the original casts of *The Time of Your Life, Three Men on a Horse, The Righteous Are Bold,* and *Shadow and Substance.*

DREYFUSS, MICHAEL, director, d. New York, March 30, 1960, age 32. A director for many television shows, he began his career as an actor in *Life with Father,* later appeared in *The Traitor, Joy to the World,* and the revival of *Babes in Arms.*

DRUMMOND-GRANT, ANNE, d. London, Sept. 11, 1959. A contralto, she spent twenty-six years with the D'Oyly Carte Opera Company, appearing in various Gilbert and Sullivan operettas.

DUNCAN, ROSETTA, actress, d. Chicago, Dec. 4, 1959, age 58. One of the famed vaudeville act, the Duncan Sisters, she appeared on Broadway in *Topsy and Eva, Tip Top,* and in 1936, in the revue *New Faces.*

EL BAKKAR, MOHAMMED, d. Pawtucket, R.I., Sept. 8, 1959, age 46. A specialist in the songs of the Middle East, he appeared on Broadway in *Fanny.*

EYRE, LAWRENCE, playwright, d. New York, June 6, 1959, age 78. He was the author of *The Things That Count, The Merry Wives of Gotham,* and *Mis' Nelly of N'Orleans.*

FIELDS, BENNIE, actor, d. New York, Aug. 16, 1959, age 65. A vaudeville and night-club performer, he appeared on Broadway in the revue, *Star Time.*

FISKE, DWIGHT, d. New York, Nov. 25, 1959, age 67. A night club entertainer, he was an accomplished pianist who composed his own music and wrote his own lyrics.

FLYNN, ERROL, actor, d. Vancouver, Canada, Oct. 14, 1959, age 50. A motion picture actor for fifteen years, he began his professional career in an English repertory company. In Hollywood, he appeared in *Captain Blood, Robin Hood, The Prince and the Pauper,* and *Objective Burma.*

FLYNN, JOE, d. Philadelphia, Pa., Feb. 29, 1960, age 73. A theatrical press agent and advance agent for the Shuberts and *The Ziegfeld Follies,* he started his career as a boy magician in vaudeville and served as assistant to Nellie Revell, newspaperwoman and theatrical entrepreneur.

FOX, HARRY, actor, d. Hollywood, July 20, 1959, age 76. A featured performer in vaudeville with the Dolly Sisters, he also appeared in motion pictures.

GEOLY, CHARLES, d. Great Neck, L.I., June 16, 1959, age 78. He was president of Eaves Costume Co., theatrical costumers.

GILLMORE, LAURA, actress, d. New York, Oct. 21, 1959. Widow of Frank Gillmore, former president of Actors' Equity, she appeared with Mrs. Minnie Maddern Fiske's company in *Hedda Gabler, Becky Sharp,* and *Tess of the D'Urbervilles.*

GLASER, VAUGHAN, actor, d. Van Nuys, Calif., Nov. 23, 1958, age 86.

He appeared on Broadway in *Many Mansions, What a Life* and in several motion pictures.

GOLDSTEIN, JENNIE, actress, d. New York, Feb. 9, 1960, age 63. A leading tragedienne of the Yiddish theater, she appeared on Broadway in *The Number* and *Camino Real.*

GOLDEN, JOSEPH M., d. Grand Rapids, Mich., Dec. 9, 1959, age 84. He was a veteran actor and vaudevillian.

GORDON, LEON, playwright, d. Hollywood, Jan. 4, 1960, age 64. A producer and scenarist for motion pictures, he was the author of numerous plays including *White Cargo, Watch Your Neighbor,* and *The Piker.*

GRANVILLE, SYDNEY, actor, d. Stockport, England, Dec. 23, 1959. He appeared in numerous Gilbert and Sullivan operettas with the D'Oyly Carte Company and toured the United States in 1936 and 1939 as a member of that company.

GRAY, GILDA, dancer, d. Hollywood, Dec. 22, 1959, age 60. Creator of the "shimmy," she appeared on Broadway in *The Ziegfeld Follies* and *George White's Scandals.*

GREGH, FERNAND, author, d. Paris, Jan. 4, 1960, age 87. A poet and dramatist, he was a member of the French Academy.

GROCK, clown, d. Imperia, Italy, July 14, 1959, age 79. He was one of Europe's most famous clowns for over 50 years. He played the Palace in New York.

GWENN, EDMUND, actor, d. Hollywood, Sept. 6, 1959, age 83. A stage and screen actor for over 60 years, he appeared in the original cast of six of George Bernard Shaw's plays in London, and in New York in *Laburnum Grove, The Three Sisters* and *The Wookey.* He won a motion picture Academy Award in 1948 for his part in *Miracle on 34th Street.*

HALE, SONNIE, actor, d. London, June 9, 1959, age 57. A favorite on the British stage for over twenty-five years, he appeared in many motion pictures.

HANLEY, WILLIAM B., actor and director, d. Los Angeles, Oct. 2, 1959, age 59. He appeared on Broadway in *Paris Bound* and was director of numerous radio and television shows.

HELBURN, THERESA, d. Norwalk, Conn., Aug. 18, 1959, age 72. Actress, playwright, critic and production manager, she was co-founder and executive director of the Theatre Guild and as such was responsible for the production of *The Philadelphia Story, Oklahoma!, The Ice-*

man *Cometh, Come Back Little Sheba,* and *Picnic* among others.

HEYDT, LOUIS JEAN, actor, d. Boston, Mass., Jan. 29, 1960, age 54. He appeared in over 150 motion pictures, and on Broadway in *The Trial of Mary Dugan, Strictly Dishonorable,* and *Happy Birthday* among others.

HILLIAS, MARGARET, actress, d. Kansas City, March 18, 1960. A performer on television, radio and in motion pictures, she appeared in *A Streetcar Named Desire.*

HOLMES, TAYLOR, actor, d. Hollywood, Sept. 30, 1959, age 80. He appeared in numerous motion pictures, both silent and talking, and on Broadway in *A Day in the Sun, Marriage à la Carte, I'd Rather Be Right,* and *Woman Bites Dog,* and in the touring companies of *Tobacco Road* and *The Man Who Came to Dinner.*

HOPPER, EDNA WALLACE, actress, d. New York, Dec. 14, 1959. She appeared in numerous Broadway plays, including *Florodora, Lend Me Your Wife, The Club Friend* and *The Girl I Left Behind Me.*

HOWARD, OLIN, actor, d. Hollywood, Sept. 21, 1959, age 63. A character actor in many films, he appeared in New York in *The Warrens of Virginia, Leave It to Jane* and many others.

HUBER, HAROLD, actor, d. New York, Sept. 29, 1959, age 49. He appeared in motion pictures, on radio and on Broadway in *A Farewell to Arms, First Night, Two Seconds,* and *Merry-Go-Round.*

JAHNN, HANS HENNY, d. Hamburg, Germany, Nov. 29, 1959, age 65. He was a noted German novelist and playwright.

JEROME, EDWIN, actor, d. Hollywood, Sept. 10, 1959, age 73. He appeared in numerous motion pictures and in *Deep Are the Roots, The Patriots, The Band Wagon,* and *Roberta.*

KEITH, IAN, actor, d. New York, March 26, 1960, age 61. He appeared in *Laugh, Clown, Laugh, He Who Gets Slapped, Edwin Booth* and many others on Broadway, and in the national company of *Long Day's Journey Into Night.* At the time of his death, he was appearing in *The Andersonville Trial.*

KELLY, ERIC, author, d. Phoenix, Ariz., Jan. 3, 1960, age 75. Former professor of journalism at Dartmouth College, he was the author of several children's books, novels, pamphlets, and dramas.

KENDALL, KAY, actress, d. London, Sept. 6, 1959, age 33. Born in England, she appeared on the stage in the revue, *Wild Violets,* and in the motion pictures *The Constant Husband, The Reluctant Débutante, Genevieve, Les Girls,* and *Once More, With Feeling.*

KLIEGL, JOHN, d. New York, Sept. 30, 1959, age 89. President of the Kliegl Brothers Universal Stage Lighting Co., developers of the klieg light used in motion pictures, he also assisted in the development of the disappearing footlight, remote color changer spotlight, pinhole downlight for auditoriums and a wide-angle scenic projector.

KLINE, HARRY, manager, d. Dallas, Tex., July 3, 1959, age 80. Born in Cleveland, he served as general manager for the Chanin organization and opened the Biltmore, Mansfield, Royale, Golden and Majestic Theaters.

KRUGER, ALMA, actress, d. Seattle, Wash. April 5, 1960, age 88. A radio and motion picture actress, she had appeared on Broadway in *Daisy Mayne, Camille, Hedda Gabler,* and *Few Are Chosen.*

LANE, LUPINO, d. London, Nov. 10, 1959, age 67. An actor and theatrical manager, he directed several motion pictures and appeared on Broadway in *The Ziegfeld Follies* in 1924 and in *The Mikado.*

LANNING, DON, actor, d. Miami, Fla., Feb. 14, 1960, age 65. He appeared in several Broadway shows including *Good News.*

LANZA, MARIO, actor, d. Rome, Italy, Oct. 7, 1959, age 38. An operatic tenor, he appeared on Broadway in *Winged Victory* and in the motion pictures, *The Great Caruso, That Midnight Kiss, Serenade* and many others.

LARDNER, JOHN, author, d. New York, March 24, 1960, age 47. A columnist for *Newsweek* magazine and *The New Yorker,* he was the author of several books and had served as drama critic for the New York *Star* and *The New Yorker.*

LEWIN, SAMUEL, author, d. New York, June 3, 1959, age 69. Author of several novels and books of poetry as well as the plays, *In Exile* and *The Holocaust.*

LILLY, PAUL, actor, d. New York, Oct. 19, 1959, age 50. He appeared on Broadway in *Auntie Mame, Street Scene, The Shrike,* and *My Three Angels,* and was a member of the executive board of the Catholic Actors Guild.

LONERGAN, LESTER, actor, d. New York, Dec. 23, 1959, age 65. He made his stage debut at the age of 5 in *The Heart of the Klondike,* appeared on Broadway in *Good Earth, Live Life Again* and *Bruno and Sydney* among others.

LUBIN, DAVE, actor, d. Seattle, Wash., Sept. 23, 1959, age 55. A singing and dancing comedian, he appeared on the Yiddish stage under the name of Dave Lubritsky with Molly Picon, Ludwig Satz, and Menasha Skulnik.

LUPINO, CONNIE, actress, d. Barstow, Calif., Dec. 26, 1959, age 68. Mother of actress Ida Lupino, she appeared on the British stage as Connie Emerald and was the widow of Stanley Lupino, actor, playwright, and producer.

MACDONALD, DONALD, actor, d. New York, Dec. 9, 1959, age 61. He appeared on Broadway in numerous plays including *Deep Are the Roots* and in the touring companies of *Brigadoon* and *Arsenic and Old Lace*.

MANN, CLAIRE, d. New York, De. 30, 1959, age 48. She was an actress, writer, and beauty consultant.

MARSH, MAYBELLE, actress, d. New York, Dec. 7, 1959, age 71. She was an actress and dancer in the early 1900s.

MATTHEWS, MAURINE, actress, d. New York, Sept. 14, 1959. She appeared in *Ramshackle Inn* on Broadway and on several television shows.

MILES, MURIEL, actress, d. New York, August 10, 1959, age 59. She appeared on Broadway in *The Ziegfeld Follies*.

MILLER, KATHERINE BROWNING, playwright, d. Berkeley, Calif., March 24, 1960, age 101. She was the author of *The Delinquents* and *Help Yourself*.

MITCHELL, ABBIE, actress, d. New York, March 16, 1960. Widow of composer Will Marion Cook, she appeared in *Porgy and Bess*, *The Little Foxes*, *In Dahomey*, and *The Red Moon*.

MINSKY, HERBERT KAY, d. New York, Dec. 21, 1959, age 68. With his three brothers, he founded a coast-to-coast chain of burlesque houses.

MOOERS, DE SACIA, actress, d. Hollywood, Jan. 11, 1960, age 72. A leading actress in over 100 silent movies, she appeared in *The Great Train Robbery*, *Potash and Perlmutter*, and in many films opposite Tom Mix.

MORGAN, CAREY, song writer, d. Pittsburgh, Jan. 6, 1960, age 75. A writer of special material for vaudeville acts, he composed the scores for musical comedy shows including the *Greenwich Village Follies*, *The Honeymoon Cruise*, and *Fifty-Fifty*.

NELMES, HARRY B., d. New York, Jan. 4, 1960, age 81. A former vaudeville actor, he was a member of the box-office staffs of Broadway theatres for over 50 years and a charter member of the Treasurers Club of America.

NORTON, WILLIAM, manager, d. New York, June 27, 1959, age 73. He was company manager for several Michael Todd productions and for the touring company of *A Raisin in the Sun*.

NORTHWORTH, JACK, actor and songwriter, d. Laguna Beach, Calif., Sept. 1, 1959, age 80. He appeared on radio, television and in vaudeville as well as in *The Ziegfeld Follies* and on Broadway in *The Fabulous Invalid*. He composed over 3000 songs, including "Take Me Out to the Ball Game."

O'NEIL, PEGGY, actress, d. London, Jan. 7, 1960, age 61. She appeared in many musical comedy productions including *Peg O' My Heart*, *The Flame*, and *Paddy the Next Best Thing*.

PARK, SAMUEL J., d. Keansburg, N.J., Jan. 15, 1960, age 72. A playwright, actor and script writer for radio and stage comedians, he was the author of *Philadelphia* and *Black Water* and co-author of *Black Widow* and *The Sheriff*.

PEARSON, BUD, d. New York, Nov. 21, 1959, age 62. A former vaudevillian, he was a gag writer for Bob Hope, Eddie Cantor and other comedians, and co-author of the stage productions *Around the World in Eighty Days*, *Too Hot for Maneuvers*, and *As Long as You're Healthy*.

PECKHAM, FRANCES, actress, d. New York, June 7, 1959, age 66. She appeared in vaudeville and on Broadway in *The Ziegfeld Follies*.

PHILIPE, GERARD, actor, d. Paris, Nov. 25, 1959, age 36. A noted actor in French motion pictures, he appeared in New York in two productions of the Théâtre National Populaire of Paris, *Lorenzaccio* and *Le Cid*.

PICKARD, HELENA, actress, d. Reading, Eng., Sept. 27, 1959, age 59. She appeared in many plays on the English stage, and on Broadway in *The Country Wife*, *Time and the Conways*, and *Flare Path*.

PINSKI, DAVID, playwright, d. Haifa, Israel, Aug. 11, 1959, age 87. He was the author of 38 plays, mostly for the Yiddish theater, including *The Eternal Jew*, *King Solomon*, and *The Final Balance*.

RELPH, GEORGE, actor, d. London, April 24, 1960, age 72. A British character actor, he appeared on Broadway with the Old Vic Company, in *The Gioconda Smile*, and in *The Entertainer*.

ROBBINS, JACK, song publisher, d. New York, Dec. 15, 1959, age 65. A publisher of popular songs, he operated J. J. Robbins, Inc., which handled scores for Broadway shows; he had a partnership in Word & Music, Inc., music publishers.

ROBINSON, GEORGE M., actor, d. New York, July 30, 1959, age 69. He appeared in the 1909 *Ziegfeld Follies.* ·

ROLLAND, WILLIAM, producer, d. Dallas, Tex., Jan. 16, 1960, age 73. He operated several Yiddish theaters, including the Liberty and the Second Avenue.

ROSENFELD, ARTHUR, d. New York, July 24, 1959, age 74. He was a manufacturer of picture frames for theater lobbies.

ROSS, THOMAS W., actor, d. Torrington, Conn., Nov. 14, 1959, age 86. He appeared in many plays on Broadway including *Our Town, Your Uncle Dudley* and *The Fortune Hunter* and in the motion picture *The Remarkable Andrew.*

SELWYN, ARCH, producer, d. Hollywood, June 21, 1959, age 82. Producer of many plays on Broadway, including *Smilin' Through, Private Lives,* and *Bittersweet,* he was co-founder of the Goldwyn Pictures Corporation, which later became Metro-Goldwyn-Mayer.

SHANNON, ELIZABETH, d. New York, Aug. 18, 1959. A showgirl in the Ziegfeld-White-Carroll era, she was known as Betty Sundmark.

SMART, J. SCOTT, actor, d. Springfield, Ill., Jan. 15, 1960, age 57. Actor in motion pictures and on radio, he appeared in *The Pirate.*

SMITH, G. ALBERT, actor, d. New York, Sept. 3, 1959, age 61. In motion pictures, on television and on Broadway he did *Coquette, The Wisteria Trees, State of the Union,* and *The Animal Kingdom.*

STEWART, CECIL, composer and director, d. Hollywood, Jan. 18, 1960, age 61. He was musical director for the plays, *The Desert Song, Hit the Deck,* and *New Moon* and composer of the songs, "In Old Monterey" and "Dusty Saddles."

STURGES, PRESTON, d. New York, Aug. 6, 1959, age 60. Author, director and producer of many films, including *Christmas in July, The Lady Eve, Miracle of Morgan's Creek,* and *Hail the Conquering Hero,* he won an Academy Award in 1940 for his script of *The Great McGinty* which he also directed. He was the author of the Broadway play, *Strictly Dishonorable.*

SULLAVAN, MARGARET, actress, d. New Haven, Conn., Jan. 1, 1960, age 48. She made her Broadway début in 1931 in *A Modern Virgin,* later appeared in *Stage Door, The Voice of the Turtle, Deep Blue Sea* and *Sabrina Fair* and many motion pictures.

SUTHERLAND, ELIZA, actress, d. New York, Feb. 28, 1960, age 41. Wife of actor Melville Cooper, she appeared on Broadway in *The Wookey, Autumn Hill,* and *The Haven* and several others.

SWEET, CHANDOS, d. New York, March 1, 1960, age 77. A stage manager, scenic designer, and theatrical manager, he was associated with the productions of *Many Mansions, Three Men on a Horse, The Consul,* and *A Roomful of Roses.*

THAYER, TIFFANY, author, d. Nantucket, Mass., Aug. 23, 1959, age 57. Author of more than nineteen novels, he began his career acting in stock companies, later spent some years in Hollywood as a scenarist.

THROPP, CLARA, actress, d. New York, Feb. 29, 1960, age 88. She made her stage début in *Rip Van Winkle* at the age of eight, appeared in *Little Johnnie Jones, The Field God,* and *The Mountain.*

TREVELYAN, HILDA, actress, d. London, Nov. 11, 1959, age 79. She was the original Wendy in Sir James Barrie's *Peter Pan.* -

VAIL, LESTER, actor and director, d. Hollywood, Nov. 28, 1959, age 59. An actor in early motion pictures, he directed several Broadway plays and television series.

VERNON, NELL, actress, d. New York, Oct. 19, 1959, age 74. A performer in vaudeville, on the screen and stage, she appeared in *Shepherd of the Hills* and *Sunup.*

WALLACE, FAYE, actress, d. New York, Dec. 8, 1959, age 70. She appeared on the Broadway stage for over twenty-five years.

WHITE, SAMMY, actor, d. Beverly Hills, Calif., March 3, 1960, age 65. A musical comedy star, he appeared in *Show Boat* and *The Girl Friend* on Broadway and in many motion pictures.

WINTON, JANE, actress, d. New York, Sept. 22, 1959, age 51. She appeared in the *Ziegfeld Follies* and in many motion pictures, including *Don Juan* in 1926, one of the first pictures to synchronize sound with action. A soprano, she appeared in various operatic roles here and abroad, and was the author of two novels.

WOLIN, DONALD, producer, d. New York, Aug. 21, 1959, age 33. He was formerly one of the operators of the Theatre-by-the-Sea, Matunuck, R.I.

YEAGER, EDITH, actress, d. Mount Kisco, N.Y., Sept. 1, 1959, age 69. She played on Broadway in the companies of Daniel and Charles Frohman and under the direction of Arthur Hopkins. She was author of the play, *Sugar,* produced by William A. Brady.

YOUNG, ADAH, d. Columbus, Ohio, Sept. 9, 1959. One of vaudeville's "Bubbling Youngs," she was featured in several *Ziegfeld Follies.*

INDEX

Abbott, George, 41–50, 76, 151, 152, 153, 203–4
Abie's Irish Rose, 253
Actman, Irving, 191
Actors Equity, 13, 21, 24
Adams, Franklin P., 290
Adams, Jacqueline, 259
Adams, Lee, 73, 261–63
Adams, Samuel Hopkins, 17, 25, 42, 168
Adler, William, 244
Adrian, Gilbert, 290
Adrian, Max, 91, 223
Advise and Consent, 24
Aegis Theatre Club, 153
Affairs of Anatol, The, 24
Ah, Wilderness!, 18, 188–90
Aherne, Brian, 20, 254
Albee, Edward, 22, 23
Albright, Jessica, 261
Alda, Alan, 201
Aldene, Judy, 269
Aldredge, Theoni V., 186, 208, 220, 257
All the King's Men, 22
Allan, Jed, 258
Allen, Rita, 221
Allister, Claud, 218
Alloy, Albert, 246
Allwyn, Marilynn, 274
Alswang, Ralph, 174, 191
Altman, Frieda, 108, 178, 220
Alvarez, Anita, 272, 273, 274
Alvin, Robert, 253
Alvin Theatre, 191, 248
Ambassador Theatre, 167, 221, 232, 255
American National Theatre and Academy, 153, 213, 240
American Theatre Society, 251
American Theatre Wing, 42, 152
Amram, David, 169, 230
Anania, John, 276

Anatol, 24
Anders, Glenn, 251
Anders, Margo, 213
Anderson, Clinton, 215
Anderson, Johnathan, 161
Anderson, Richard, 194
Anderson, Robert, 107, 208
Andersonville Trial, The, 19, 97–106, 153, 216–17
André, 221
Andreu, Mariano, 161
Andrews, Nancy, 275
Anouilh, Jean, 22, 24, 62, 213–14, 259
Ansky, S., 15, 51
ANTA Theatre, 153, 213, 240
Anthony, Joseph, 119, 120, 257
Anthony, Sal, 191
Antonio, Lou, 246
Arenton, James, 216
Aristophanes, 24
Arlecchino, Servitore di due Padroni, 236
Arlen, Harold, 210–12
Arlen, Jerry, 210
Armbruster, Richard, 228
Armstrong, R. G., 232
Armstrong, Will Steven, 98, 169, 216, 230
Arnett, Chuck, 227, 229
Aronson, Boris, 140, 186, 205, 253
Aston, Frank, 97–98, 140
At the Drop of a Hat, 18, 19, 174–75
Atkinson, Brooks, 31, 74, 130, 182, 199, 221
Aumont, Jean Pierre, 259
Austin, Patty, 272
Aveilhe, Art, 234
Avian, Robert, 269
Axelrod, George, 215
Ayler, Ethel, 234
Aymé, Marcel, 176–77

B & M Productions, 171
Bacall, Lauren, 215